I0810580

IMAGES
of America

1957 Fargo Tornado

On the Cover: Days after the devastating 1957 tornado, residents of the Golden Ridge neighborhood searched for any salvageable property among the ruins of their homes. Unfortunately, many found that little or nothing remained. This survivor stands near the intersection of Twenty-ninth Street North and Eighth Avenue North, looking east. (Courtesy of the North Dakota State University Archives.)

IMAGES
of America

1957 Fargo Tornado

Trista Raezer-Stursa, Lisa Eggebraaten,
Jylisa Doney, and John Hallberg

ARCADIA
PUBLISHING

ISBN 978-1-4671-2673-1

Published by Arcadia Publishing
Charleston, South Carolina

Printed in the United States of America

Library of Congress Control Number: 2017939976

For all general information, please contact Arcadia Publishing:
Telephone 843-853-2070
Fax 843-853-0044
E-mail sales@arcadiapublishing.com
For customer service and orders:
Toll-Free 1-888-313-2665

Visit us on the Internet at www.arcadiapublishing.com

We dedicate this book in memory of the 12 Fargoans who died due to the tornado, the many survivors, and those who supported recovery efforts.

Contents

ACKNOWLEDGMENTS

The authors would like to express their deep appreciation to several individuals and organizations for their support and assistance with this book. First and foremost, we would like to thank Cal Olson's family for donating his collection of negatives to the North Dakota State University (NDSU) Archives, from where we pulled the majority of images. We would also like to thank Catherine McMullen, Olson's daughter, for providing insight into her father's work during the tornado. Much appreciation goes to Matt Von Pinnon, editor of the *Fargo Forum*, for his support of this publication. In addition to Cal Olson's images, we also used images from *Forum* photographers Chet Gebert and Alf T. Olsen. These three documented the tornado, and with the rest of the *Forum* staff, received a Pulitzer Prize for their efforts. All images appear courtesy of the North Dakota State University Archives.

Introduction

The tornado that struck Fargo, North Dakota, on June 20, 1957, left a path of destruction and devastation in its wake. Of the five tornadoes that traveled through North Dakota and Minnesota on that day, the one that hit Fargo was the most severe in terms of lives lost and injuries as well as the number of dwellings damaged and destroyed.

In total, the tornado killed 12 people, seven children and five adults, and injured numerous residents. One family, the Munsons, lost six of their seven children: Phyllis, Darwin, Bradley, Jeanette, Lois Ann, and Mary Beth. Their mother, Mercedes, was at work waiting for a coworker to cover the rest of her shift; Gerald, the father, was in Bismarck, North Dakota, on business; and the surviving child, LeRoy, was babysitting at another house. The Munson house, which was in the most devastated area of the Golden Ridge neighborhood, did not have a basement for the children to seek shelter, resulting in the home collapsing on them. The entire Udahl family, Theodore and Theresa Udahl along with their adopted daughter Mary Jean, was killed when the tornado wiped out their home. Don Titgen was killed by the tornado while his wife, Betty, died almost three years later in 1960 after being in a coma since the disaster. Laura Schoenherr sustained injuries that led to a leg amputation and paralysis of an arm; she later died on July 15, 1957, from her injuries. Within this devastation, there were many miraculous incidents of survival. One incident relayed in the *Fargo Forum* detailed the story of the infant Jon Davenport, who was torn from his mother's arms by the tornado. Jon was found by an unidentified stranger and brought to a hospital where, after brain surgery, he survived his injuries and was eventually reunited with his parents, Jerry and LuVerne Davenport.

The recovery needs of survivors became clear in the aftermath of the tornado. Local police and emergency departments, the National Guard, and other local, state, and national emergency workers responded to the disaster and addressed the urgent needs of the community. The Red Cross and local churches, service groups, and individuals arranged food, shelter, and access to other goods and services necessary to move toward recovery. Neighbors, friends, and family members supported each other throughout this crisis.

Mayor Herschel Lashkowitz proclaimed the Red Cross the official disaster relief agency. According to the Red Cross, 329 dwellings were destroyed, leaving approximately 2,000 residents displaced due to the disastrous tornado. Additionally, 356 dwellings suffered major damage, 679 dwellings had minor damage, and 4 churches, 3 schools, and 15 commercial buildings were ripped apart. The total estimated damage was reported to be around $20 million. Nine families were taken in at Concordia College in Moorhead, Minnesota, and the North Dakota Agricultural College, now North Dakota State University, provided housing for other displaced families as they searched for more permanent residences. Over 100 tons of clothing and bedding were donated to the Red Cross and distributed to tornado victims. Red Cross volunteers at Plymouth Congregational Church served approximately 57,000 cold lunches and 40,000 hot meals to tornado victims and workers while volunteers at Agassiz Junior High School provided meals to the National Guard. The Red Cross also established 24 mobile canteens to feed victims and volunteers in the disaster area. In total, 225 families applied for assistance from the Red Cross. Of those, 188 met the Red Cross's requirements and these survivors received a total of $286,777 for medical care as well as rebuilding and repairing homes and purchasing household furnishings. Family-owned businesses were also able to purchase tools, instruments, and the supplies needed to reestablish themselves.

Donations for survivors poured in from around the country and Canada. Individuals, companies, and nonprofit organizations empathized with the plight of survivors and wanted to help them rebuild. One such example was Winnipeg, Manitoba, whose citizens gave $40,000. Grateful for the assistance Fargo gave them during the disastrous 1950 flood, the citizens of Winnipeg wanted to reciprocate the kindness they were shown.

In the wake of this disaster and mere minutes after the devastating tornado hit, the *Fargo Forum*'s 20-member staff all reported to work, unasked, and started gathering information and taking photographs to ensure that their community remained informed. At 1:09 a.m. on June 21, only 5 hours and 29 minutes after the tornado struck, a special edition of the *Fargo Forum* went to press, containing 24 columns of print and many photographs. If a single image was to be selected as representative of the *Fargo Forum*'s reporting on the tornado, it would have to be chief photographer Cal Olson's iconic image of Richard Shaw carrying the body of Jeanette Munson (see page 26). This photograph appeared on the front page of the next issue of the *Fargo Forum* and showed the devastating impact of this natural disaster. The *Forum*'s photographs and reporting in the days, weeks, and months following the tornado helped the newspaper win the Pulitzer Prize for Local Reporting on May 5, 1958, "for its swift, vivid and detailed news and picture coverage of a tornado which struck Fargo on June 20 . . . under considerable difficulty and overcoming many handicaps, a small but skilled staff put out a complete tornado edition within five hours after the disaster." On the day after the award was announced, *Forum* publisher Norman D. Black Jr. proclaimed in the May 6, 1958, issue of the *Fargo Forum*, "It was with great enthusiasm and understandable pride that I heard yesterday of our receiving the coveted Pulitzer Prize . . . Every newspaper publisher dreams that the efforts of his fellow workers might someday make such an award possible. Monday my dream came true. Congratulations to all of you for a job well done under terrific handicaps." The *Forum* staff dedicated the prize to the recently retired editor-in-chief H.D. "Happy" Paulson, who worked for the *Forum* for 41 years.

The photographs in this book illustrate how the residents of Fargo, and individuals across North Dakota and the United States, banded together to respond and recover from tremendous hardship following this disaster. This is truly a story of strength, hope, and a vibrant community coming together to rebuild in the wake of devastation.

One

The Tornado

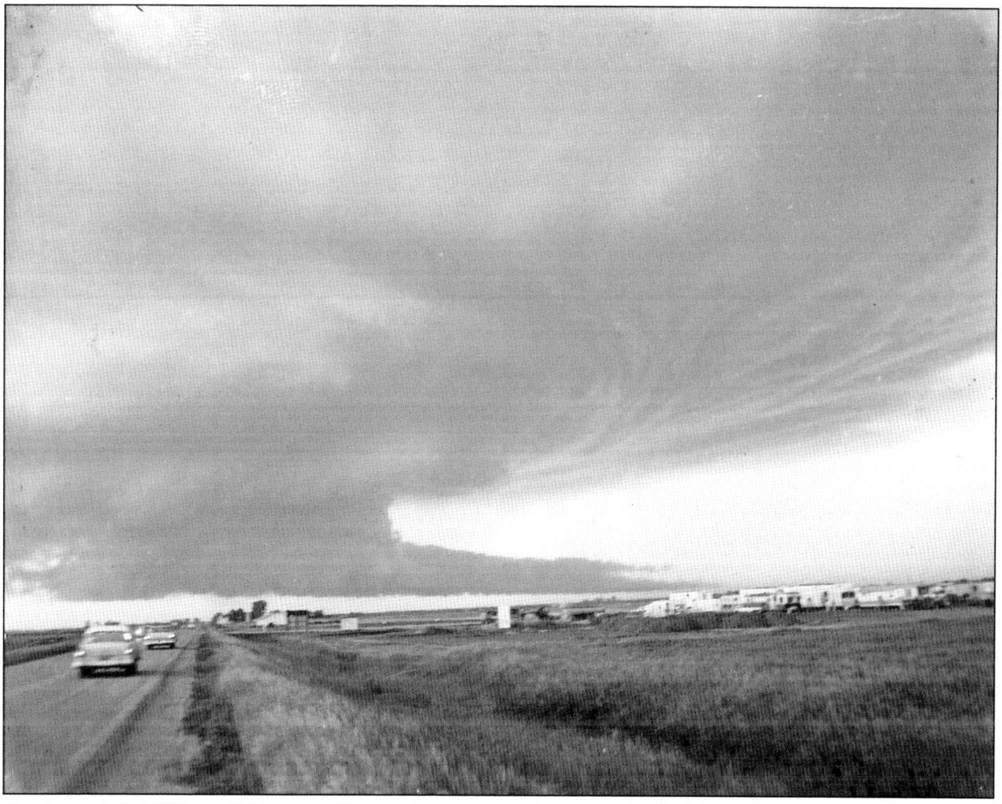

On June 20, 1957, at 7:14 p.m., Dewey Bergquist photographed this ominous wall cloud about six miles west of Fargo. The wall cloud sprouted a long tail cloud. As seen here, a collar cloud surrounds the top of the wall cloud, and a disc cloud streaks across the sky. This picture was taken from Nineteenth Avenue North, near the old Hector Airport.

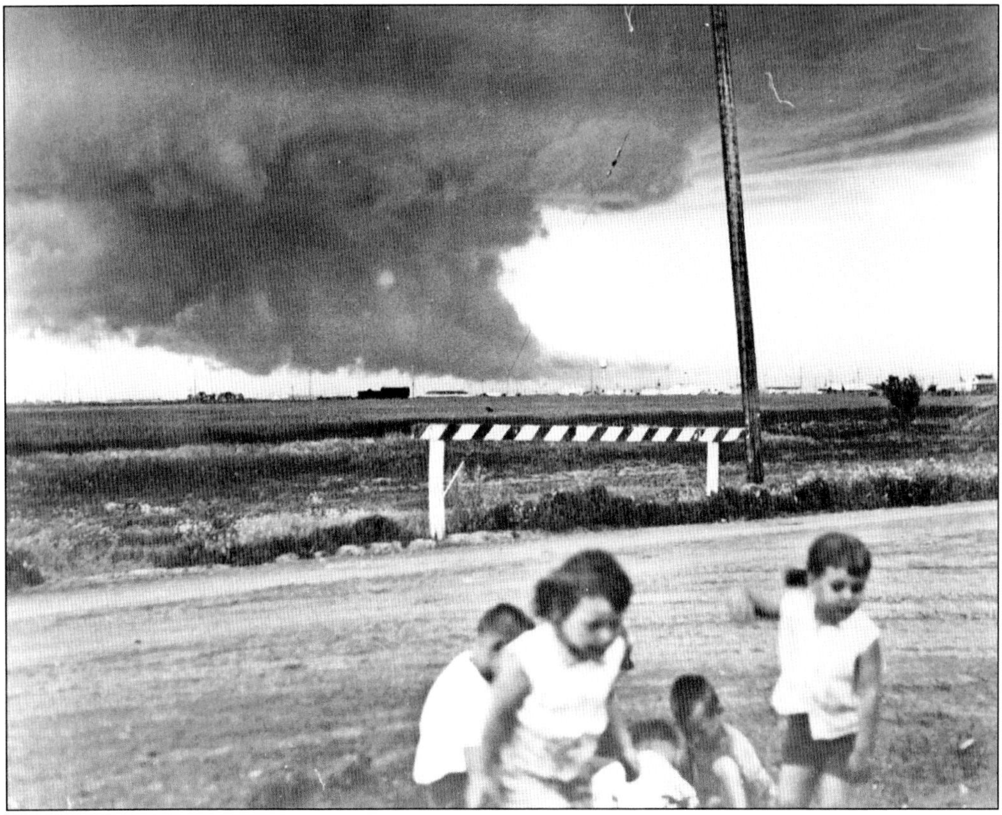

At 7:23 p.m., *Fargo Forum* photographer Alf T. Olsen grabbed his camera and photographed the wall cloud from near his home on Twenty-first Street South. His and his neighbors' oblivious children—from left to right, Michael J. Olsen, Carol Betz, Terry Farley, Patrick T. Olsen, and Barbie Betz—were too busy examining a dead parrot in the ditch to notice the ominous cloud.

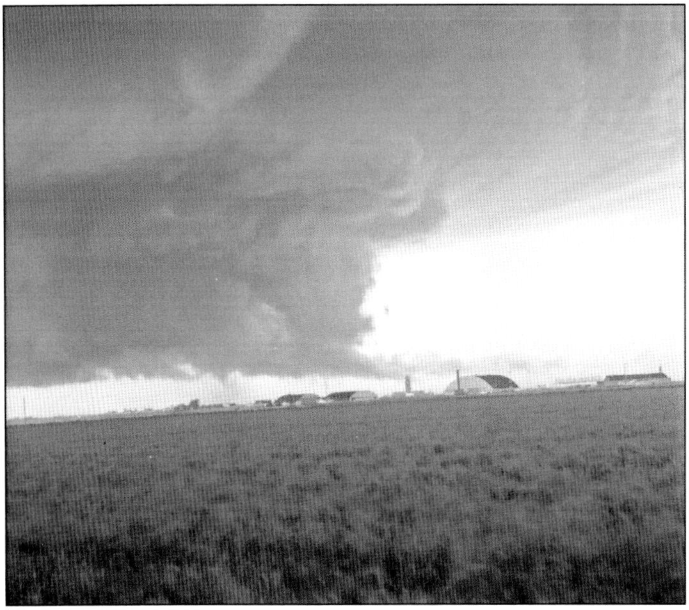

At 7:25 p.m., the wall cloud could be seen quickly approaching Hector Airport. *Fargo Forum* photographer Chet Gebert also got straight to work when he heard about the approaching tornado and took this photograph from near his home in north Fargo, close to the intersection of Tenth Street North and Twenty-second Avenue North.

Three minutes later, the new funnel can be seen southwest of the original Hector Airport. It took only 30 seconds for the funnel to reach the ground after it appeared from the cloud. The airport started hosting commercial flights in 1931 and constructed a new terminal and administrative building in 1953. Despite the appearance in this photograph, the airport was not in danger of being hit.

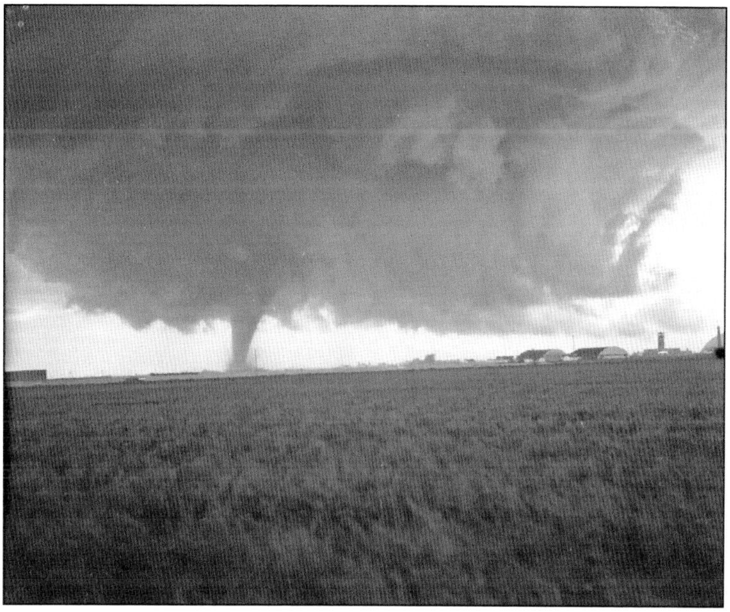

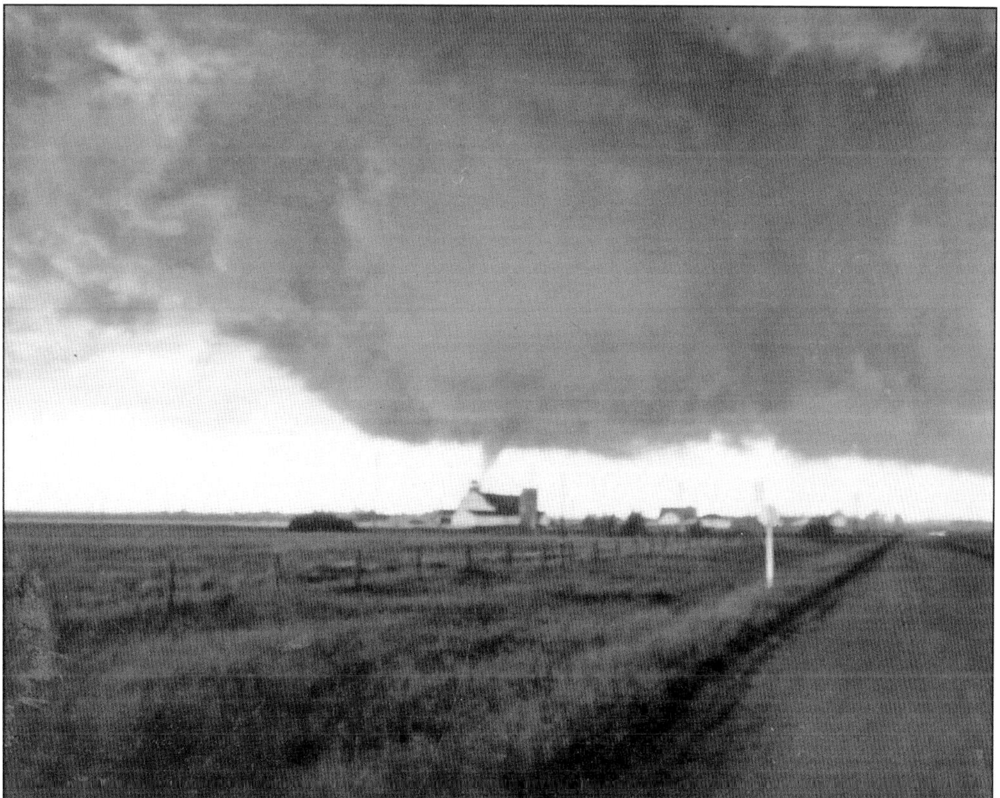

Dewey Bergquist took this picture on Nineteenth Avenue North looking southwest. Barns that belonged to the North Dakota Agricultural College, now North Dakota State University, can be seen in the background. The barn was not damaged. This tornado was the third of five that traveled 64 miles through North Dakota and Minnesota.

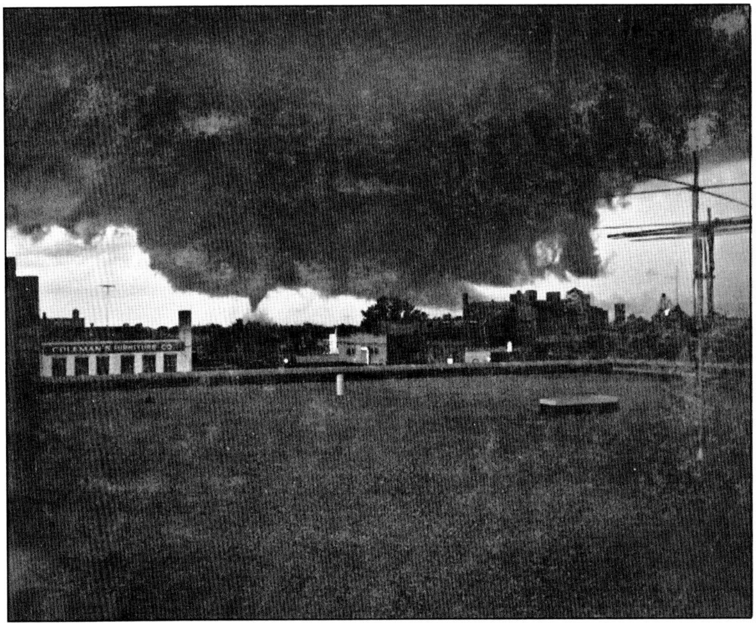

This photograph was taken from the top of the WDAY television station building at 207 Fifth Street North, looking northwest. Coleman's Furniture Company is in the background to the left, and the rest of downtown Fargo is to the right. Downtown was a safe distance from the tornado.

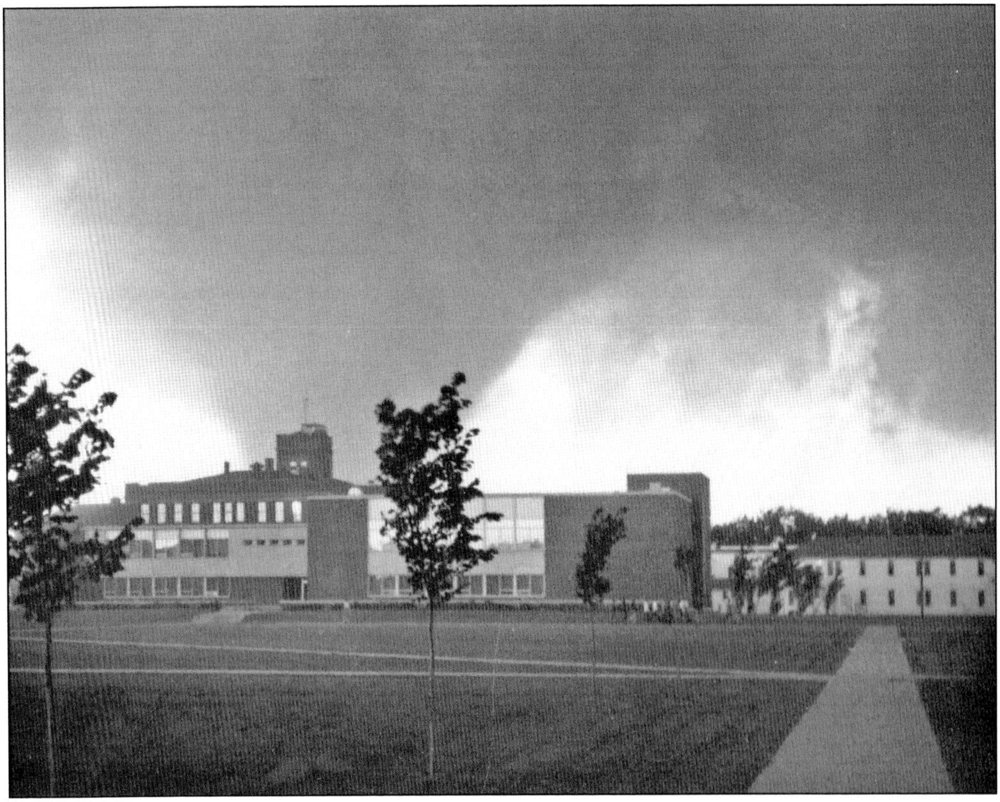

Elwin E. Hutchinson photographed the menacing funnel cloud of the tornado seen behind the North Dakota Agricultural College campus, near the Memorial Union. Fortunately, there was very little damage on campus. The campus gates and health center were heavily damaged, but other buildings only suffered broken windows. The gates and health center were quickly repaired.

Elwin E. Hutchinson continued to take photographs as the tornado descended upon north Fargo. This photograph was also taken from the North Dakota Agricultural campus. The tower of Old Main is at lower right. Debris flies through the sky. The tornado grazed the edge of campus and damaged many buildings across the street on Thirteenth Street North, now University Drive.

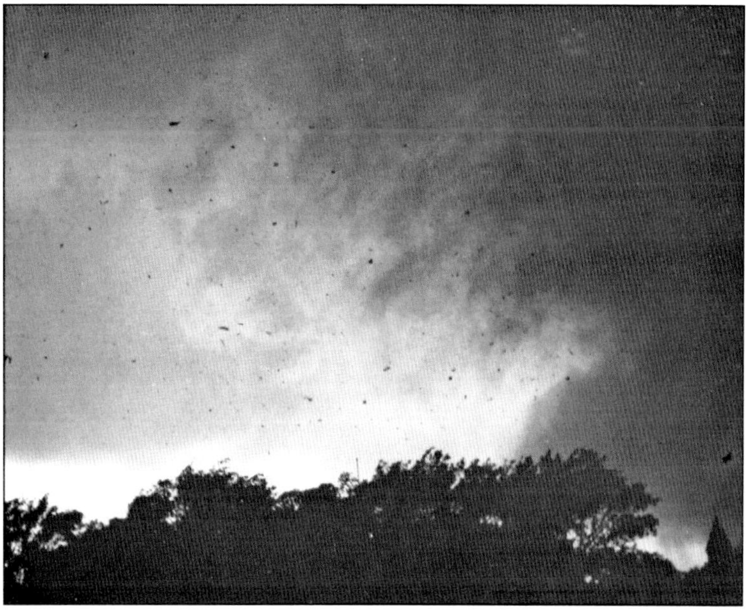

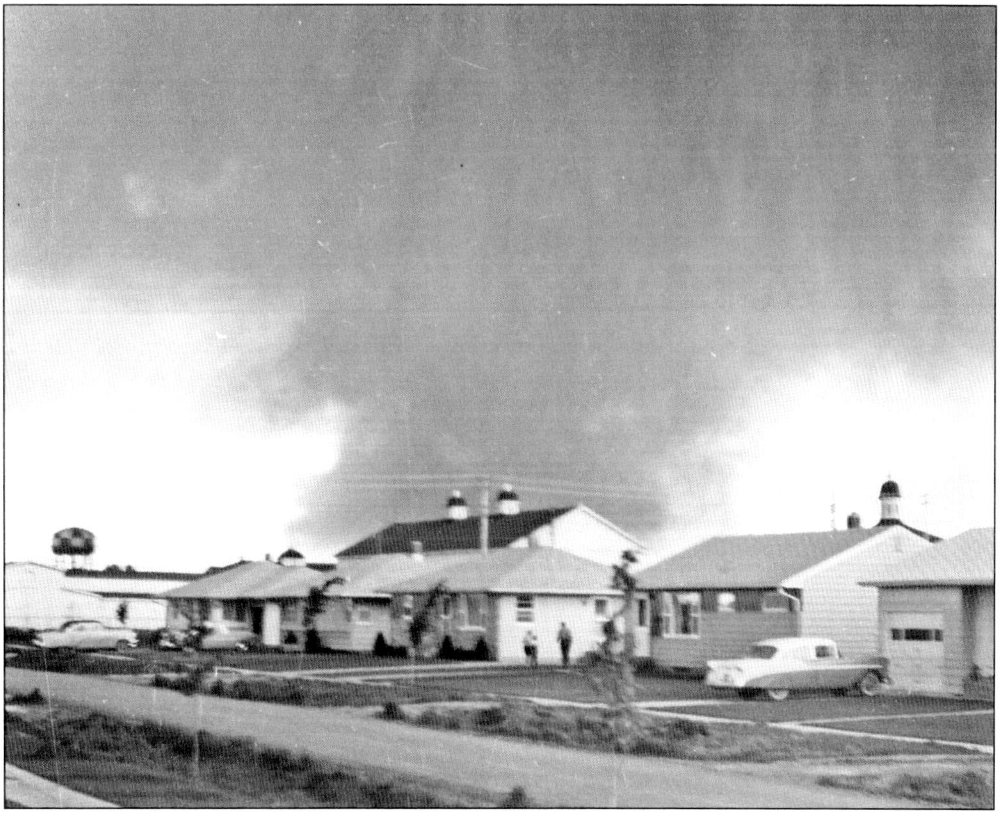

Some Fargoans did not seem to be deterred by the approaching tornado. As Chet Gebert bravely photographed the swirling funnel cloud, neighbors across the street stood in their yard to get a view as well. Gebert lived at 2009 Ninth Street North. The old Red River Valley Fairgrounds, then located on Nineteenth Avenue North, can be seen in the background.

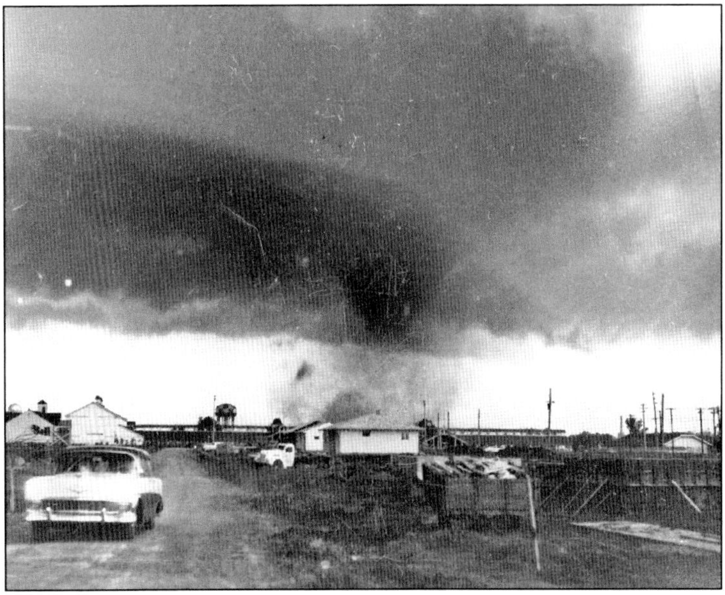

This view of the Red River Valley Fairgrounds shows how massive the funnel was. The funnel measured about 700 feet wide and spun at about 230 miles per hour at its peak. However, the funnel moved through Fargo at only 16 miles per hour. While Chet Gebert captured this image, people fled past in their cars.

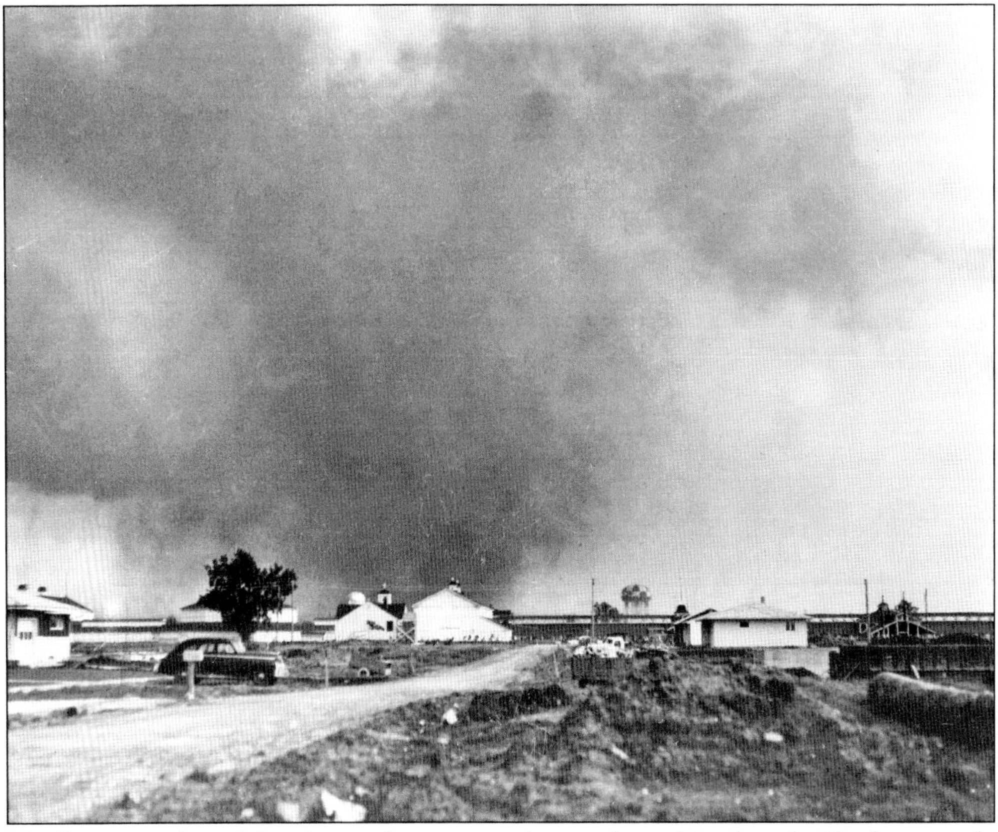

The Fargo tornado took less than an hour to complete its almost 10-mile path. The five-tornado system lasted about three and a half hours; the Fargo tornado was the third and worst. Climatologist Tetsuya Fujita studied the Fargo tornado while he created the Fujita Scale (F-Scale), which measures tornado intensity. He rated the Fargo tornado an F5, the highest rating.

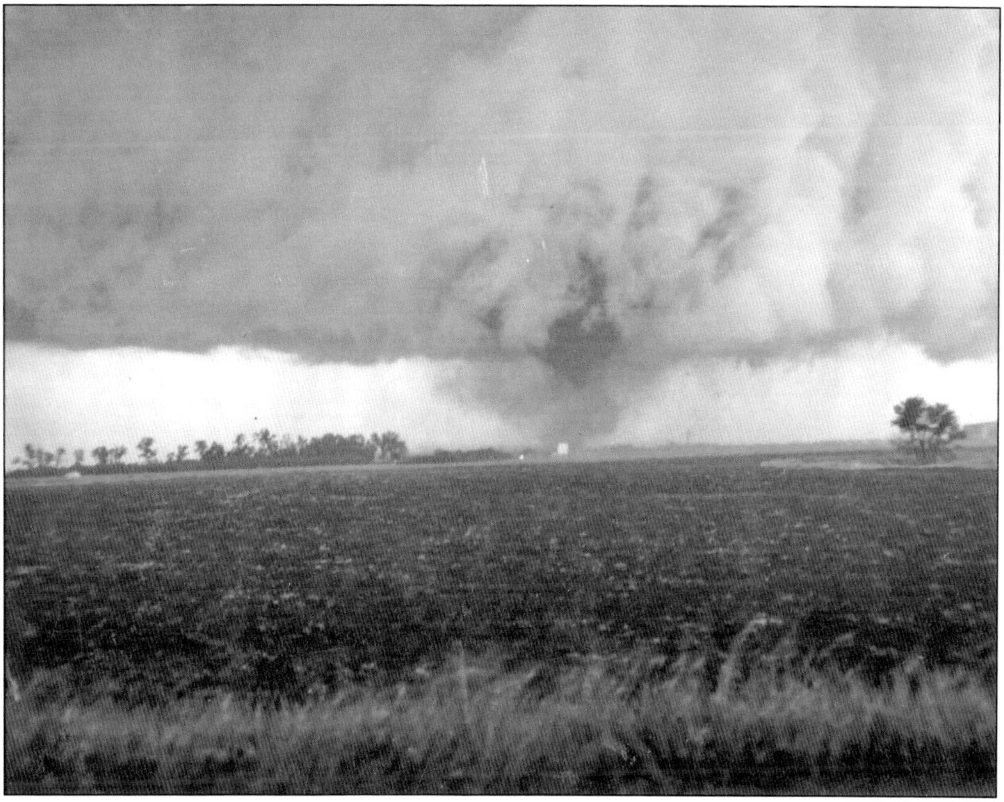

Dewey Bergquist was the first weatherman for WDAY, so he was keen to get as many pictures of the tornado as possible. He drove north of Nineteenth Avenue near Holy Cross Cemetery to capture this picture of the tornado, looking south. The tiny white square at the bottom of the tornado is the screen for the Starlight Drive-In movie theater. It was not damaged.

Dewey Bergquist followed the tornado and captured a photograph of the rope funnel cloud dissipating as it entered Minnesota. This photograph was taken looking northeast from near the El Zagal Bowl, which is now the El Zagal golf course. Fortunately, Moorhead did not sustain much damage. The tornado ended at 7:50 p.m.

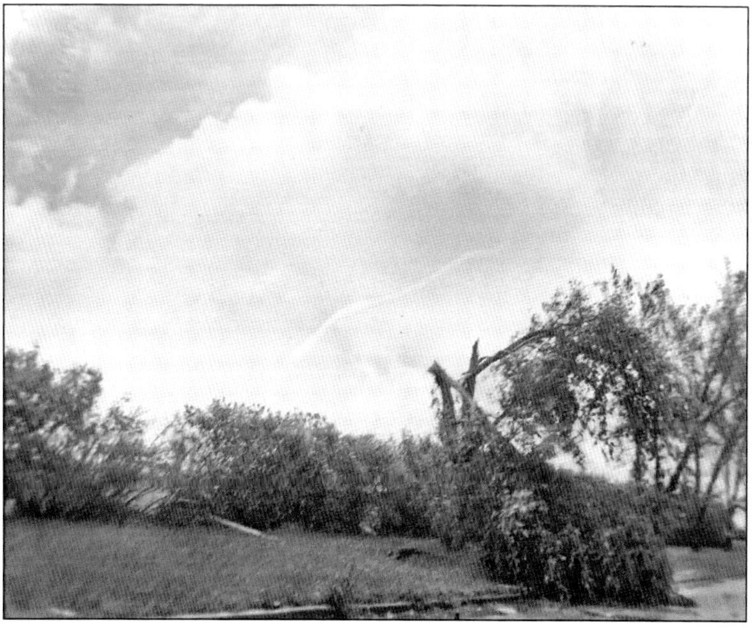

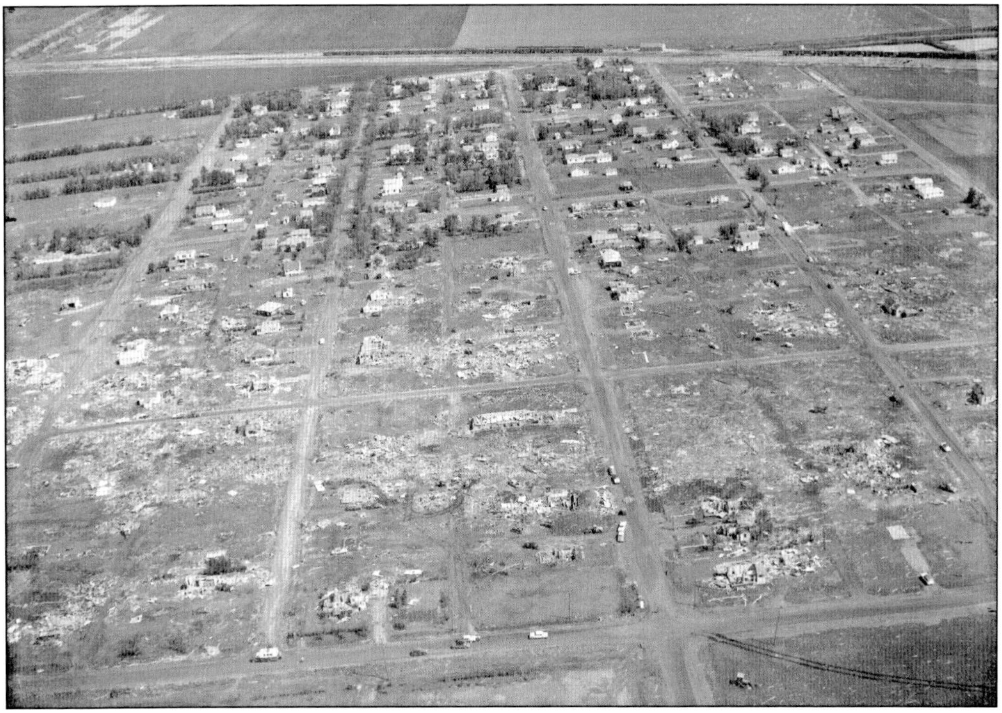

The following aerial photographs show the path of the tornado. The first neighborhood of Fargo to get hit was Golden Ridge. This working-class neighborhood was made up of small, poorly constructed homes, many without basements. This view is looking north with Seventh Avenue North in the foreground. The Golden Ridge School is at far left, and the Golden Ridge Lutheran Church is at center.

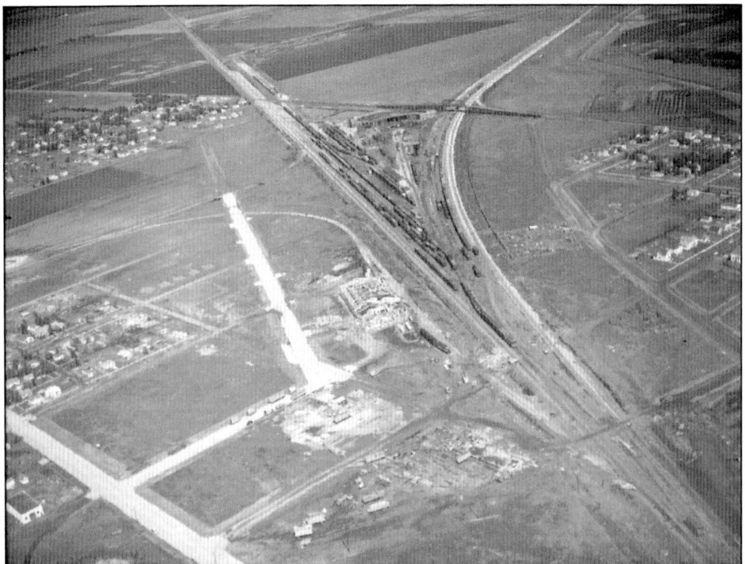

The next area affected was an industrial area that was home to several warehouses. This view looking northwest from near the intersection of Seventh Avenue North and Seventeenth Street North shows destroyed industrial facilities belonging to Peavey Fertilizer Plant, Red Truck Line, and Hart Motor Express. The Great Northern Railroad yards are also visible in this view.

This view looks north over the Roosevelt neighborhood, just south of the North Dakota Agricultural College. The path of the tornado can clearly be seen running from lower left to right center. The open area at left is Johnson Soccer Complex today; in 1957, it was a swampy area used as a location to dump tornado debris.

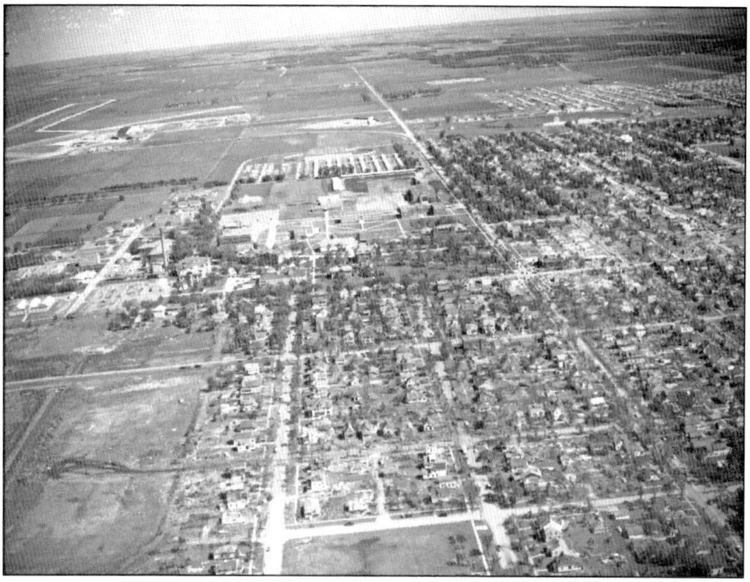

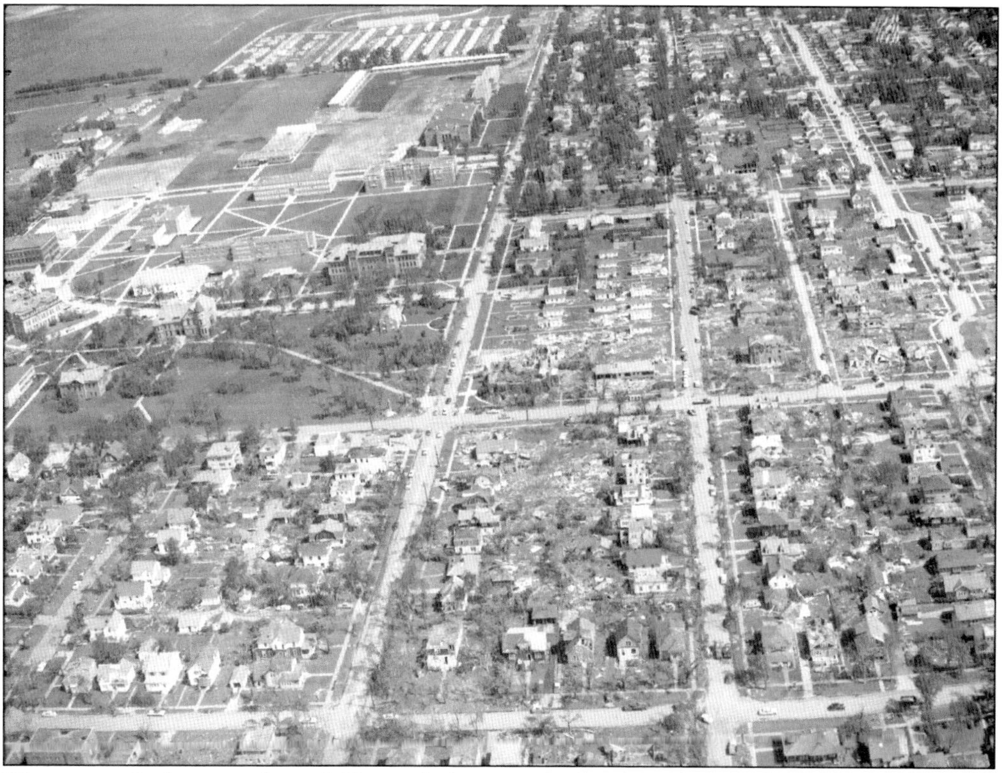

This view is looking north, with Eleventh Avenue North running along the bottom. The North Dakota Agricultural College, in the upper left corner, was barely grazed by the tornado. The destroyed Young Men's Christian Association building, Hasty Tasty restaurant, and faculty campus housing complex, called Silver City, are visible at center.

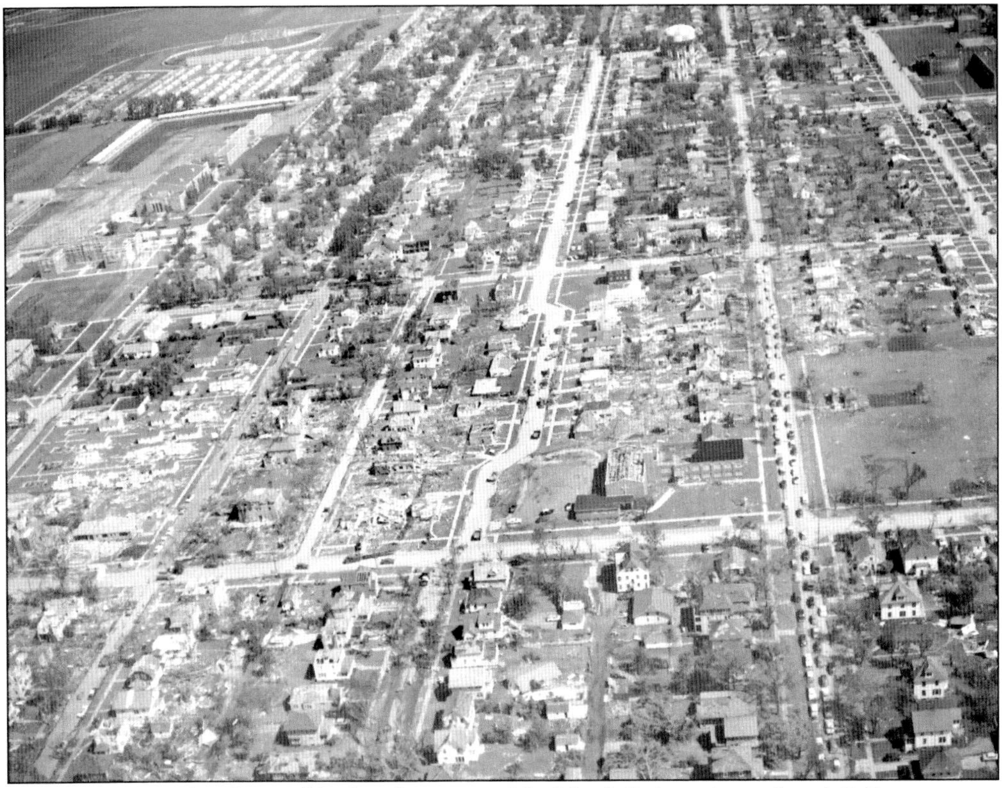

The tornado then hit the neighborhood just east of the North Dakota Agricultural College campus. The Alpha Tau Omega fraternity house and American Lutheran Church are visible along Twelfth Avenue North, running horizontally in the foreground. Tenth Street North, running vertically, appears to be bumper-to-bumper cars, likely people surveying the damage.

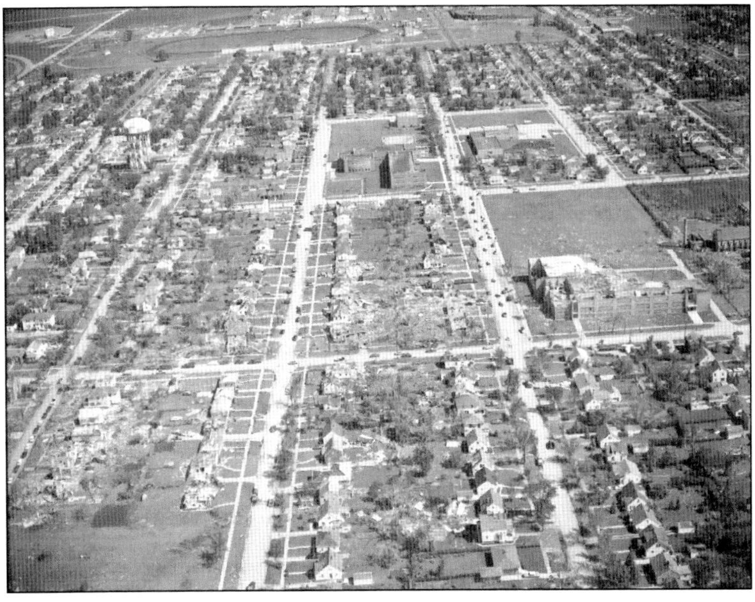

This view shows the next neighborhood struck by the tornado; it was between Tenth and Seventh Streets North. Thirteenth Avenue North runs horizontally across the center. The damage in this area was quite severe. Visible at right is Shanley High School, which is missing most of its roof.

This view looking north shows Broadway running through the center of the image. Shanley High School is at lower left, and Sacred Heart Convent is just to its right. The convent received irreparable damage in the storm. The Immanuel Lutheran Church, just to the south of the convent, lost most of its roof, and many homes in the area were heavily damaged.

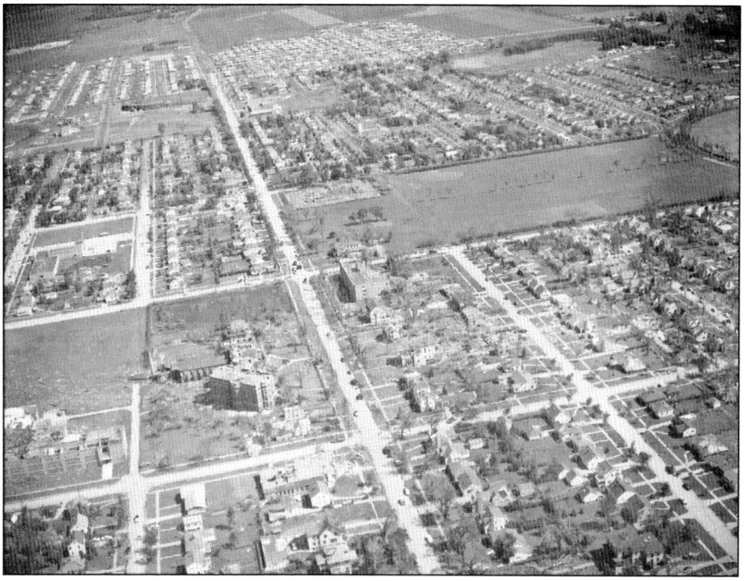

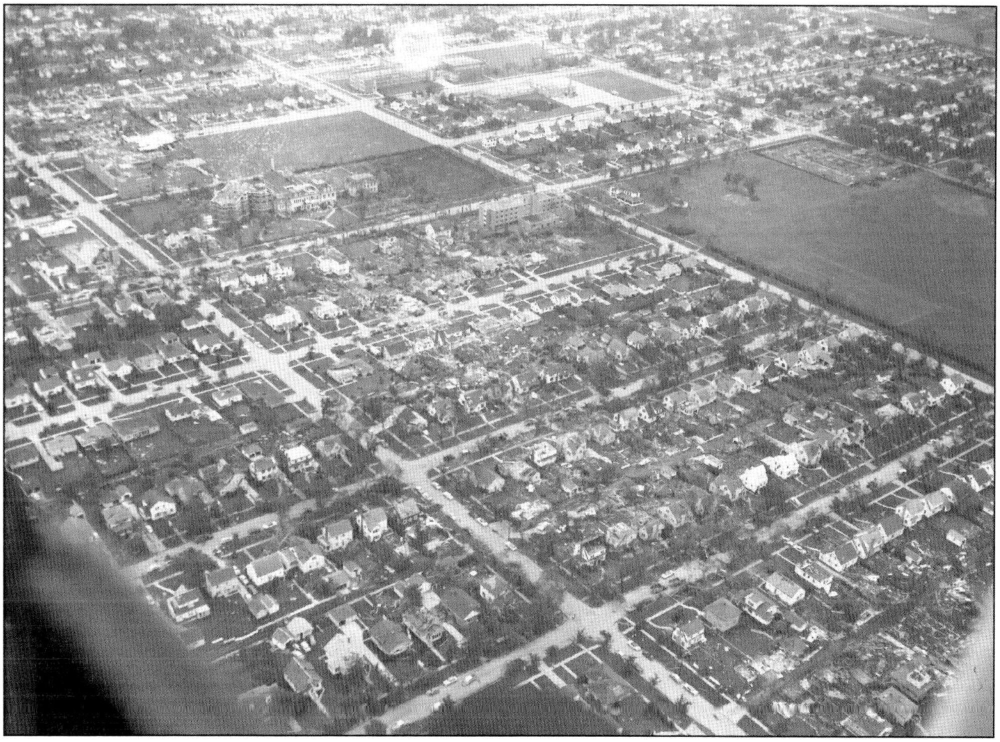

The next area hit was the northernmost section of the Horace Mann neighborhood, north of Thirteenth Avenue North and east of Broadway. Many of the homes in this area were either heavily damaged or destroyed. This aerial view is looking northwest, with Sacred Heart Convent and Shanley High School in the background.

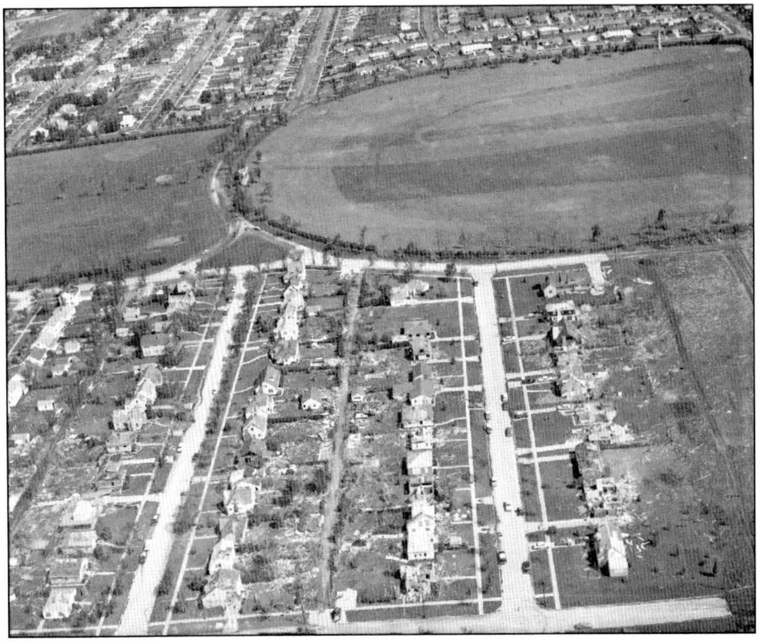

This view looking north from Thirteenth Avenue North, between First and Second Streets North, shows the last area of Fargo affected by the tornado. Most of the homes in the neighborhood were of newer construction, and most had basements for the victims to ride out the storm. El Zagal Bowl, the open park area at top, lost a number of trees around its southern perimeter.

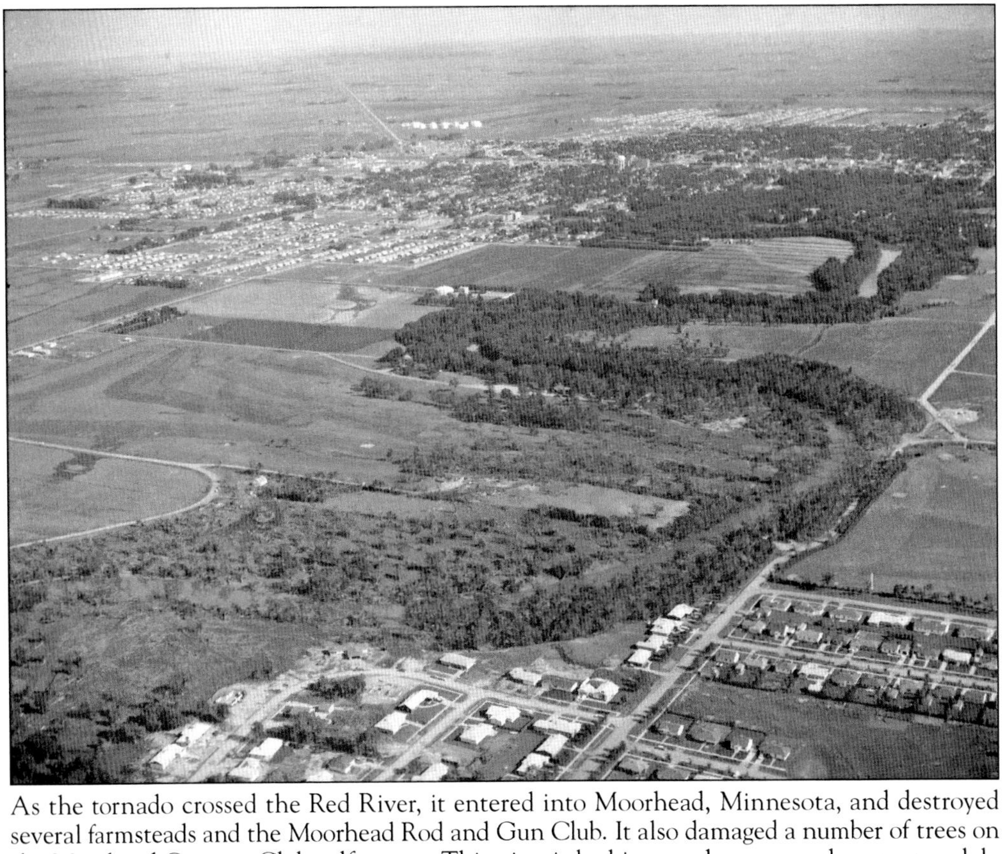

As the tornado crossed the Red River, it entered into Moorhead, Minnesota, and destroyed several farmsteads and the Moorhead Rod and Gun Club. It also damaged a number of trees on the Moorhead Country Club golf course. This view is looking southeast over the country club, with Moorhead in the distance.

Two

The Victims

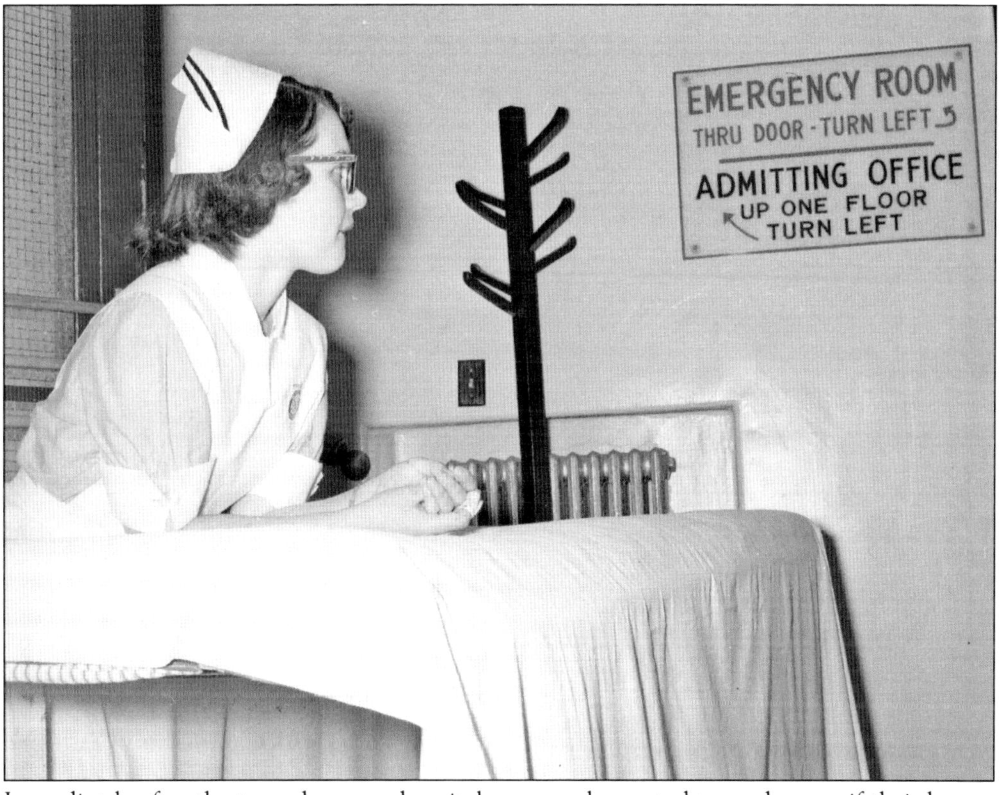

Immediately after the tornado, many hospital personnel reported to work, even if their homes were damaged. This photograph was likely taken at St. Luke's Hospital, now Sanford Hospital, at 801 Broadway in Fargo. A nurse in uniform stands next to a gurney awaiting the arrival of patients at the emergency room.

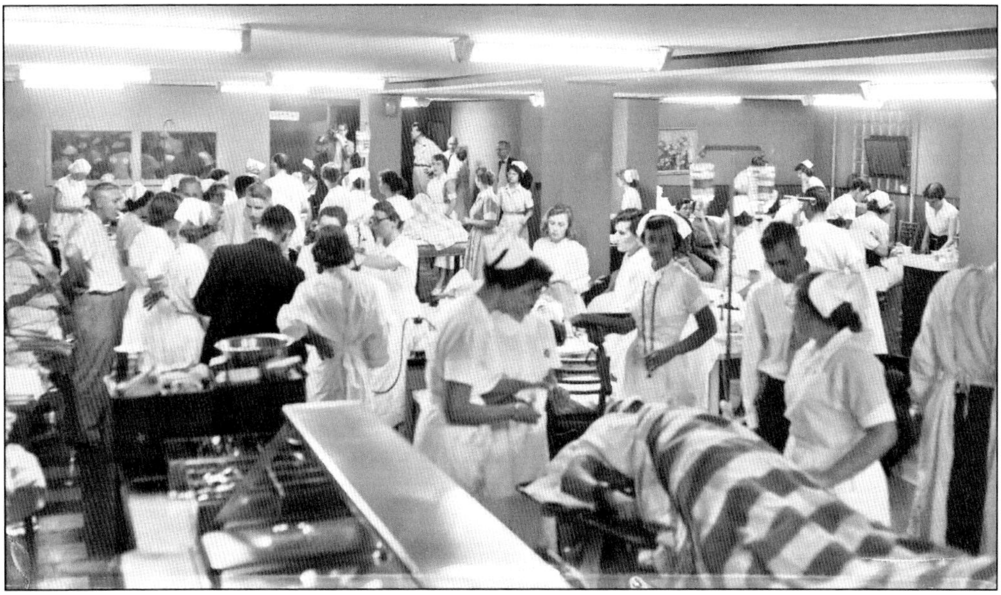

Due to the number of injuries, the St. Luke's Hospital cafeteria was converted to an emergency room after the tornado. St. Luke's Hospital treated 35 patients and St. Luke's Clinic treated 47 for injuries. Attending nurses, doctors, and civilians are seen around hospital beds. Fr. William C. Sherman, wearing black, is looking down at a patient at left.

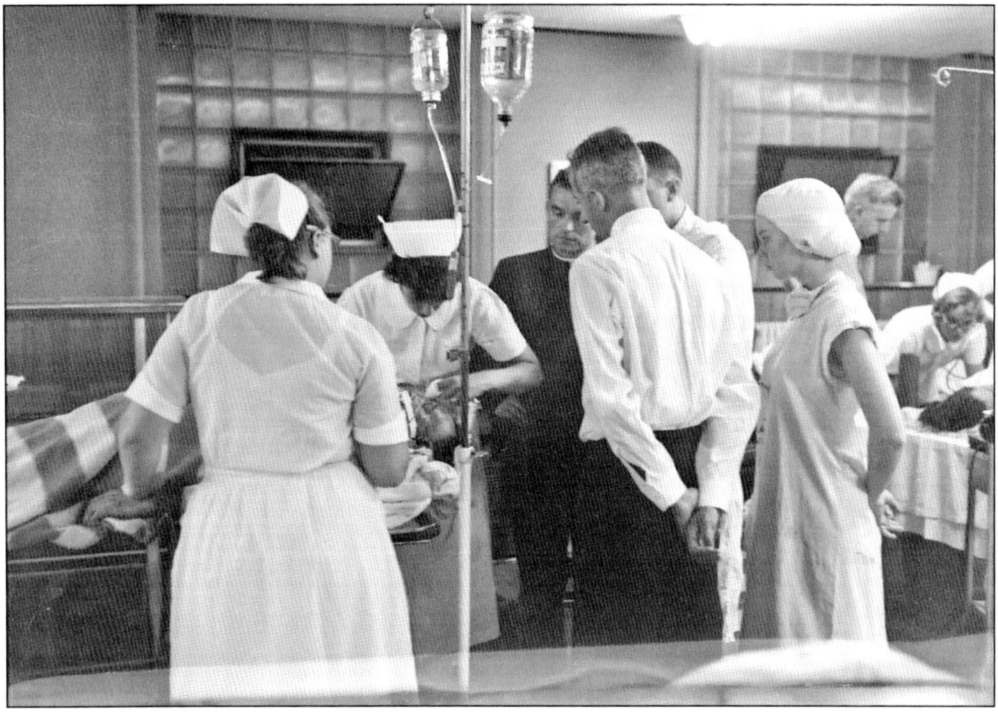

At St. Luke's Hospital, possibly in the cafeteria, three nurses and three men, one a priest, stand around a patient on a hospital bed. Father Sherman was brought to the hospital to administer last rites to seriously injured patients after the tornado. In the background, there looks to be another patient on the right.

Three men remove two deceased tornado victims from the back of a hearse. All 12 people killed as a result of the tornado resided in Golden Ridge, the neighborhood that suffered the most damage. It is unknown exactly where this picture was taken, but it was likely near a hospital or morgue.

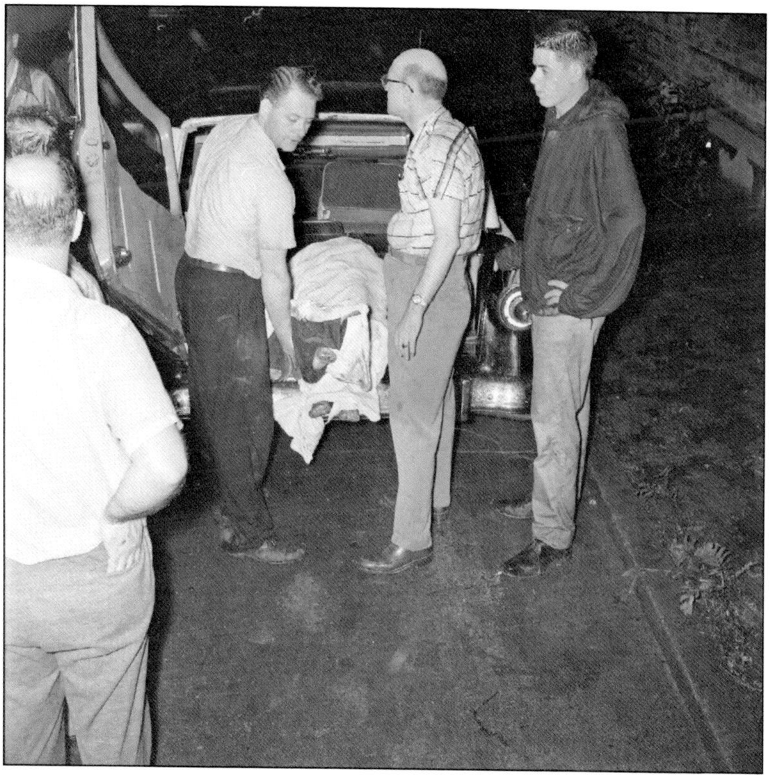

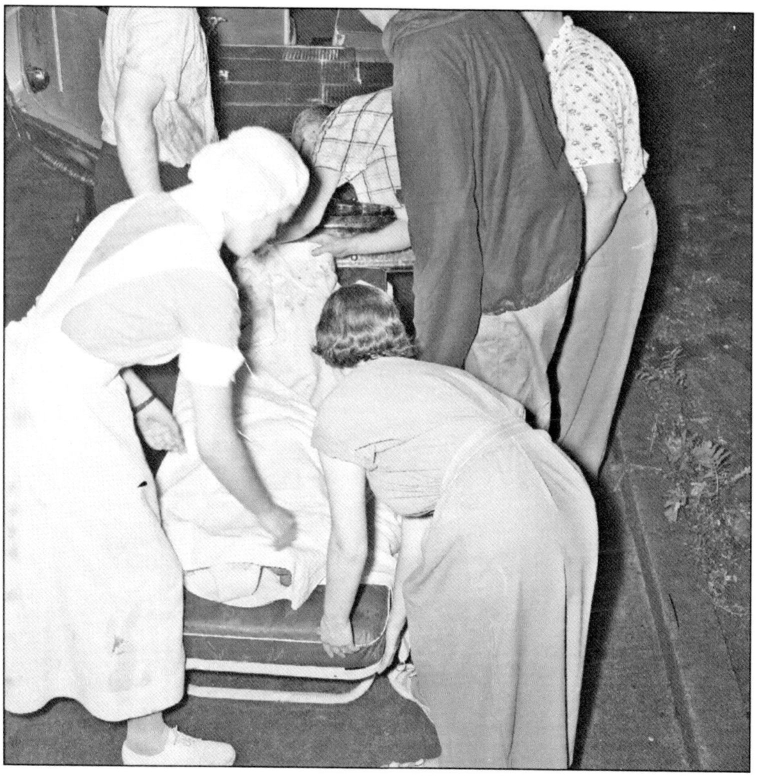

Four men, likely volunteers, and two women, one a nurse, are unloading the body of a victim from the back of a hearse. The victim is covered by a sheet or blanket.

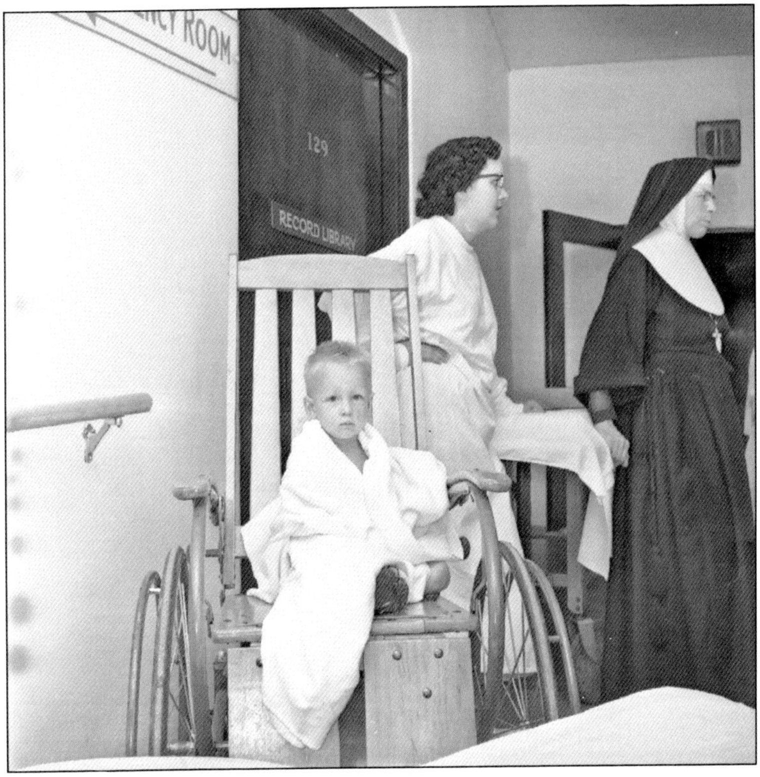

Mike Naylor, age two, waits for his parents, Daryle and Janet Naylor, in a wheelchair at St. John's Hospital. His father, a student at the North Dakota Agricultural College, worked with other volunteers to help bring in the injured, and his mother, a nurse, worked to treat incoming victims. Behind him stand a nun and a nurse.

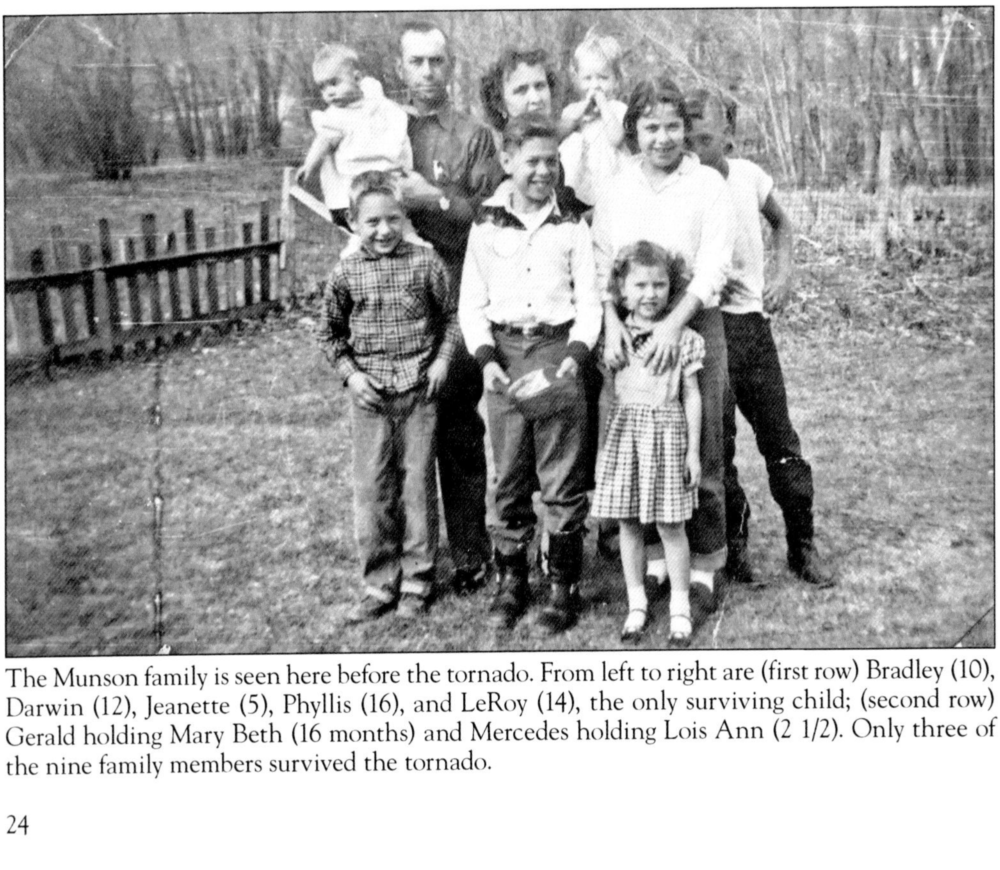

The Munson family is seen here before the tornado. From left to right are (first row) Bradley (10), Darwin (12), Jeanette (5), Phyllis (16), and LeRoy (14), the only surviving child; (second row) Gerald holding Mary Beth (16 months) and Mercedes holding Lois Ann (2 1/2). Only three of the nine family members survived the tornado.

Gerald and Mercedes Munson are pictured after the tornado. Mercedes was suffering from shock. Gerald had been in Bismarck, North Dakota, when the tornado struck, and Mercedes was at work waiting for a coworker to relieve her. According to the *Fargo Forum*, Mercedes was on the phone with her oldest daughter, Phyllis, age 16, when the tornado struck their home.

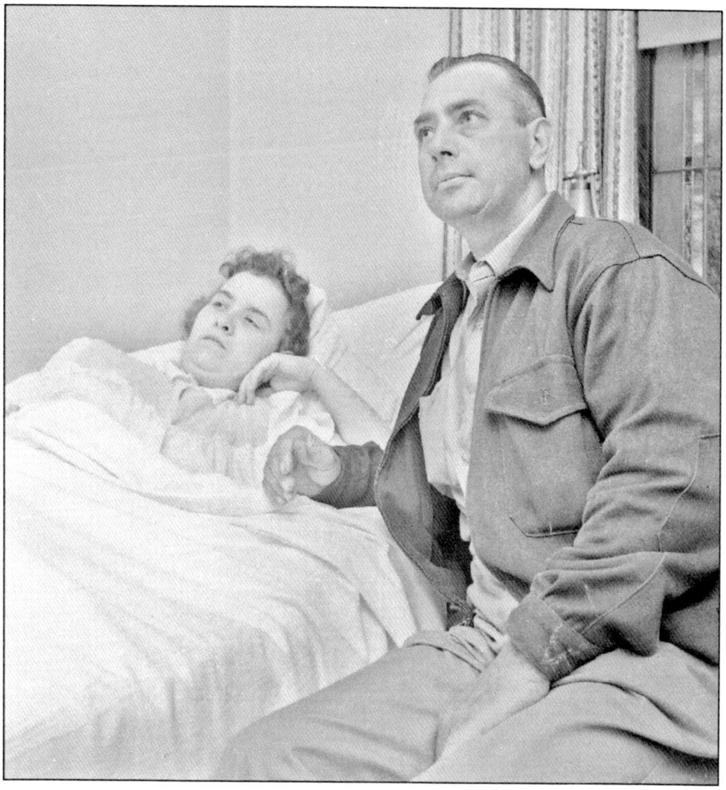

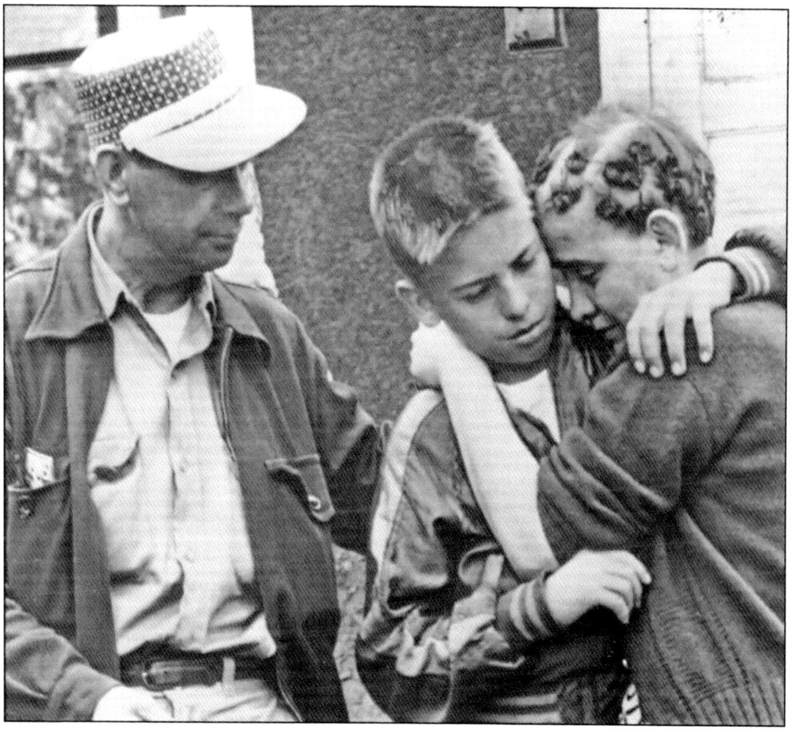

The three remaining Munson family members are pictured here. LeRoy was babysitting at another house when the tornado hit. Mercedes was trying to leave work early to celebrate her birthday with her children. According to reports, Gerald found out about the deaths of his children while reading a newspaper at his hotel in Bismarck.

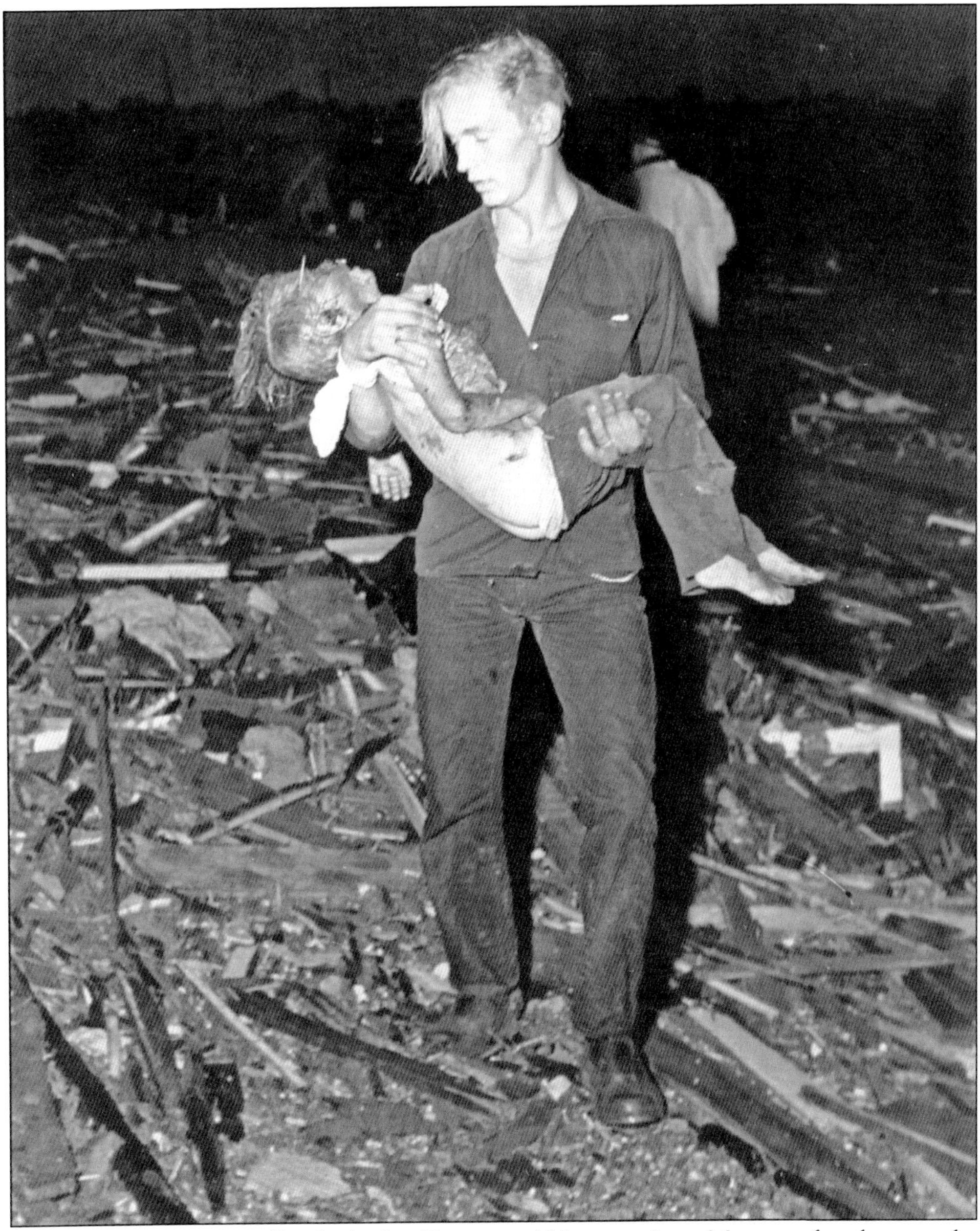

Richard Shaw, age 21, cradles the body of five-year-old Jeanette Irene Munson after the tornado. Shaw, a neighbor of the Munsons, removed her body from the destroyed home. Munson was buried with five of her siblings on June 24, 1957. The Munson family home, in the most devastated neighborhood of Golden Ridge, collapsed on the children during the tornado. Shaw was outside when the tornado hit and survived by holding onto a tree. After the tornado, Shaw tirelessly worked to free victims from the rubble of their homes and pulled out the body of one of Jeanette Munson's siblings as well. Shaw later moved to Montana and died at the age of 33 in 1969. *Fargo Forum* photographer Cal Olson took this photograph, which became the iconic image of the disaster. It symbolized the fragile nature of life. This image helped the *Fargo Forum* win its Pulitzer Prize in 1958.

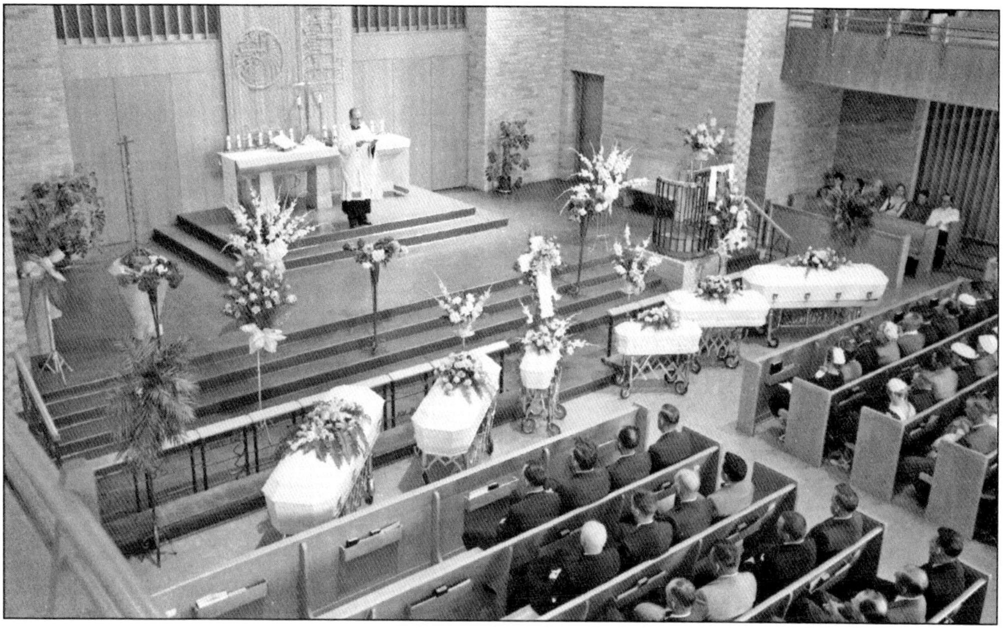

The funeral for Phyllis, Darwin, Bradley, Jeanette, Lois Ann, and Mary Beth Munson was held on June 24, 1957, at Trinity Lutheran Church in Moorhead, Minnesota, where Rev. Oscar Anderson delivered the sermon. There were over 500 friends and relatives in attendance at the funeral, including the mayor and city commissioner of Fargo. LeRoy, age 14, the only surviving Munson child, did not attend the funeral. The children were laid to rest in white coffins, each covered with a large floral arrangement, at Evergreen Cemetery in Moorhead.

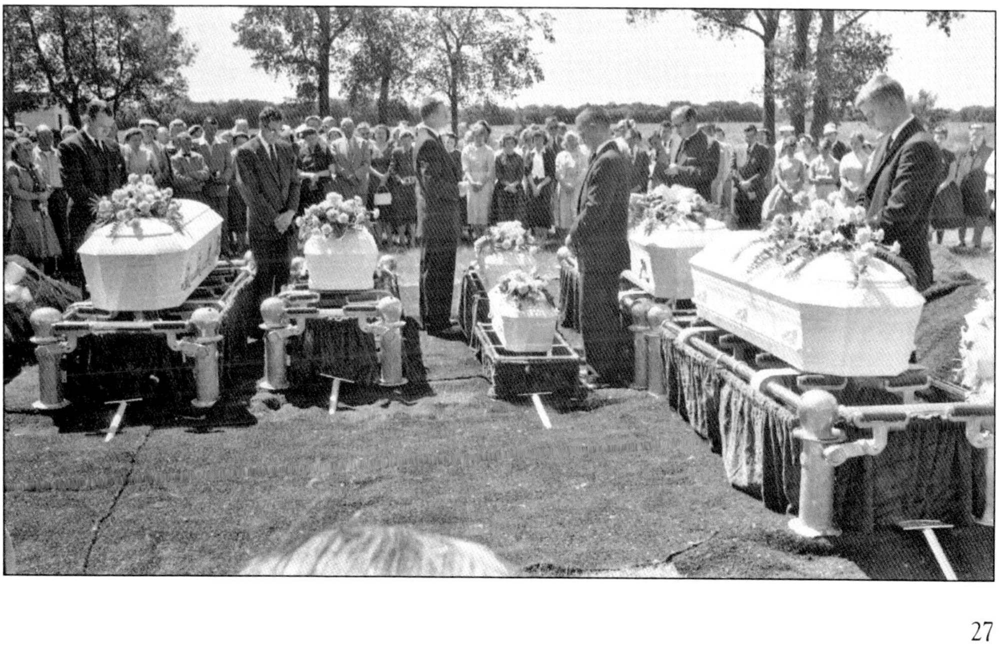

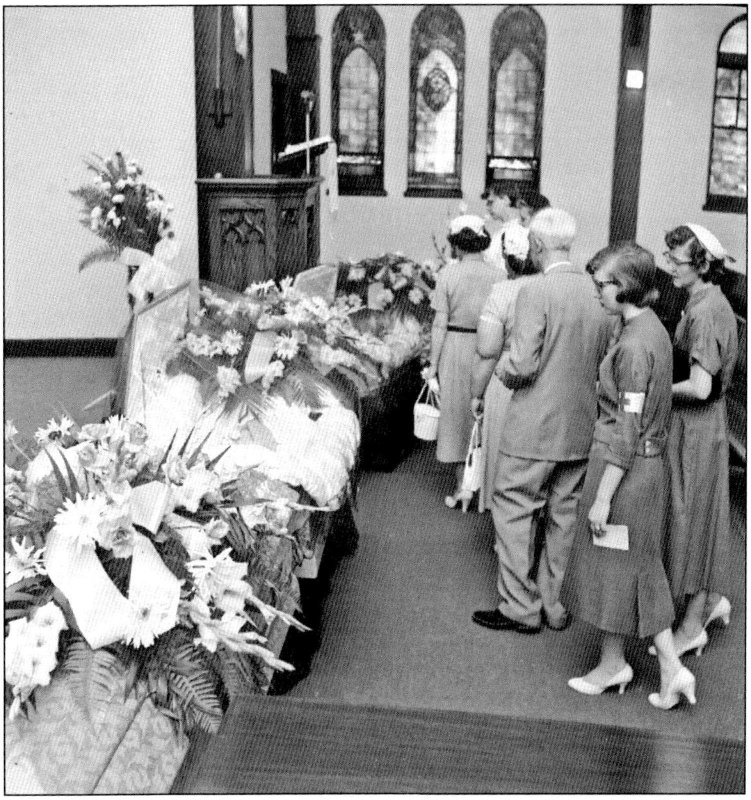

Mourners pass the caskets for Theodore and Clara Theresa Udahl and their adopted daughter Mary Jean, age eight, who died during the tornado. Their home was located at 802 Twenty-seventh Street North in the Golden Ridge neighborhood. The Udahls moved to Fargo in 1950, shortly after getting married. The funeral was held at Olivet Lutheran Church because Golden Ridge Lutheran Church was destroyed. The family was buried in Velva, North Dakota.

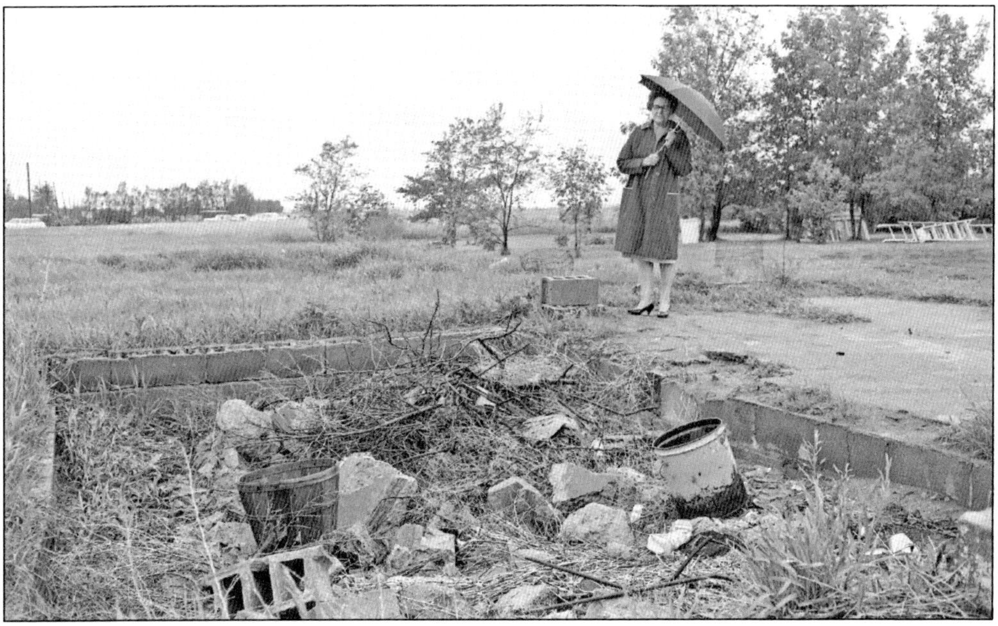

Josephine Albertson stands beside the remains of the William Farris home in 1967. According to the *Fargo Forum*, Donald and Betty Titgen lived in a trailer in the backyard of this home at 715 Twenty-ninth Street North with their two small daughters. Donald was killed, and Betty was critically injured and died in 1960 having never woken from a coma; both daughters survived.

This view is looking southeast from the 2600 block of Twenty-sixth Street North in the Golden Ridge neighborhood. The home of Laura Schoenherr, age 69, was located in this area. She lived in a trailer and sought shelter in her daughter's home next door. The home was completely destroyed, and Schoenherr suffered injuries resulting in an amputated leg. She died in the hospital a few weeks later, on July 16.

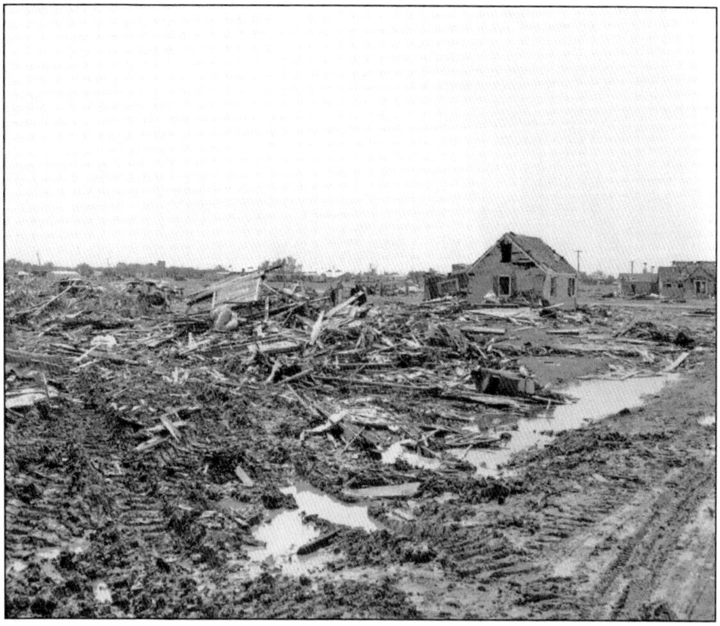

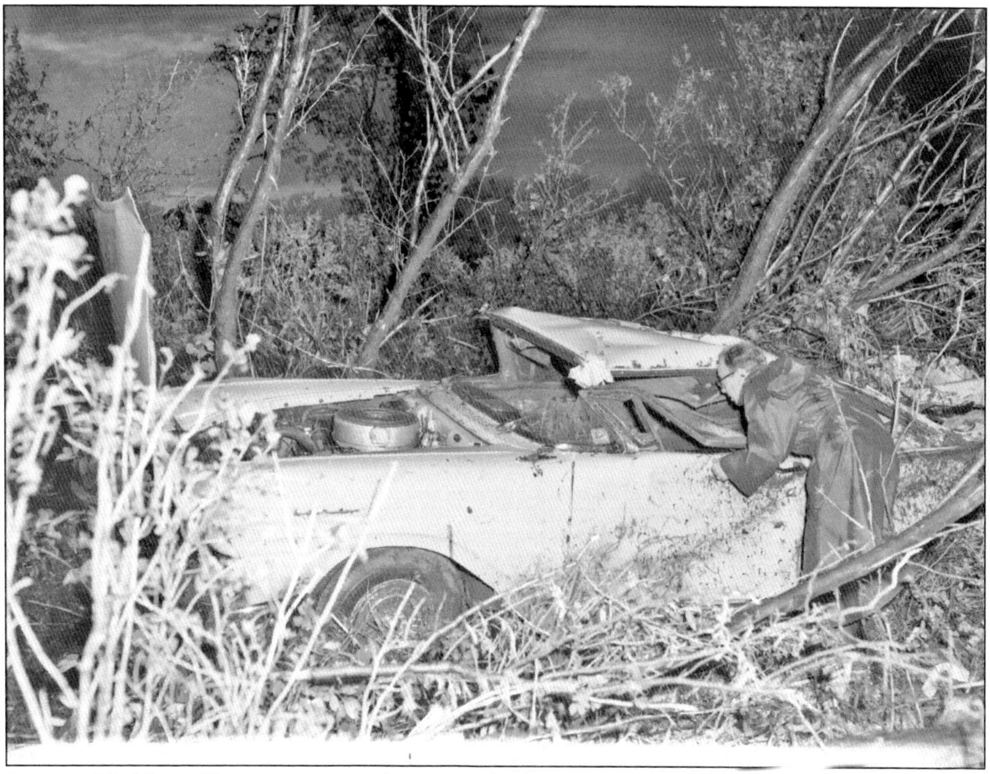

Jerry and LuVerne Davenport were driving with their two young children, Kathleen, age two, and Jon, seven months, on Oak Street when they saw the tornado approaching. While taking cover in a ditch, the tornado tore Jon from his mother's arms. Miraculously, he was brought to the hospital by a stranger and survived brain surgery. He was eventually reunited with his family. Their automobile, pictured here, was found by the golf course.

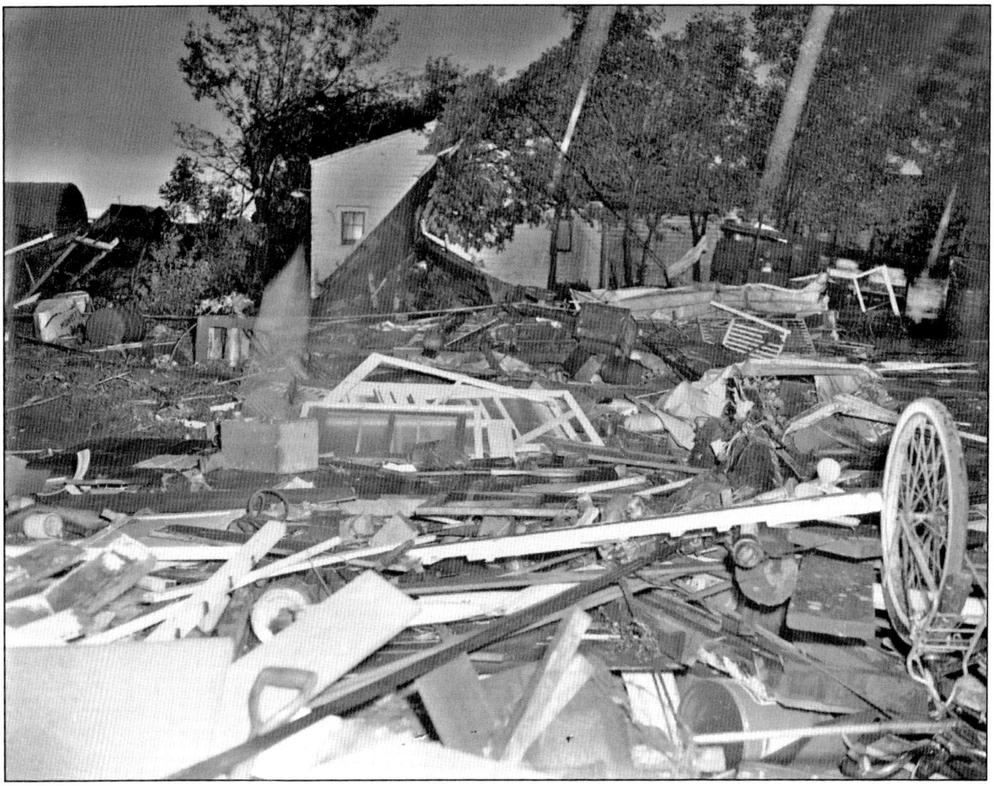

The debris from Clinton Anderson's garage at 2009 Seventh Avenue North is seen here. Half a block away, Jerry and Mary Bala and their children John, age two, and Jerry Junior, seven months, were home when the tornado hit their house. The Balas were thrown roughly 20 yards from their living room. Mary received a serious head injury and Jerry was badly bruised, but the children were not injured. Everyone was brought to the hospital.

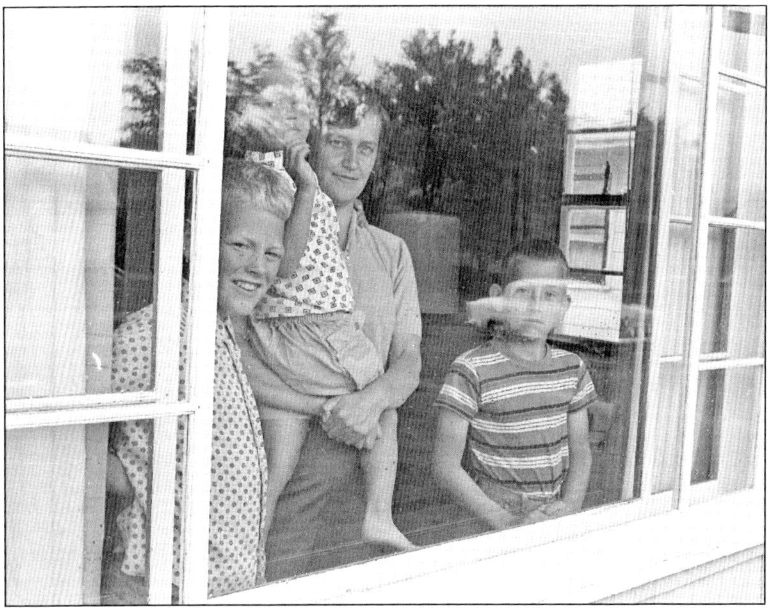

The Bala family rebuilt their home at 729 Twentieth Street North shortly after the tornado, making sure to add a basement. Mary Bala stands in her new living room with an older John and Jerry Junior 10 years after the tornado struck. She holds Jimmy, age four, who was born six years after the tornado.

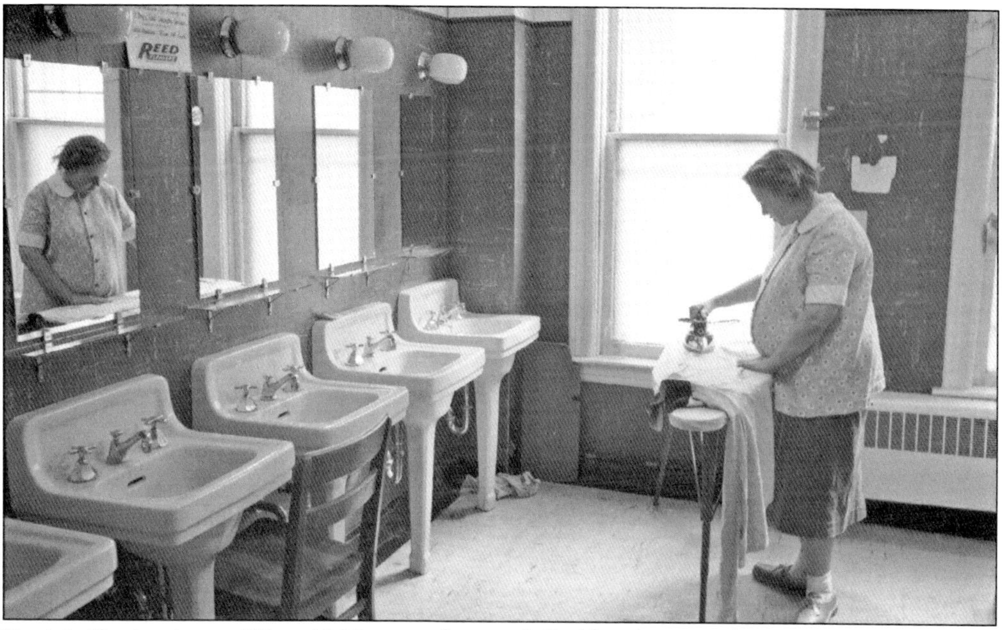

Patricia Ferris, sister of Donald Titgen, who was killed by the tornado, irons clothes while in a bathroom at Concordia College in Moorhead, Minnesota, where she and her family were relocated after the tornado. The Red Cross estimated between 1,300 and 1,400 people were displaced and in need of relocation. Concordia College provided dorm rooms for nine families, totaling 37 people.

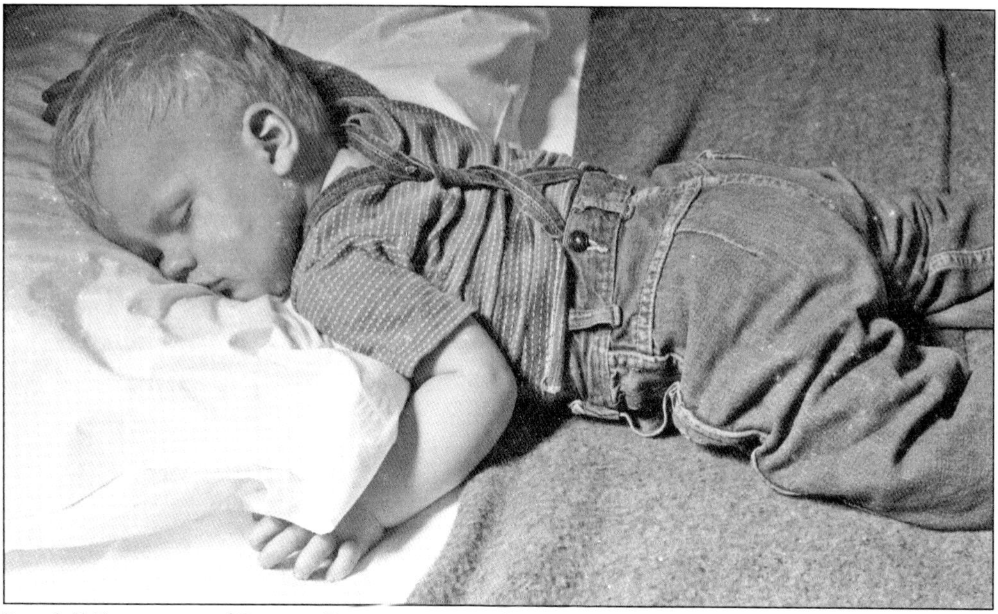

Randall Ferris, son of Patricia Ferris, is pictured peacefully napping on a dormitory bed while staying at Concordia College in Moorhead with his family after the tornado. When the tornado hit, Patricia was babysitting her two nieces, the daughters of her brother Donald Titgen. She gathered the children in a car and fled Golden Ridge.

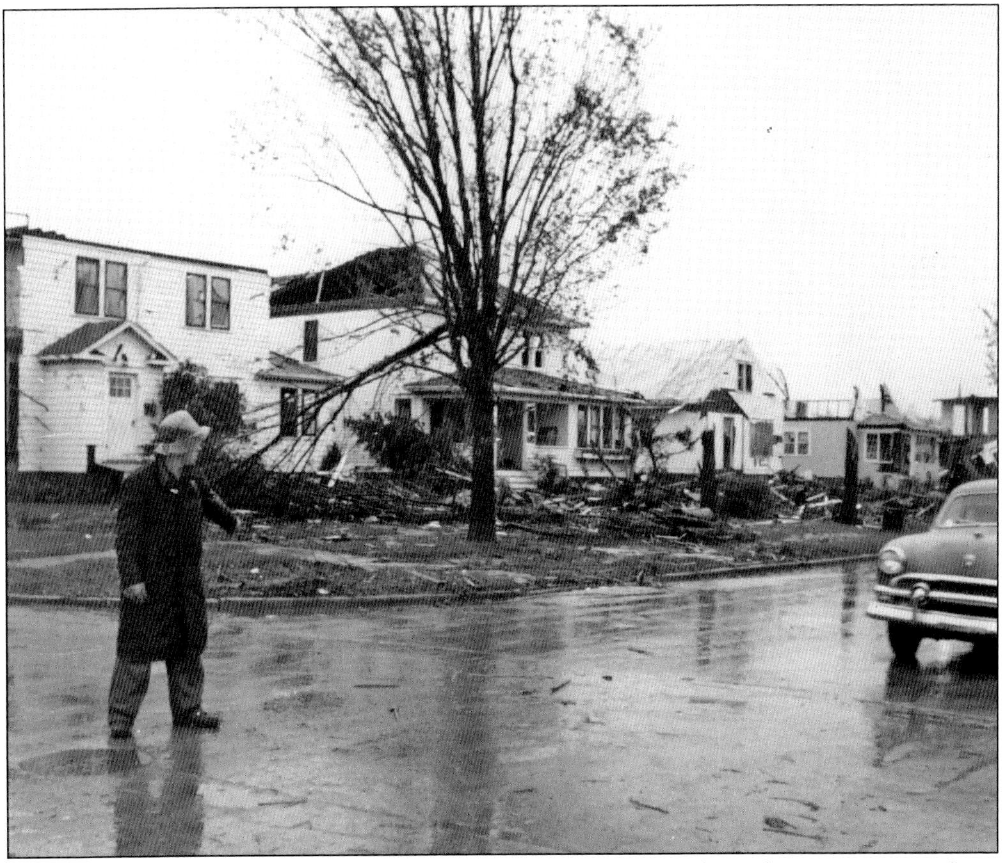

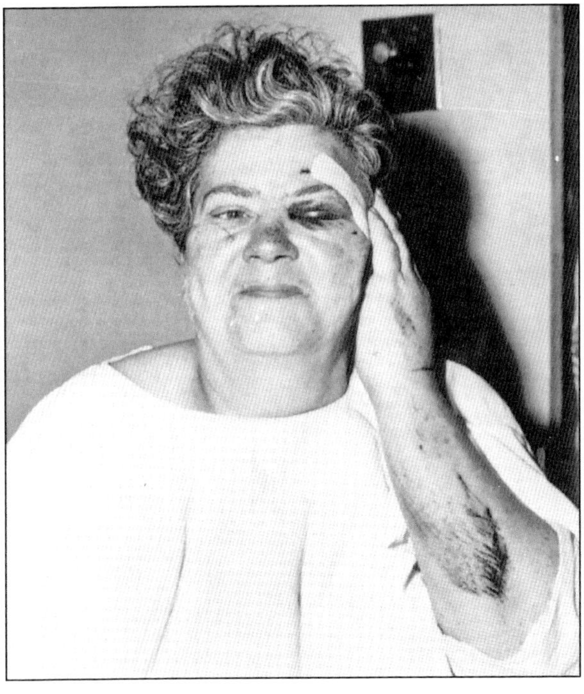

A man dressed in a raincoat and hat directs traffic at Tenth Street North and Thirteenth Avenue North. Richard Leverson and his mother were driving home when the tornado approached. They sought shelter at the third house from the left, but there was no answer. After the tornado passed, they found themselves trapped under debris at the second house from the left with no memory of what happened.

Jeanette Smith, who lived at 1226 Eleventh Street North with her sister Ella Harvey, touches her injured, swollen eye after the tornado. The large scrapes on her arm and hand, as well as some on her face, can also be seen. She was taken to St. Luke's Hospital to be treated. This photograph was taken the day after the tornado struck Fargo.

Three

DESTRUCTION

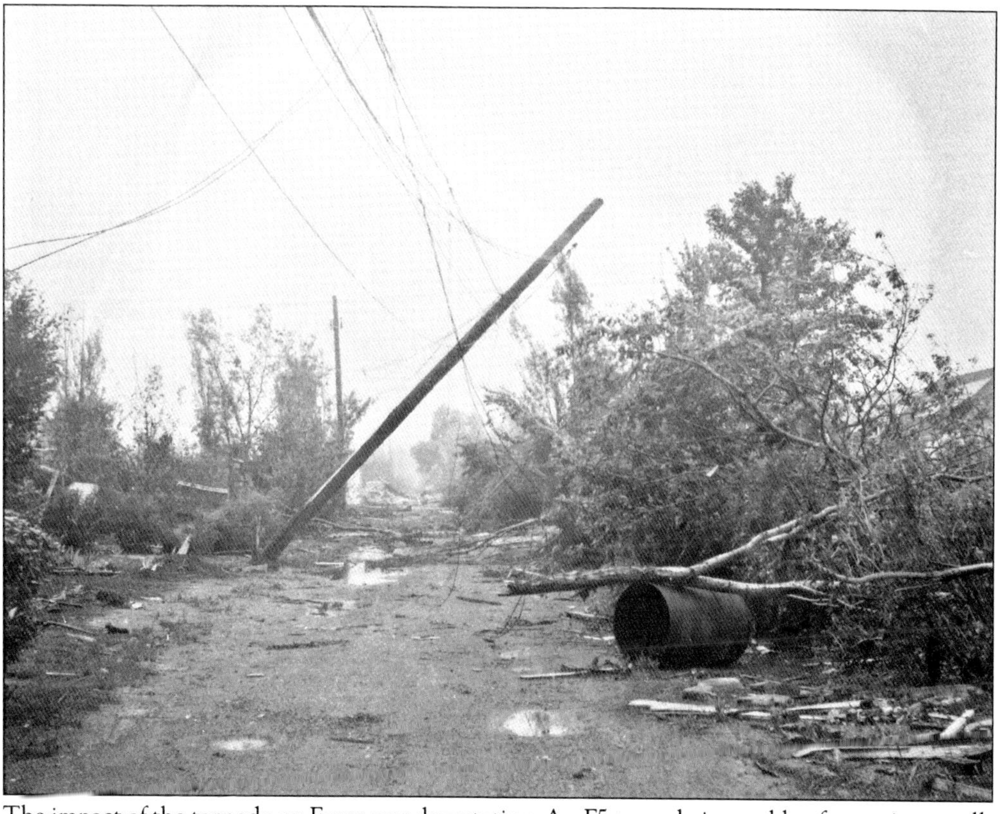

The impact of the tornado on Fargo was devastating. An F5 tornado is capable of sweeping a well-built house completely off its foundation, throwing a car over 300 feet, and debarking trees. This photograph gives a good indication of the power and force generated by the Fargo tornado.

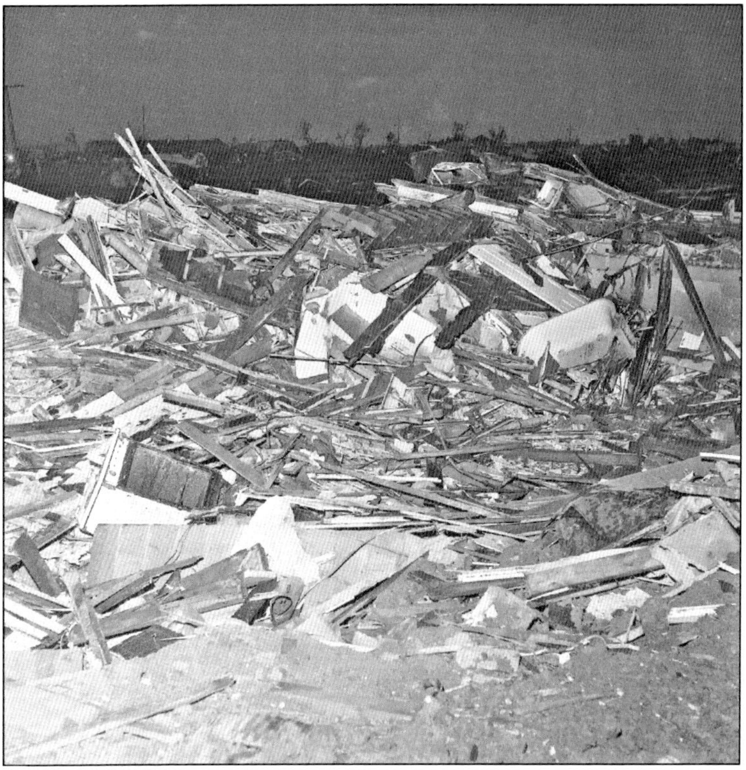

Golden Ridge was the first neighborhood to be hit and was completely devastated. This home was at the corner of Eighth Street North and Twenty-sixth Street North. A stove and bathtub sit within the rubble. The horizon line in the background, where a vibrant neighborhood once stood, is eerily empty. Many residents survived by fleeing in their cars. This photograph was likely taken shortly after the tornado.

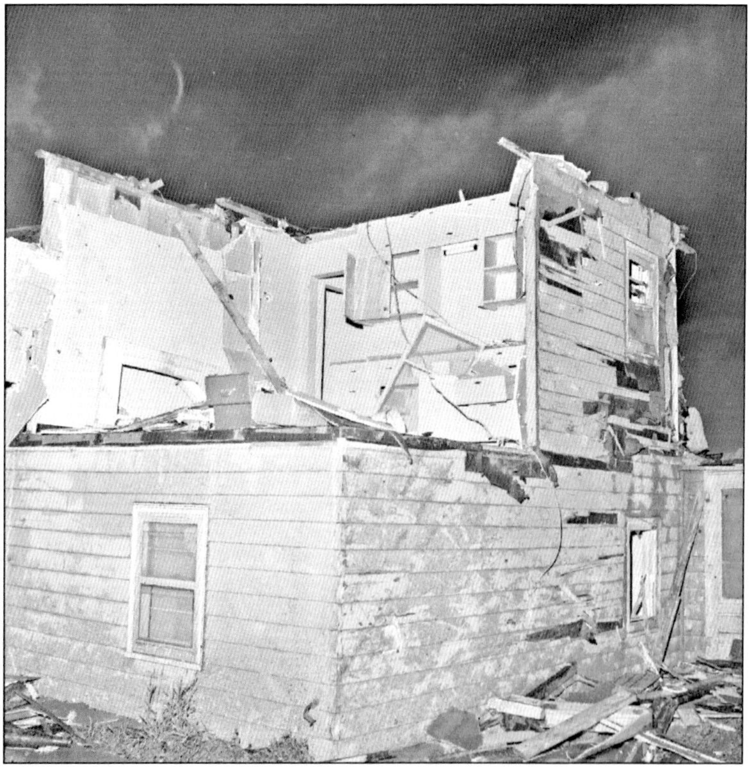

Pictured is a two-story home in the 800 block of Twenty-seventh Street North in the Golden Ridge neighborhood. The corner exterior walls of the second floor are missing, exposing a room and its cabinets. The roof is missing, and there is debris littered around the ground.

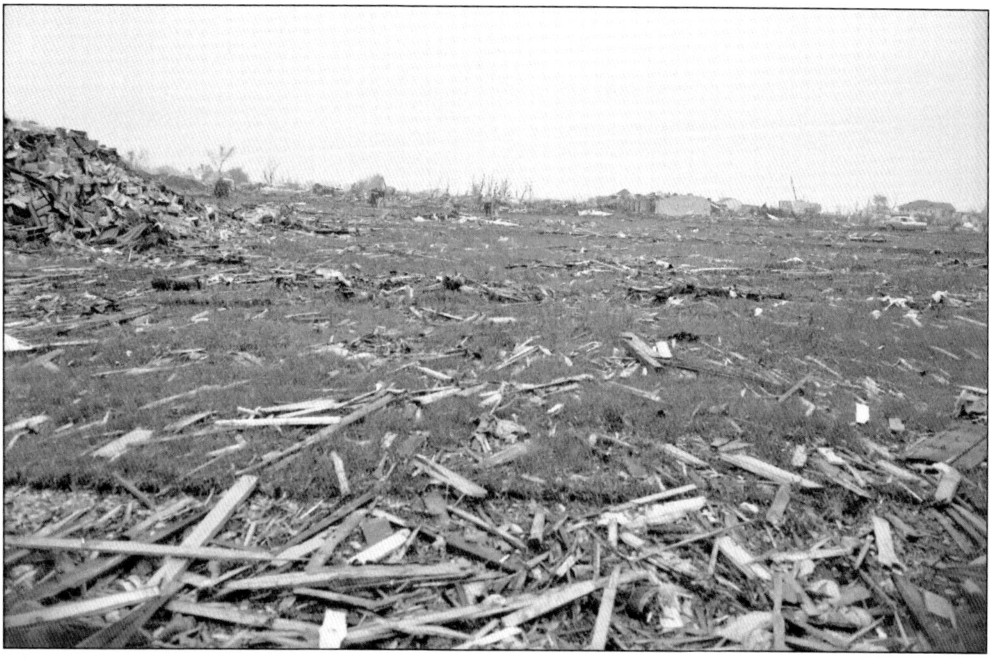

This view of the Golden Ridge neighborhood is looking west from Twenty-fifth Street North, between Seventh Avenue North and Eighth Avenue North. Debris is visible across the open area, with a large pile on the left. The remains of the Golden Ridge Lutheran Church are visible in the distance at center right. This photograph was taken near where the Munson family lived.

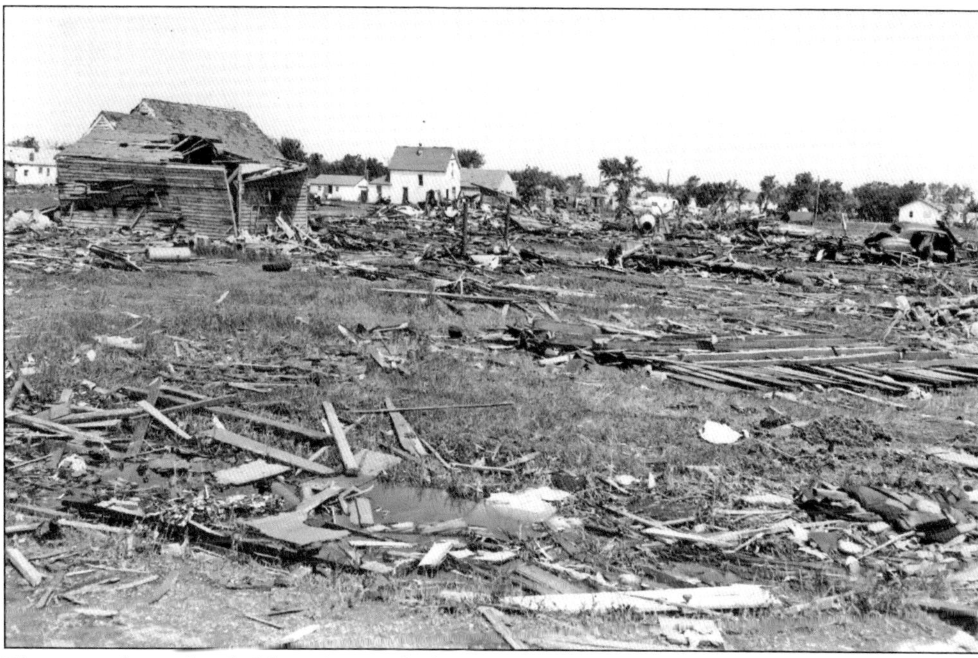

This area is littered with debris. A severely damaged home is visible at left, with unscathed houses in the distance. A damaged automobile is visible among the debris at right. The view is looking northwest from the middle of the 2500 block of Eighth Avenue North in the Golden Ridge neighborhood. At left is the back of 805 Twenty-sixth Street North.

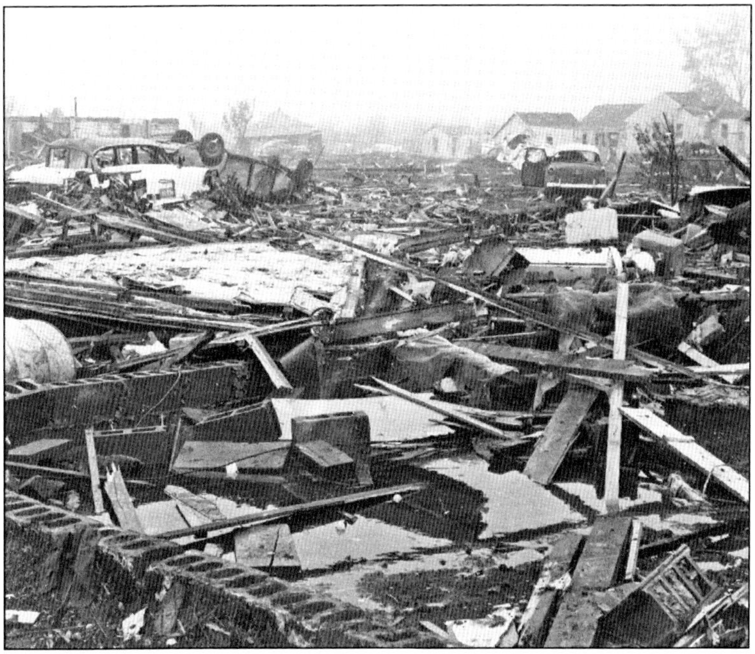

The remains of multiple homes in the 800 block of Twenty-seventh Street North in the Golden Ridge neighborhood are pictured here. In the foreground, there appears to be a cinder block foundation without a house resting on top of it. Three cars are in the background, and one is upside down. This house was close to the Udahl family home.

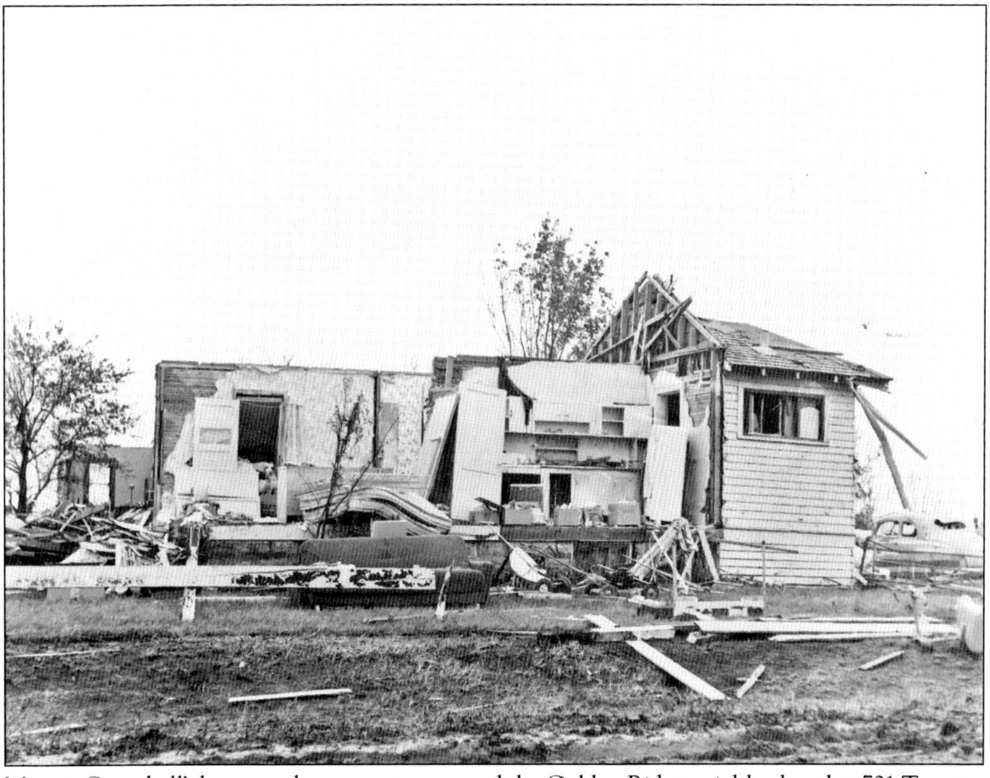

Minnie Campbell's home and grocery store served the Golden Ridge neighborhood at 701 Twenty-seventh Street North. Days after the tornado, the smells from rotting food in Campbell's Grocery and nearby homes may have attracted vermin or other pests, which concerned city officials. The roof and two exterior walls are missing, exposing the inside of the home.

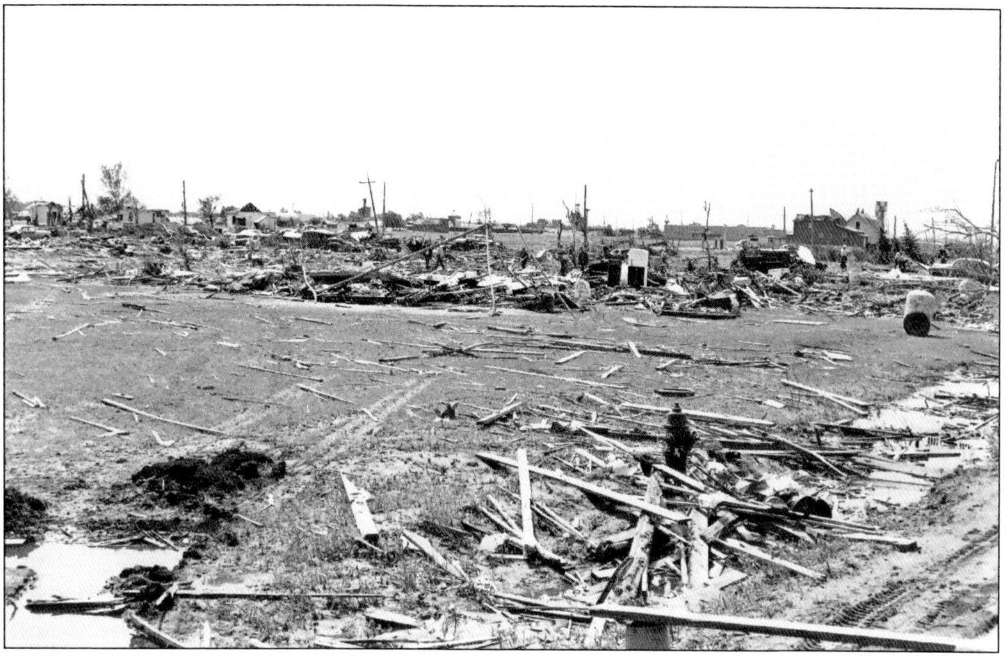

This view is looking across a landscape devastated by the tornado at the intersection of Eighth Avenue North and Twenty-eighth Street North. At center, a bent swing set and playground equipment are visible among the debris. The bulldozer in the distance indicates that cleanup has begun. This was near Golden Ridge School, which was also destroyed.

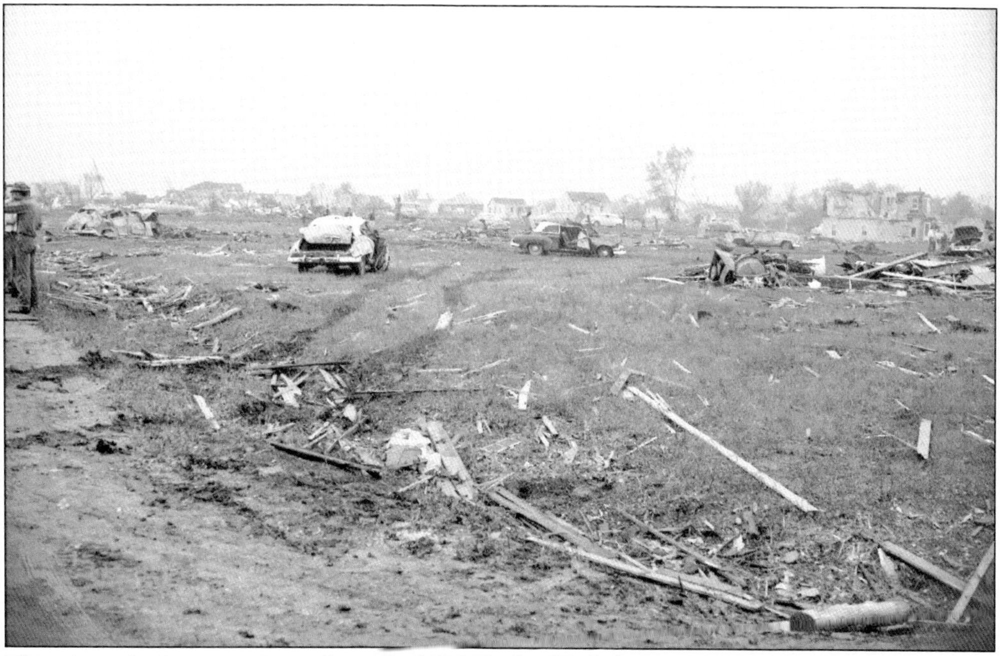

This view is looking northwest from the 2600 block of Eighth Avenue North in the Golden Ridge neighborhood. A. Gordon More of north Fargo was having his car repaired by W.P. Graffis, a resident of Golden Ridge. Nine days after the tornado, More was still searching for his missing car, though parts had been found near Graffis's garage.

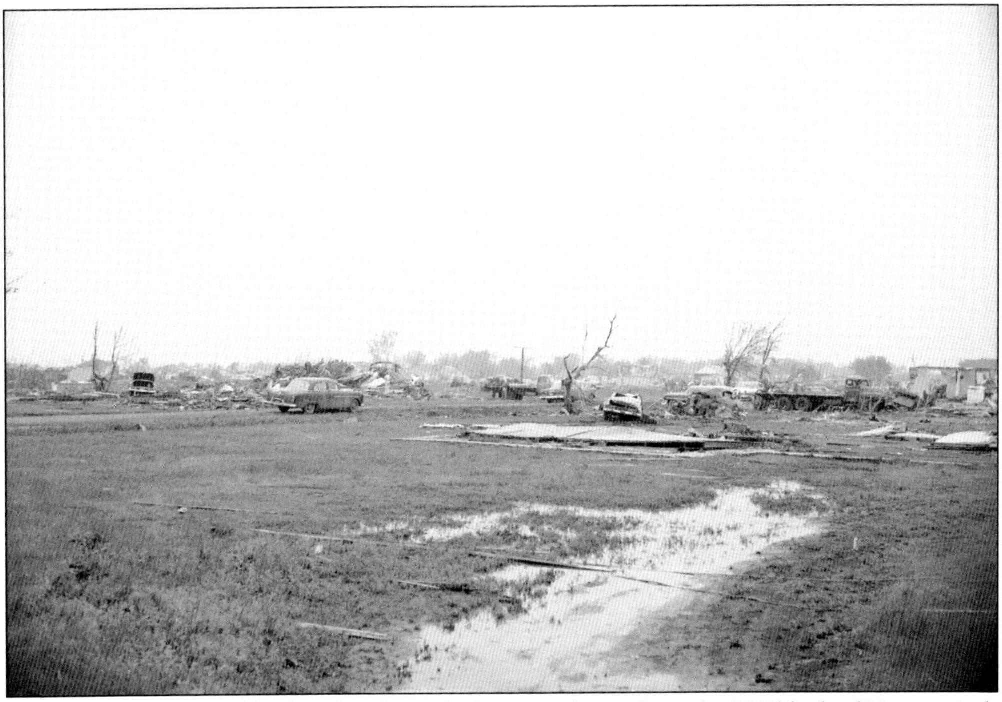

The Golden Ridge neighborhood is shown looking northwest from the 700 block of Twenty-sixth Street North. The ruins of houses and piles of rubble, as well as damaged automobiles and trucks, are seen in the background. In the distance, people are clearing the debris. A headline in the *Fargo Forum* on June 21, 1957, reported "Golden Ridge Gone" due to all the homes that were lost.

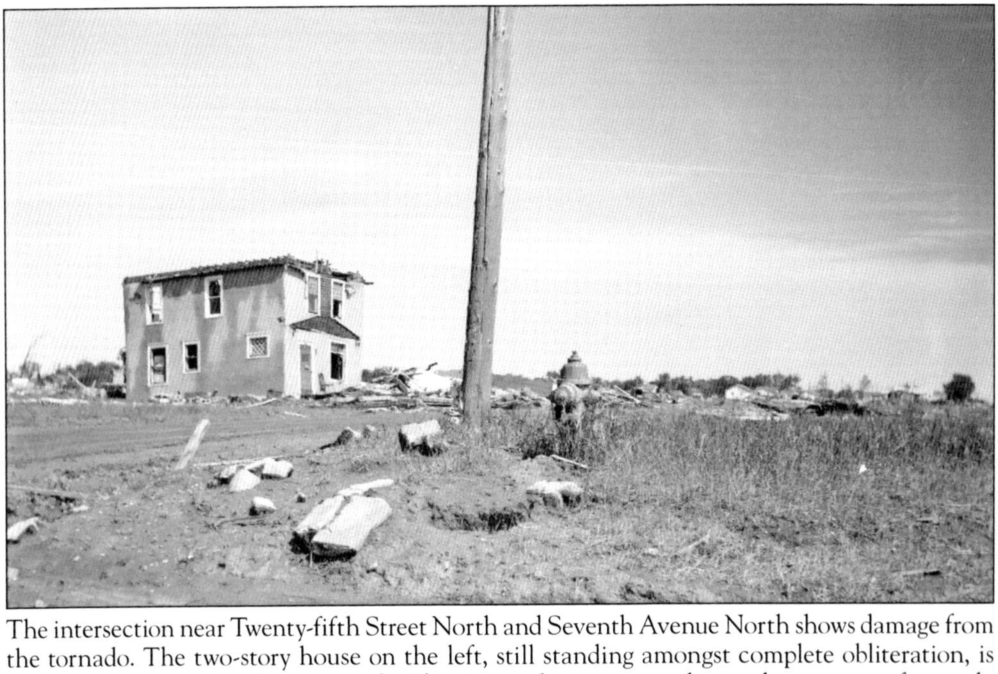

The intersection near Twenty-fifth Street North and Seventh Avenue North shows damage from the tornado. The two-story house on the left, still standing amongst complete obliteration, is missing both its roof and front porch. This image demonstrates the random nature of tornado damage. In all the debris, a utility pole and a fire hydrant can also be seen.

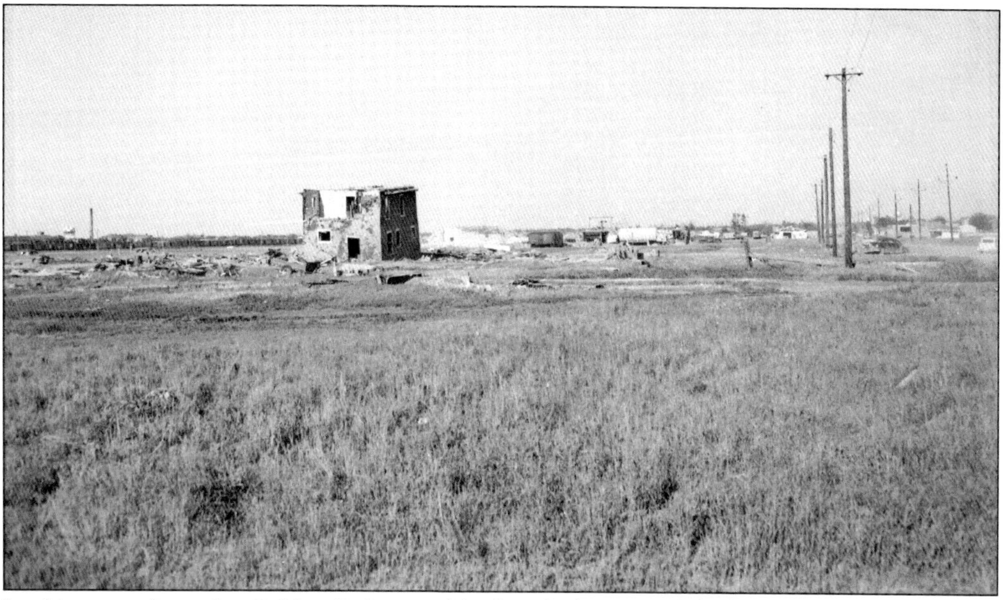

Looking east from the Golden Ridge neighborhood, the rear of the home at 704 Twenty-fifth Street North, from the previous photograph, is visible at center left. A row of utility poles are at right, and some more homes or buildings are in the distance. This view looks toward an industrial area that was hit by the tornado after it devastated Golden Ridge.

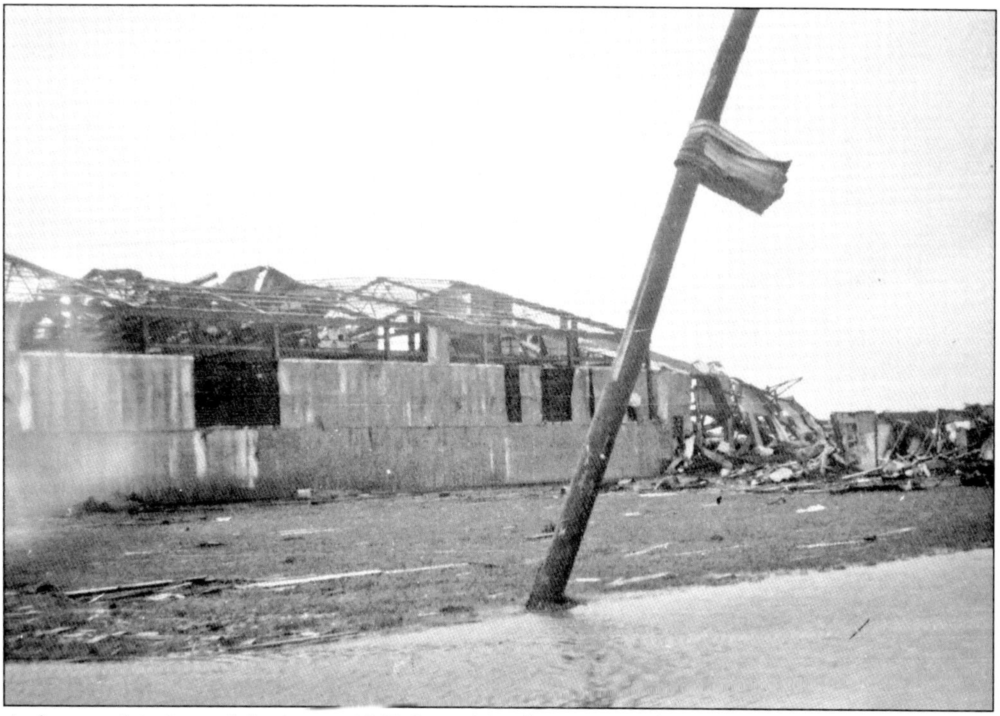

A destroyed industrial facility at 1817 Great Northern Drive, belonging to Peavey Fertilizer, is shown after the tornado. The corrugated metal roof was peeled off the building, exposing the roof beams. Part of the building at right has been badly damaged. In the foreground, a utility pole is slanted and has a sheet of metal bent around it from the extreme force of the winds.

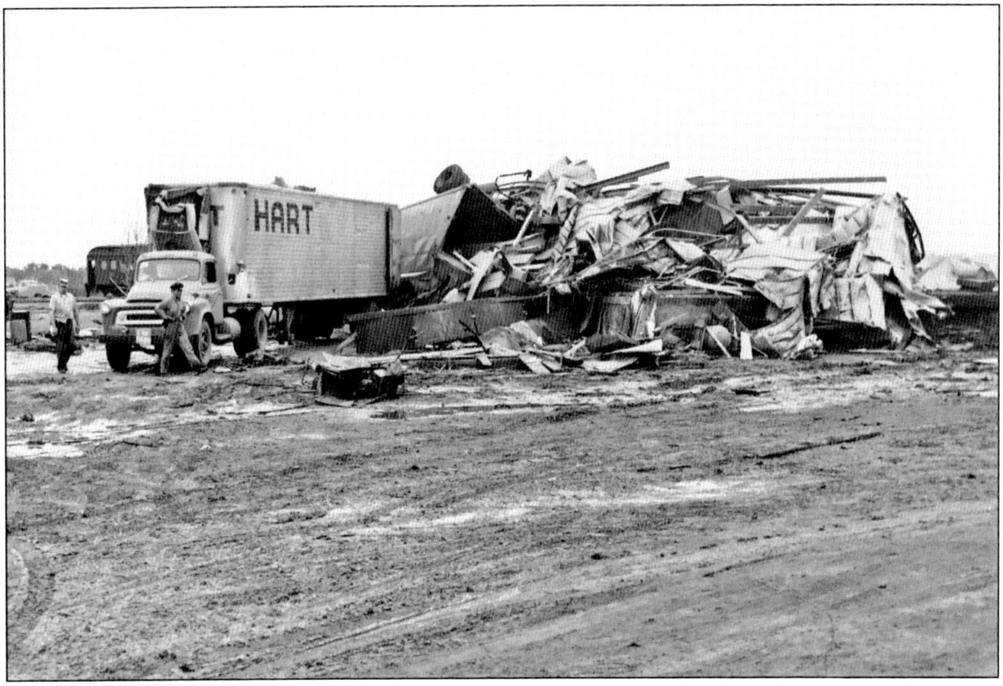

At center is a ruined warehouse with a truck parked to the left. Two men are visible by the truck. Hart Motor Express Inc. was at 715 Seventeenth Street North. The company, based out of Minneapolis, Minnesota, lost almost all of its trucks and sustained $160,000 worth of damage.

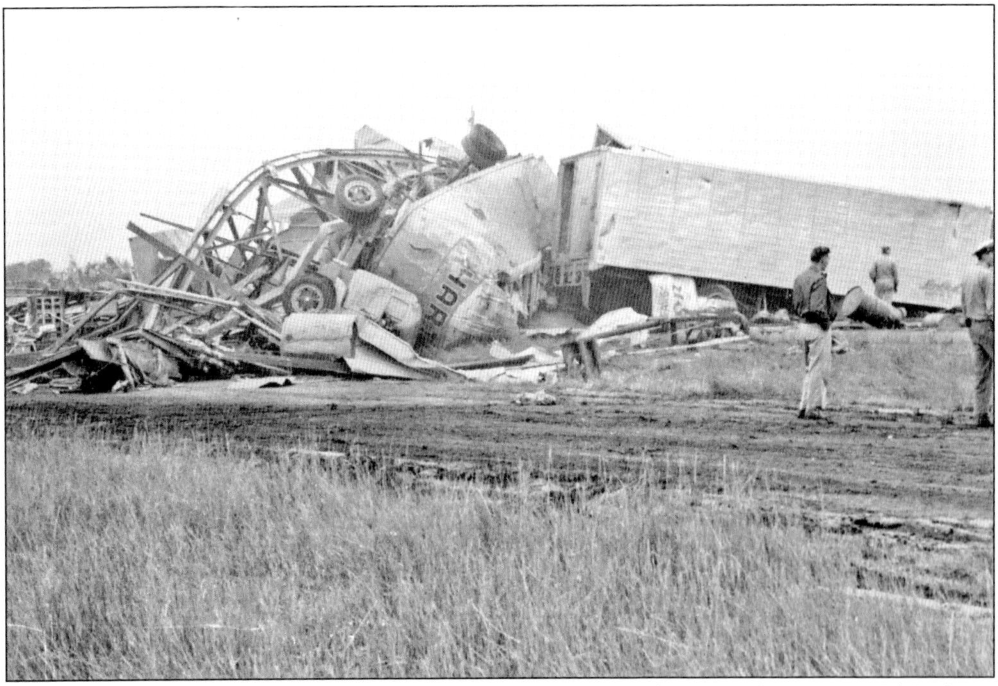

Hart Motor Express was only out of business for half a day. The general manager, Ed Rydeen, secured quarters in the Larson Building on First Avenue North, and smaller trucks were loaded in Minneapolis. Staff sent letters to customers to let them know they were still open for business.

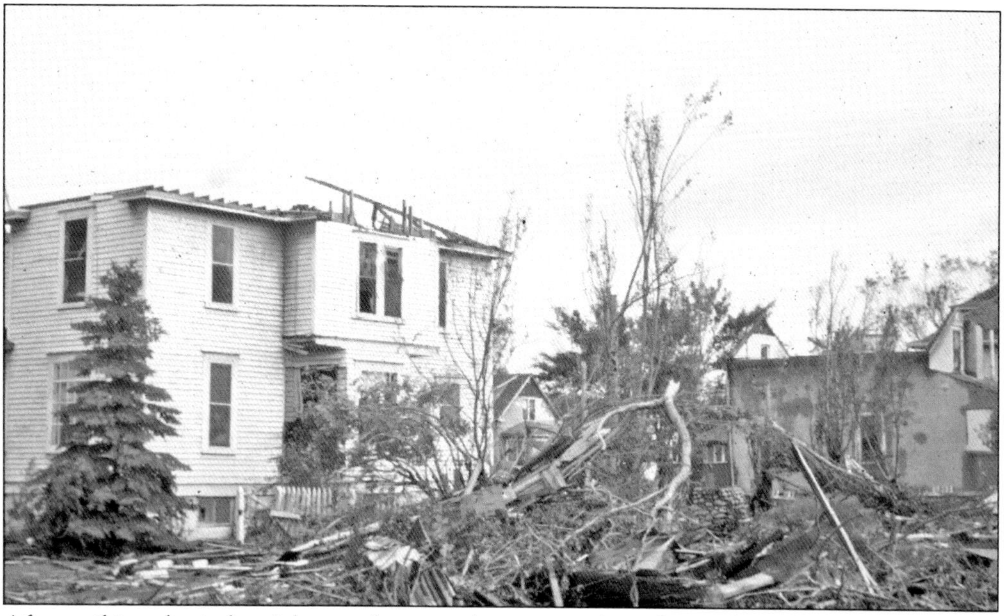

After striking the industrial area, the tornado continued northeast through Fargo, hitting the Roosevelt neighborhood south of the North Dakota Agricultural College campus. This two-story home at 1375 Tenth Avenue North shows significant damage. It is missing its roof, and some windows appear to be broken. The foreground shows broken branches and other debris. The home at right appears to be missing its roof.

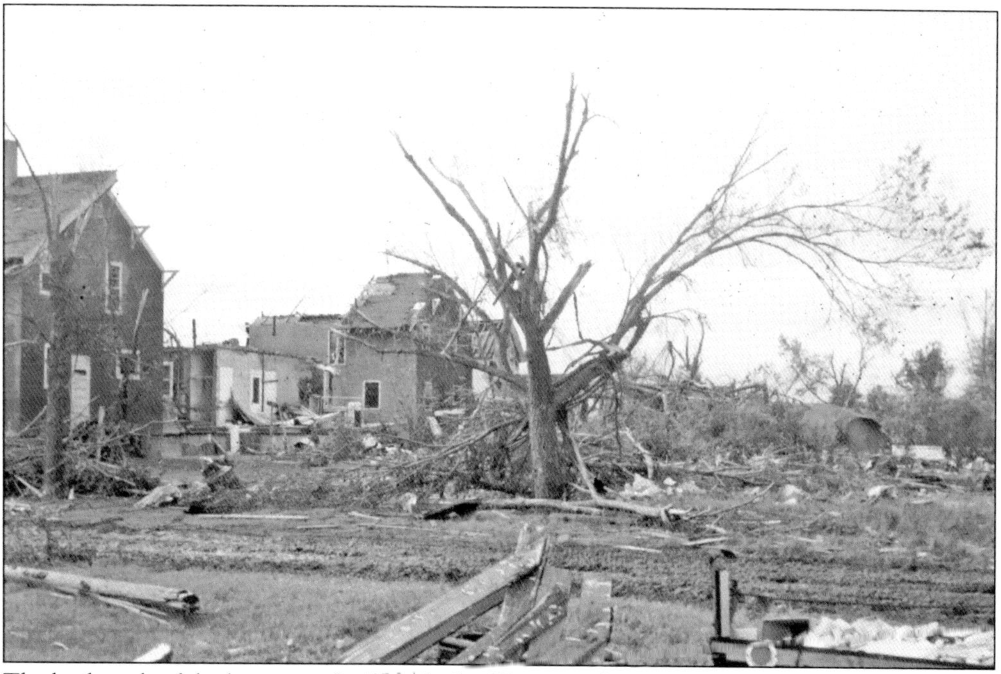

The backyards of the homes in the 900 block of Fourteenth Street North are seen here. The tree left standing at center appears to be missing many branches and leaves. The first home on the left looks to be missing half of its roof, the next home is missing its entire roof, and the home in the background is also missing half of its roof.

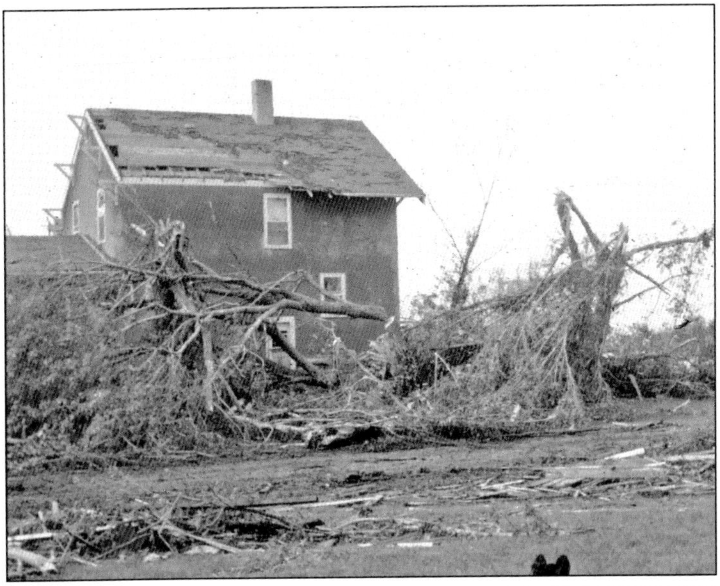

Pictured is the north side of a wooden two-story home at 920 Fourteenth Street North. The roof is showing extensive damage, the trees in the foreground have broken limbs and some are completely uprooted, and the ground is littered with debris. Photographer Frank Meyer took this picture from his yard. He wrote on the side of the photograph, "Anderson Home."

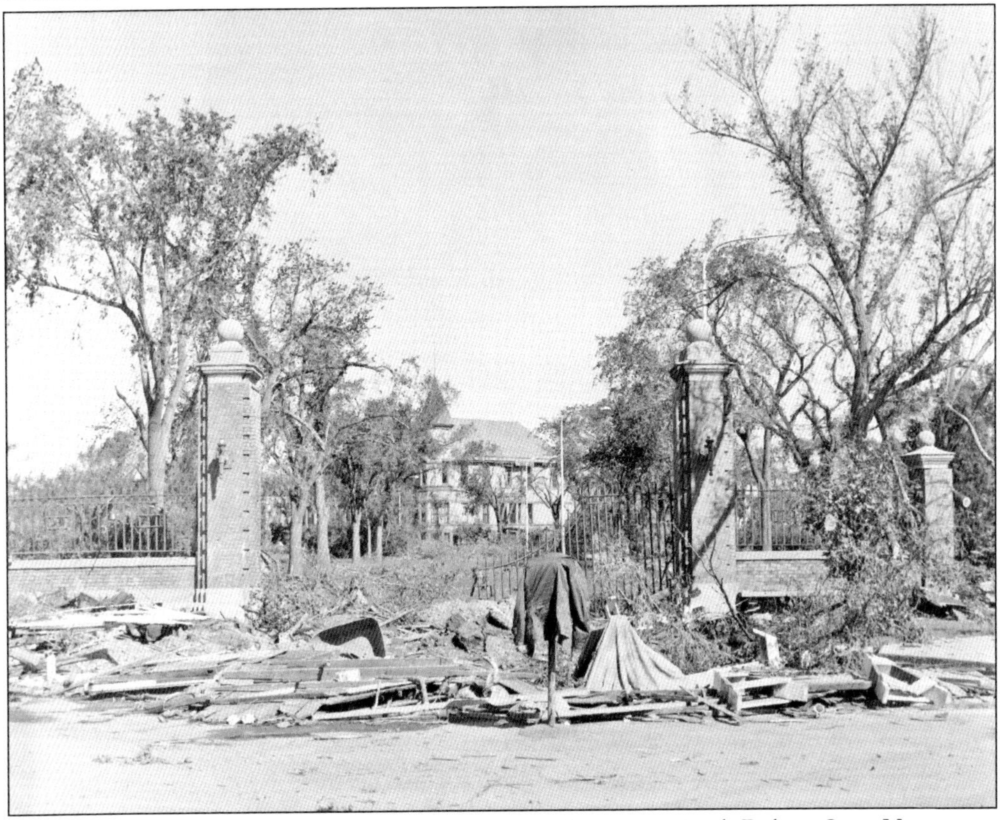

The entrance gates for North Dakota Agricultural College, now North Dakota State University, on the corner of Thirteenth Street North, now University Drive and Twelfth Avenue North, are pictured after the tornado. Old Main is visible in the background, while in the foreground there are tree limbs and other wood debris from the tornado. The gates, originally constructed in 1912 and rebuilt after the tornado, are a landmark welcoming students to campus.

An uprooted tree lies on the campus of North Dakota Agricultural College. In the background, Old Main is visible with no major damage. Old Main was the first permanent building on campus when it was constructed in 1891. The tornado spared most of campus, only hitting the southeast corner. Fortunately, no one on campus was hurt.

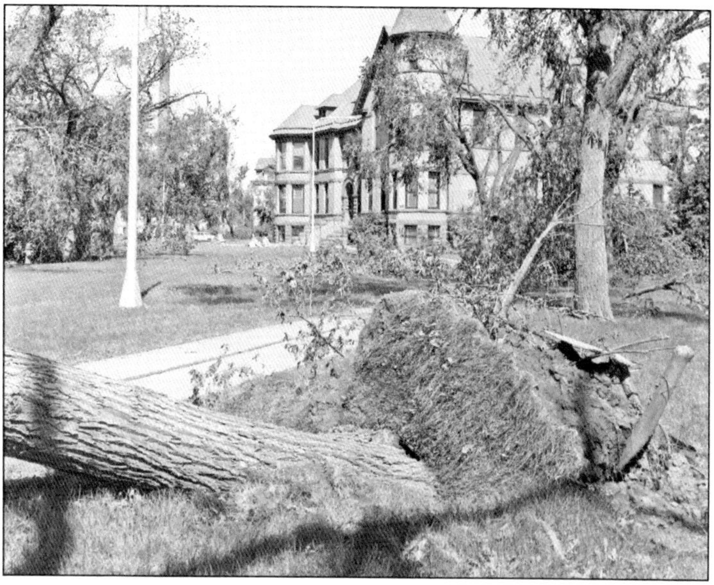

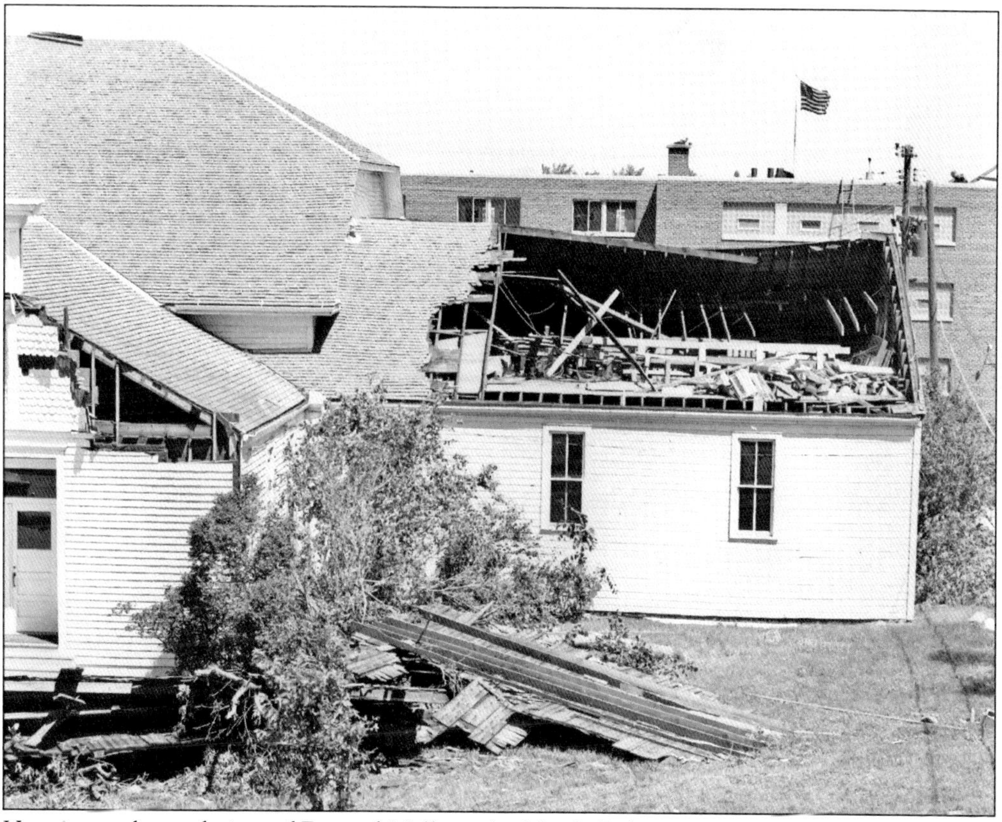

Here is an elevated view of Festival Hall on the North Dakota Agricultural College campus. Extensive damage to the roof can be seen, with part of it lying in the grass on the side of the building. The campus was hosting a Future Farmers of America convention. Moments before the tornado struck, the nearly 600 high school students in attendance were forced to seek shelter in the basement of the campus library.

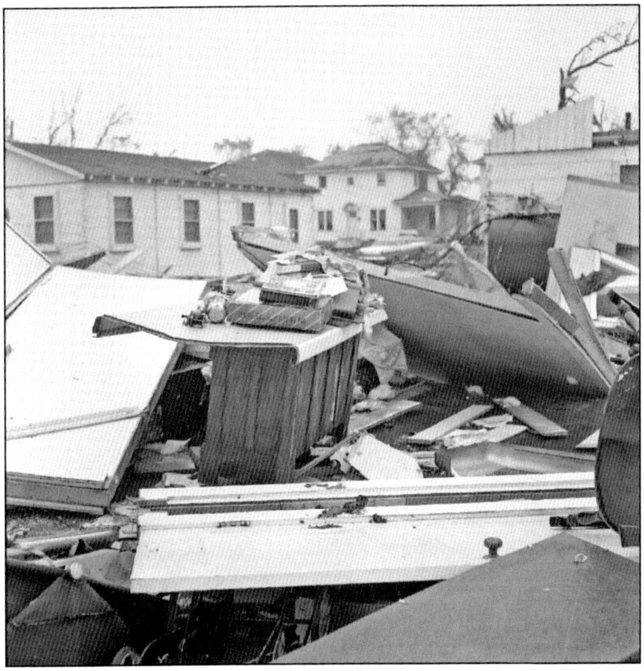

After World War II, there was a lack of homes for veterans and faculty. In 1947, on property between Twelfth Avenue North and Thirteenth Avenue North, 30 bungalows were built for faculty, which were nicknamed Silver City. All of them were destroyed by the tornado. During the storm, the residents of these homes took shelter in the nearby North Dakota School of Religion building.

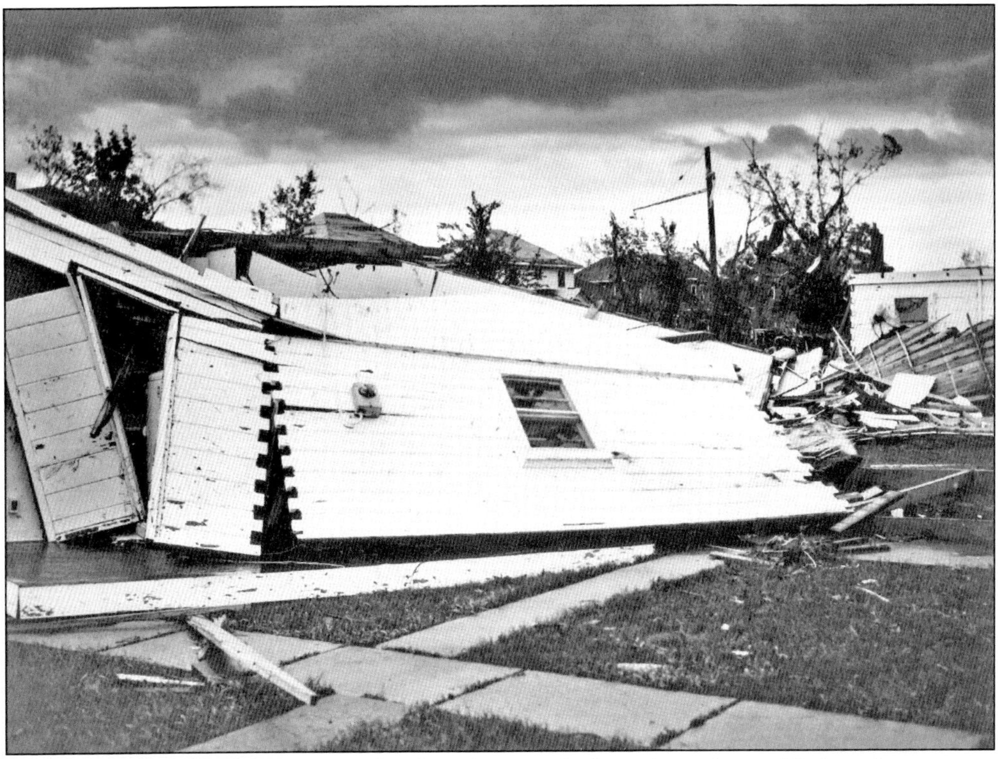

Likely taken shortly after the tornado, this photograph shows how the prefabricated temporary homes in Silver City were never meant to be permanent. This bungalow was literally torn apart at the seams. The faculty housing was not rebuilt, and the area became a parking lot between the current Alumni Center and the Bison Turf.

A broken and tangled utility pole hangs on the side of a Silver City bungalow. Other damaged homes are seen in the background, as well as pieces of debris on the lawn in the foreground. Electricity and telephone lines were cut in the area, so temporary telephones were installed around north Fargo to give residents phone access.

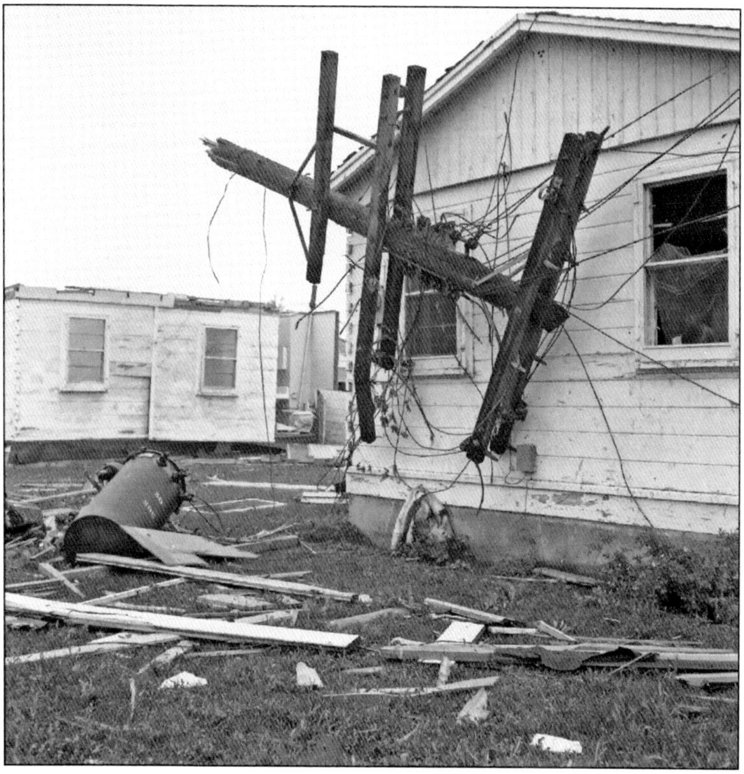

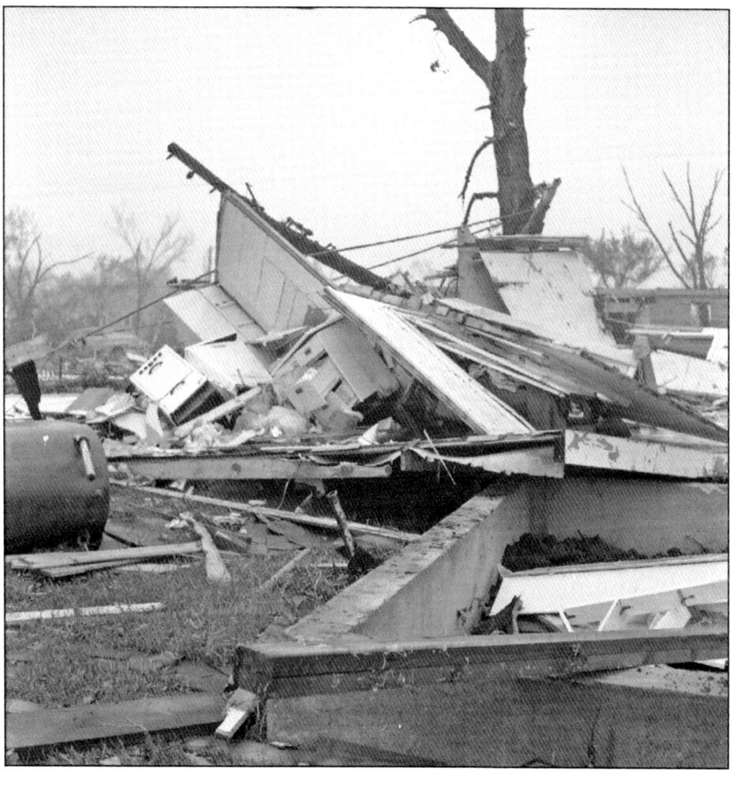

Another destroyed bungalow at Silver City is pictured here. The ground is littered with debris, including an oven, a dresser, and other household items. On the left there appears to be an oil heater tank, and at right is a foundation. The residents of Silver City had to flee because the bungalows did not have basements.

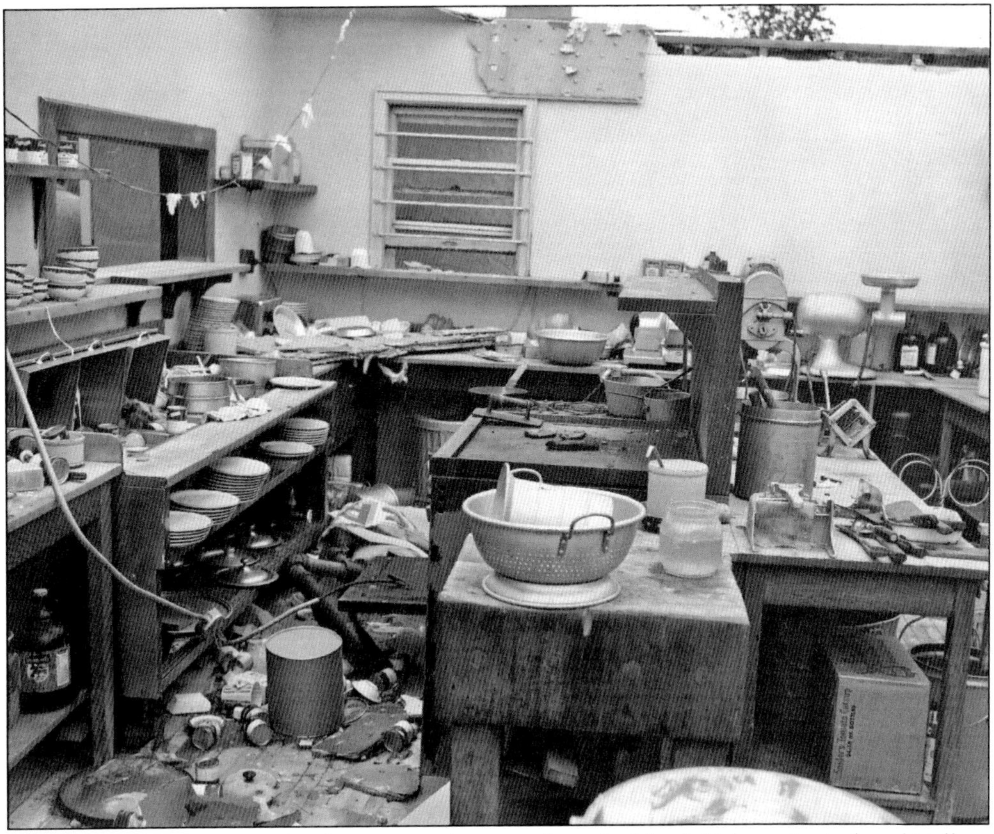

The Hasty Tasty was a popular diner across the street from the North Dakota Agricultural College campus. This is how the kitchen appeared after the tornado. In the upper right corner, a tree is visible, indicating that the roof is missing. The plates and bowls along the wall on the left are still stacked in place waiting to be used. Other kitchen equipment is strewn about the floor.

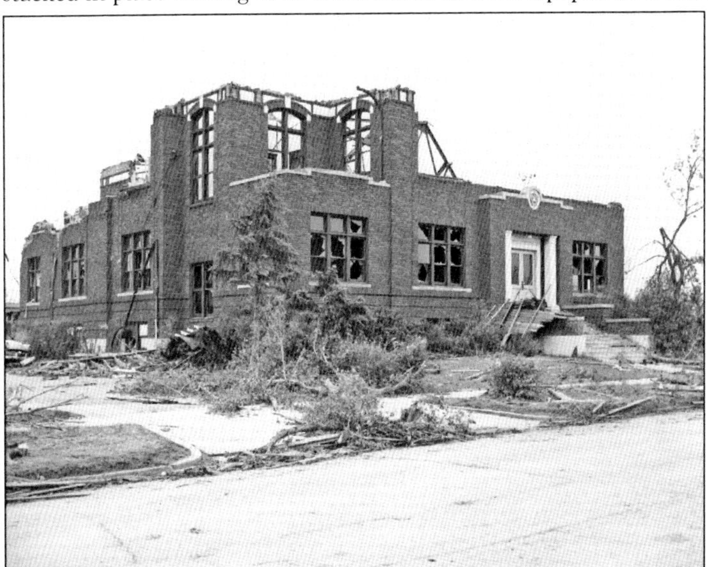

The North Dakota Agricultural College YMCA, at the intersection of Twelfth Avenue North and Thirteenth Street North, now University Drive, was a complete loss. The campus YMCA was founded in 1901, and this building was completed in 1919. Unfortunately, a new building was not constructed. A gas station now stands at this location.

The Hasty Tasty and YMCA stood side by side, making for a popular hub of student activity. The Hasty Tasty was rebuilt, eventually changing its name to Nick's Place. Nicholas Ginakes's son John took over the restaurant in 1986 and renamed it the Bison Turf. Even though the YMCA was not rebuilt, its headquarters moved to campus.

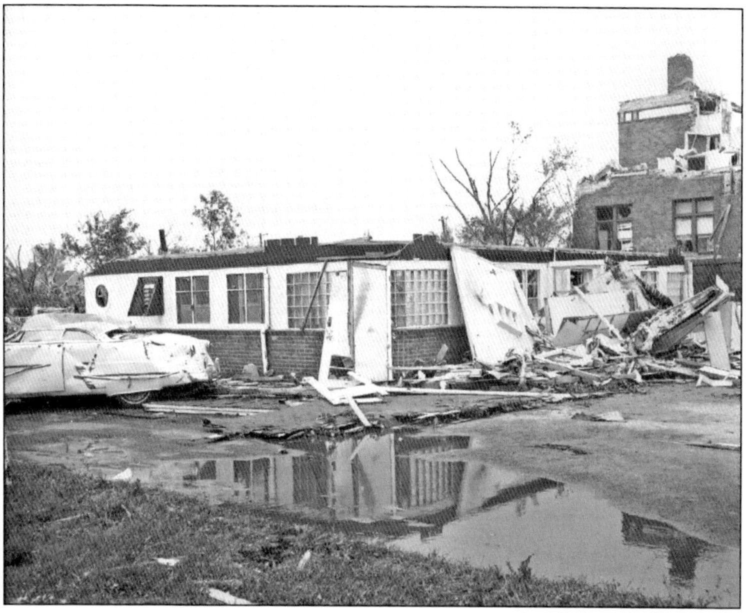

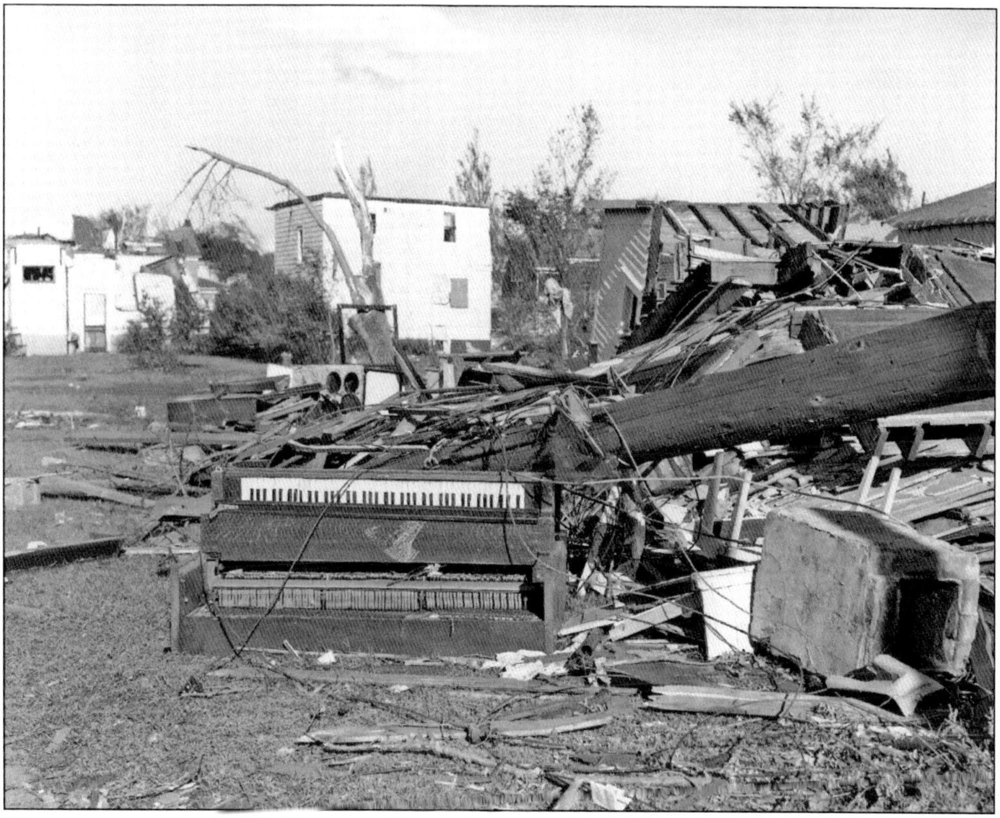

The remains of St. Paul's Newman Center litter its former lawn at 1143 Thirteenth Avenue North, now University Drive. The Newman Center served the Catholic students at the college by providing mass, gatherings, and events. This piano most likely belonged to the center. The center was rebuilt and is still serving Catholic students to this day.

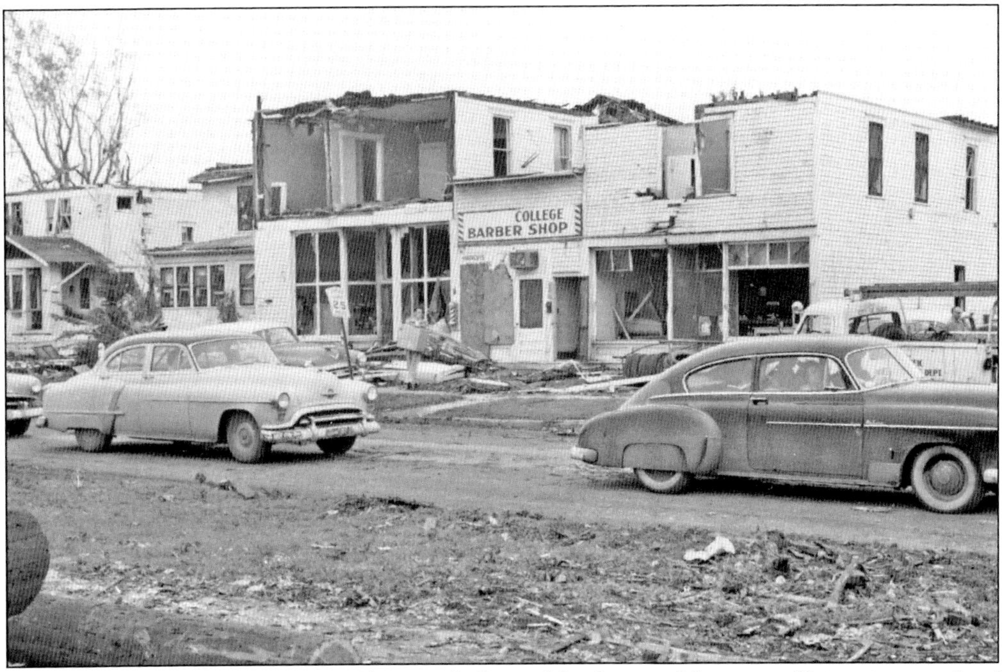

This view is looking west across Thirteenth Street North, now University Drive, just south of Twelfth Avenue North. Debris is visible along the curbside and in front of the businesses on the far side of the street. The second storefront from the right has a sign reading "College Barber Shop," and the College Grocery and College Inn restaurant on both sides show significant damage.

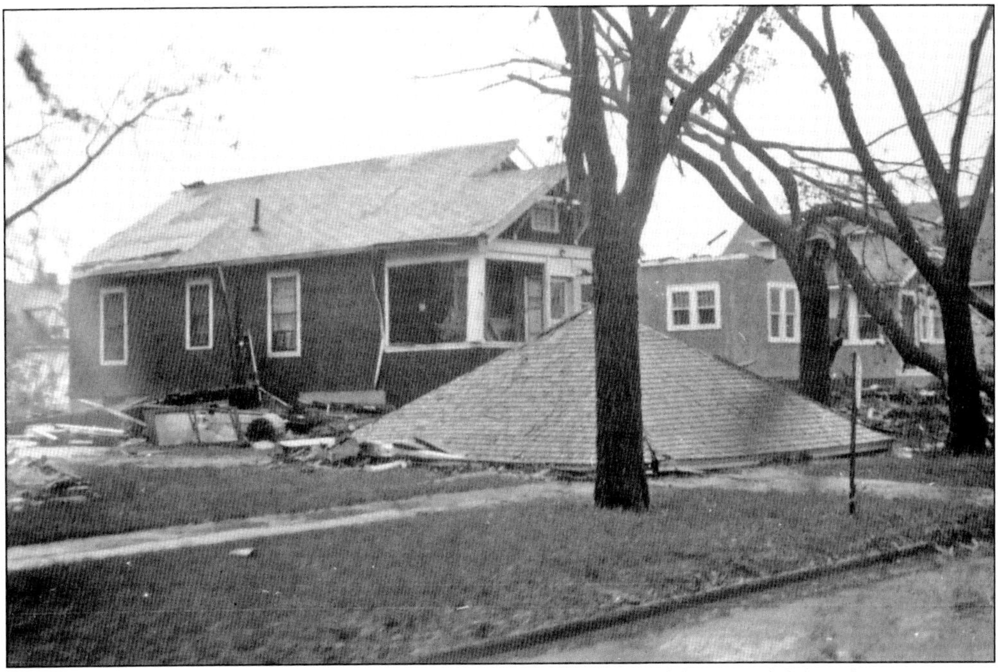

The high winds from the tornado tore apart trees and houses and deposited debris far away. Here, the owners of the home at 1035 Thirteenth Street North, now University Drive, acquired a new roof in their front yard. Their home appears to have a damaged roof as well, but it was repairable.

The Alpha Tau Omega fraternity house at 1155 Twelfth Avenue North sustained broken windows. The house was built in 1929 for the North Dakota Agricultural College local fraternity Alpha Kappa Phi, which became the Epsilon Zeta chapter of Alpha Tau Omega in 1931. The house was repaired and is still the home for Alpha Tau Omega fraternity members.

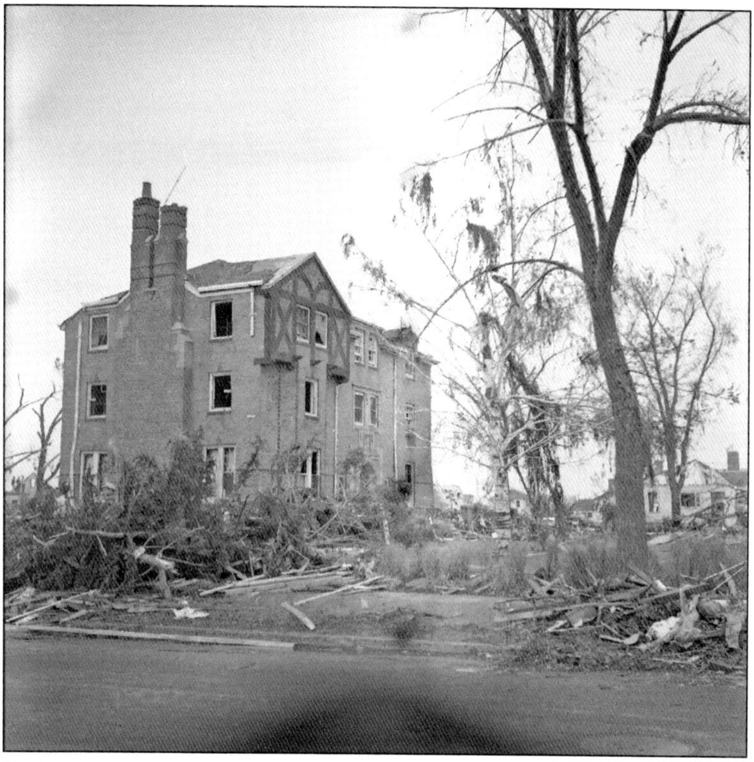

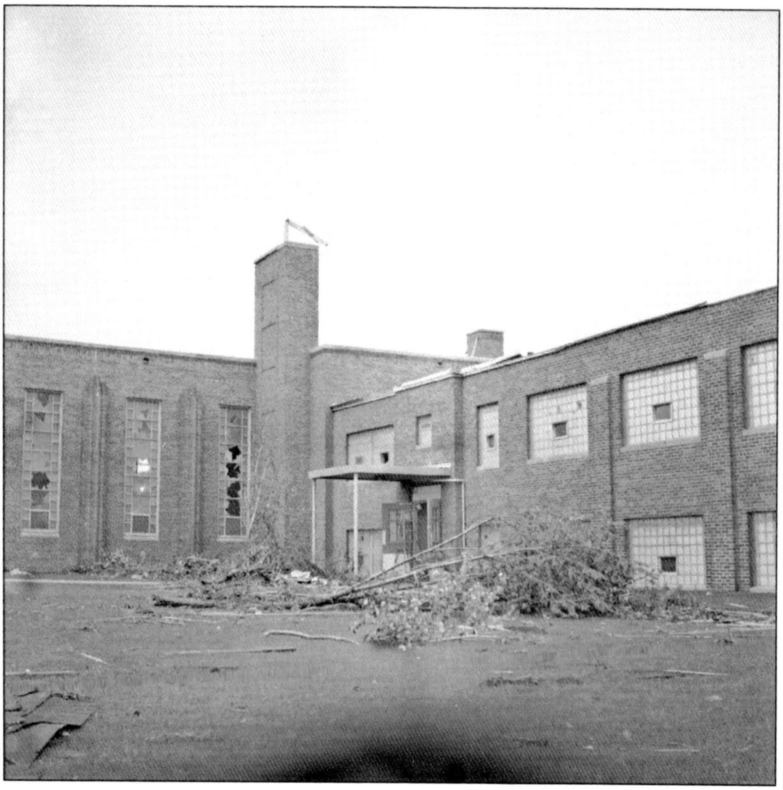

The American Lutheran Church at 1011 Twelfth Avenue North lost its roof, and many windows were broken. The church was repaired and is now called Peace Lutheran Church. When the Golden Ridge Lutheran Church was founded in 1955, a total of 67 members from the American Lutheran Church transferred to the Golden Ridge church.

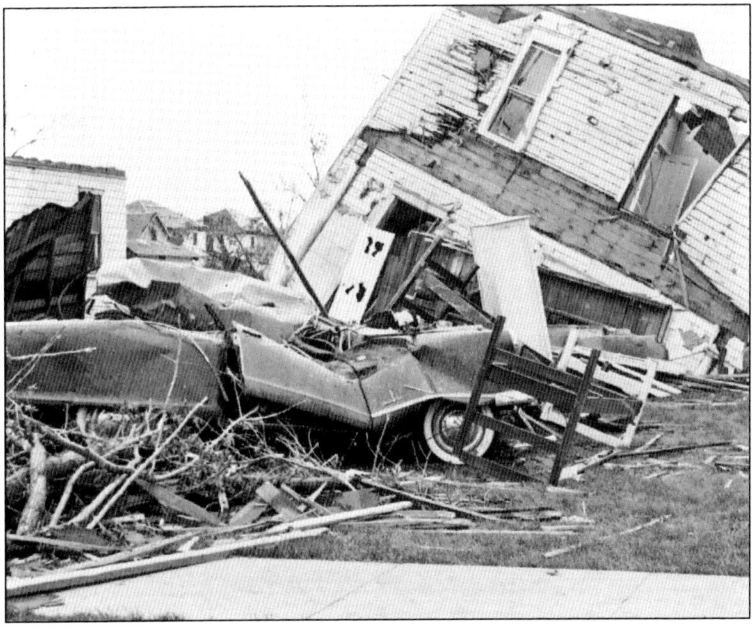

A collapsed and askew two-story, wood frame home at 1105 Twelfth Avenue North is pictured here. In addition to the damage caused by the house collapsing, the roof appears to be missing. A car in the foreground has been crushed by debris, and on the right side of the car there seems to be a twin bed frame.

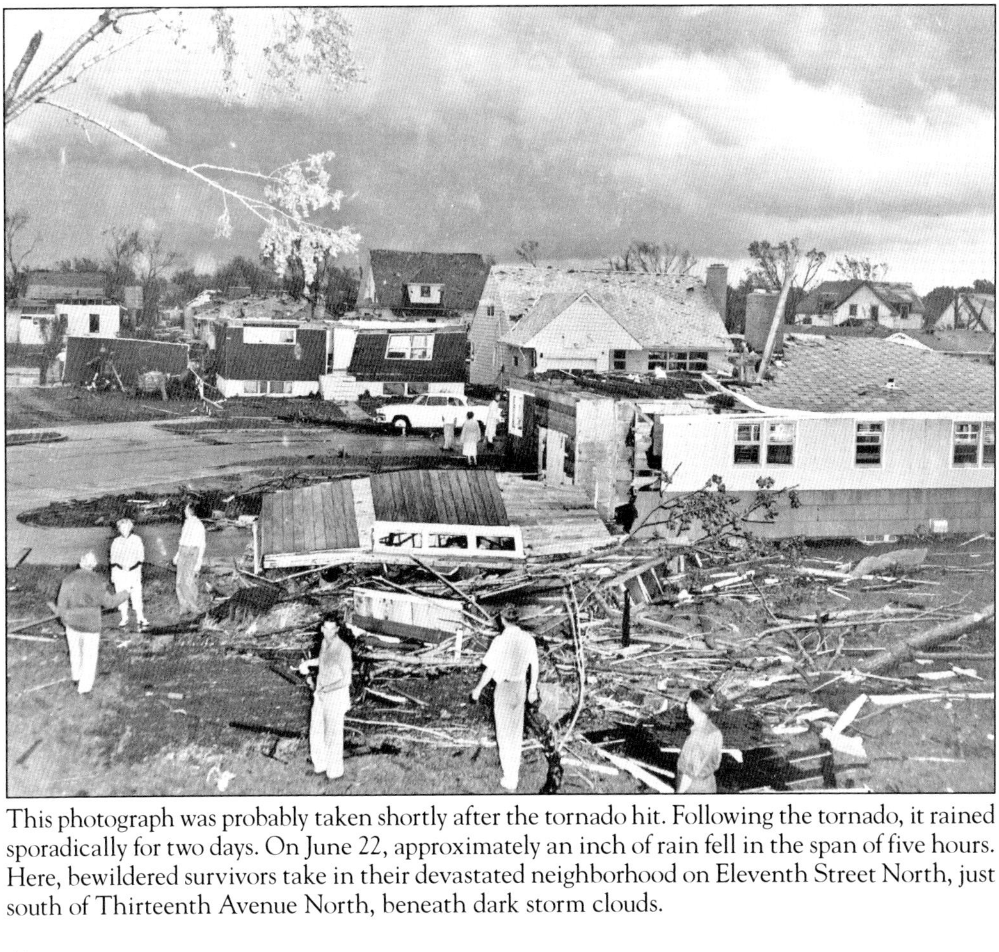

This photograph was probably taken shortly after the tornado hit. Following the tornado, it rained sporadically for two days. On June 22, approximately an inch of rain fell in the span of five hours. Here, bewildered survivors take in their devastated neighborhood on Eleventh Street North, just south of Thirteenth Avenue North, beneath dark storm clouds.

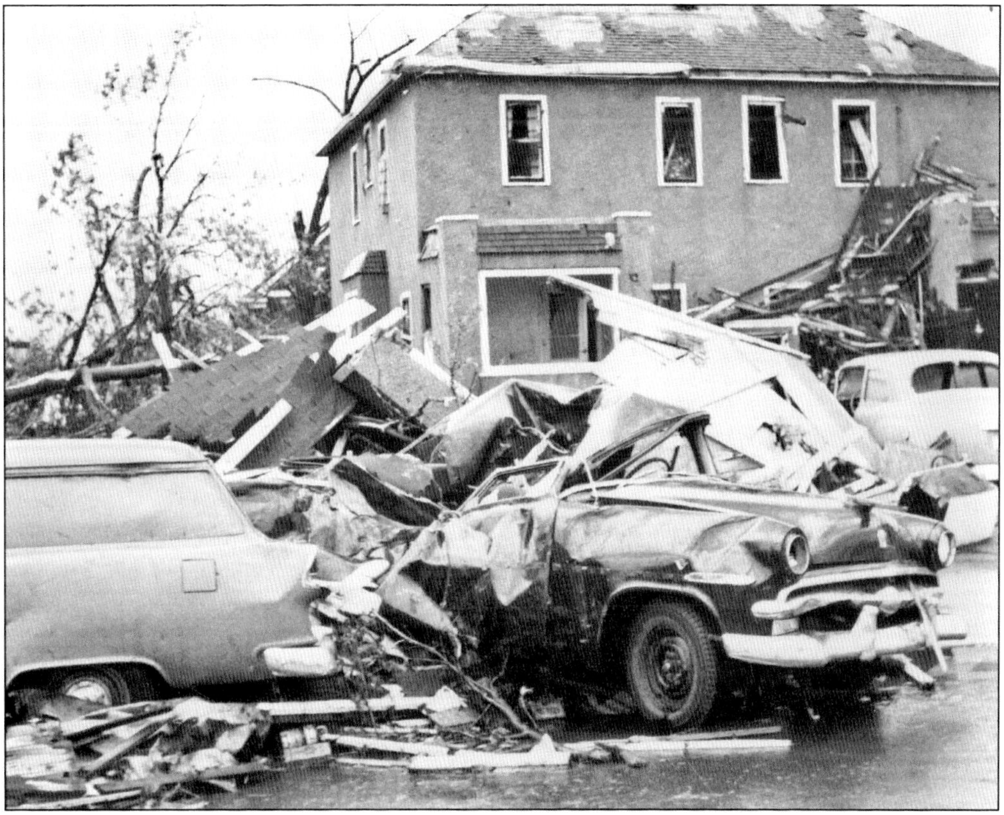

This image shows three automobiles and a home. The automobile on the left shows significant denting, the center one was destroyed by debris, and the one on the right shows little damage. The home in the background was located at 1218 Twelfth Street North behind what is now the Bison Turf.

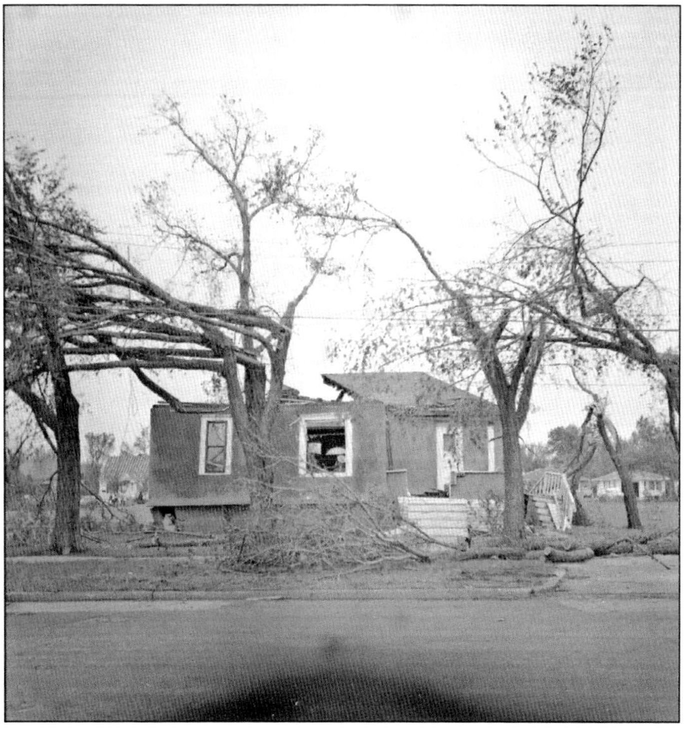

This home at 1213 Tenth Street North was shifted a few feet off its foundation by the incredible winds. To the right of the house is a staircase that no longer leads to the home. The bent trees in the front yard indicate the direction of the swirling funnel.

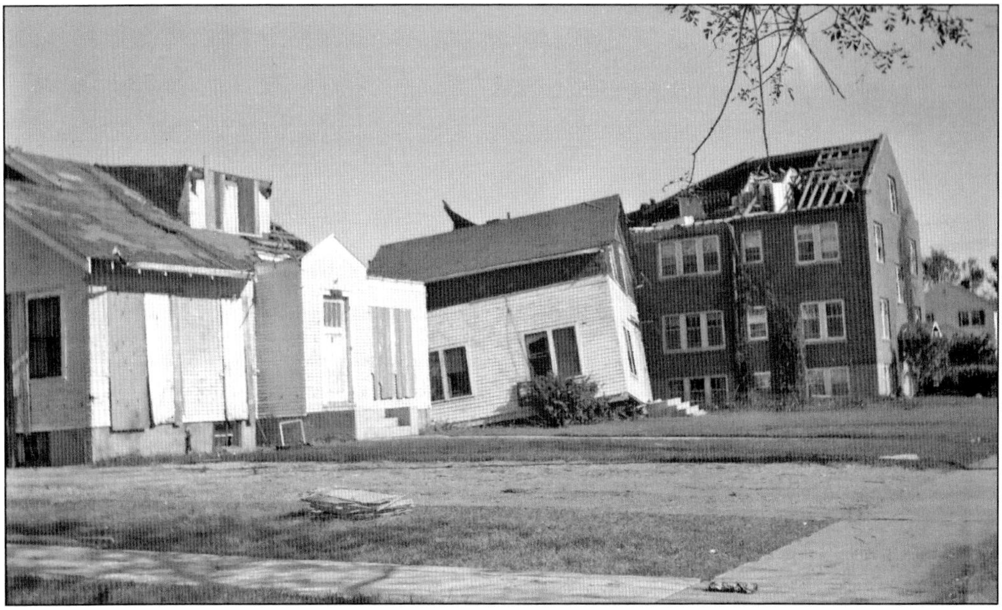

The Arbor Apartments at 1258 Tenth Street North, owned by Ina B. Lawrence, nearly lost its entire roof. Lawrence told the *Fargo Forum* that she planned on rebuilding. The apartment building still stands to this day. Miraculously, the leaning house at center was also saved and still stands. The house at left was torn down.

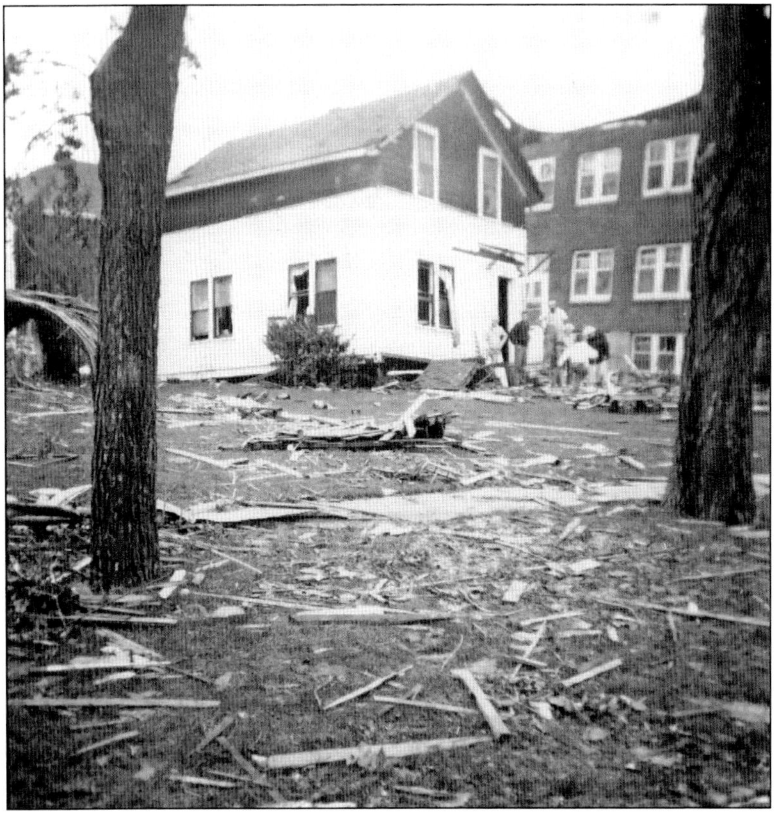

Here is a closer view of the homes in the previous image. A group of people assess the damage of the two-story, wood frame home at 1242 Tenth Street North, which appears to be blown off its foundation and is sitting upright at an angle. Debris is visible on the ground in front of the house, and the tree on the left appears to be split.

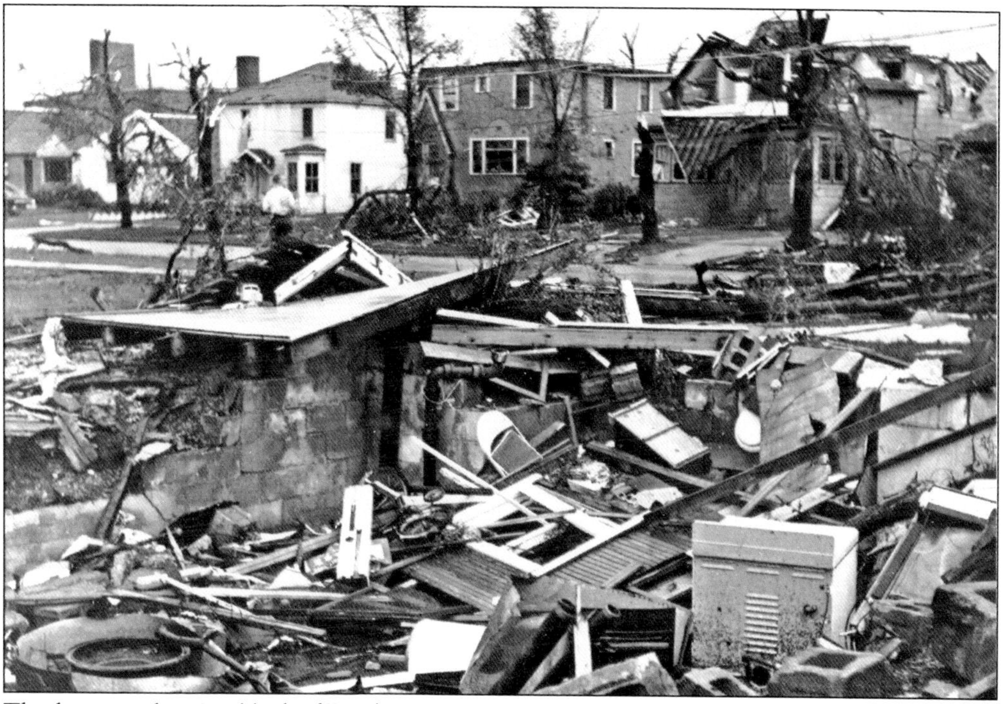

This home in the 1200 block of Tenth Street North was reduced to a pile of rubble in its basement. Among the debris is a bicycle, furniture, the rim of a car tire, a toilet, a folding chair, household appliances, and remnants of the home. Across the street is the home seen in the next image.

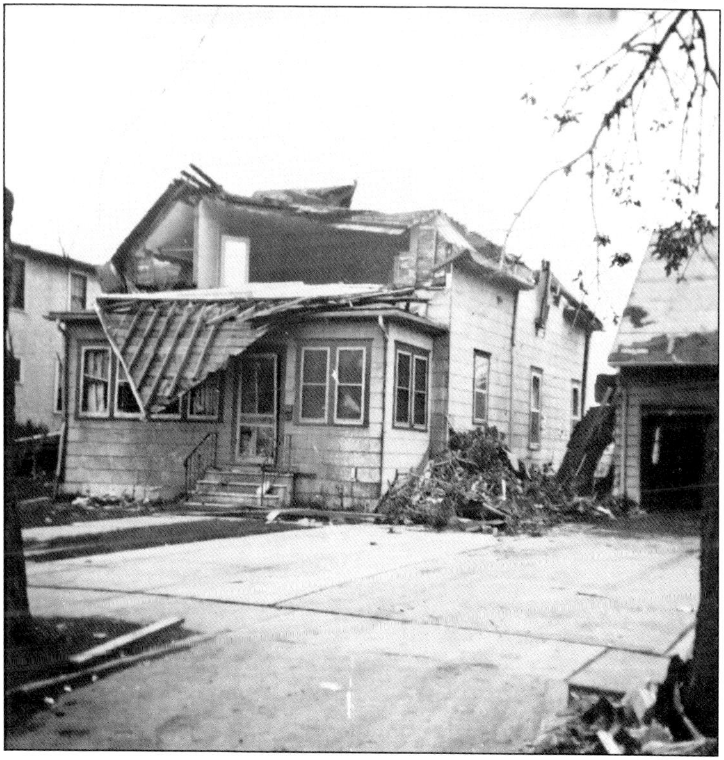

At the two-story, wood frame home at 1216 Tenth Street North, the roof is severely damaged and the exterior wall above the porch is peeled open, exposing a second-floor room. Wood debris sits on the side of the home, and the garage on the right appears to be missing most of its shingles.

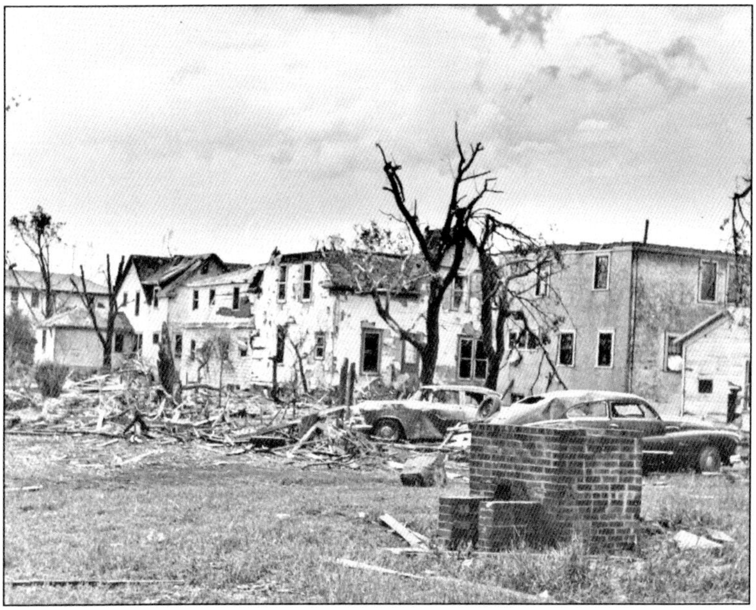

The third structure from the right is the back of the home in the previous image. Heaps of rubble, which were possibly garages or sheds, litter the backyards. The brick structure is an undisturbed barbeque pit. In this neighborhood, the average cost of the dwellings was set at $12,000–$15,000 by insurance surveyors.

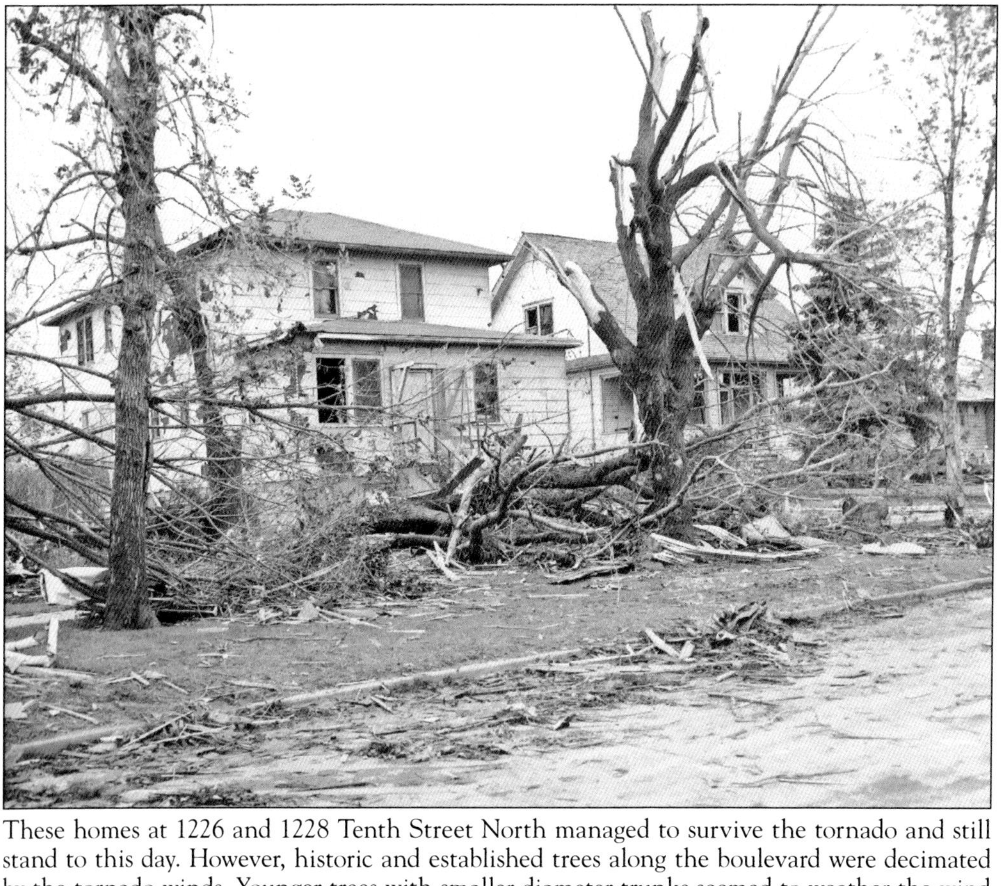

These homes at 1226 and 1228 Tenth Street North managed to survive the tornado and still stand to this day. However, historic and established trees along the boulevard were decimated by the tornado winds. Younger trees with smaller diameter trunks seemed to weather the wind better due to their greater flexibility.

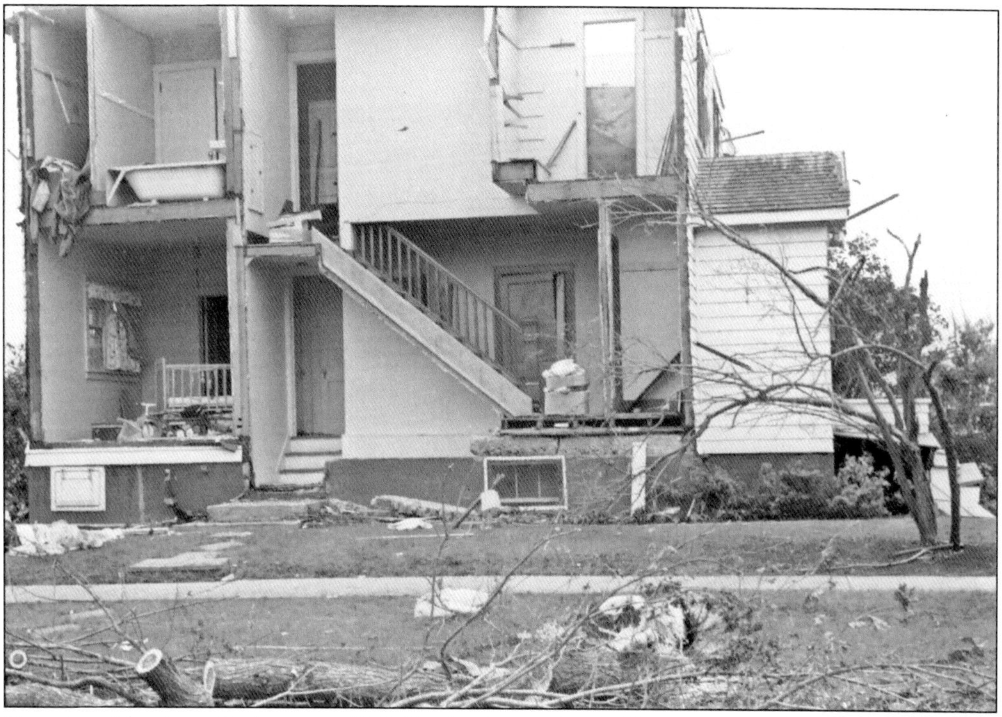

Here is a side view of a home at 1261 Tenth Street North. The exterior side wall is completely missing, exposing the interior of the home. On the second floor on the left, a bath tub, sink, and closet are visible; directly below, an infant's crib and toys are intact.

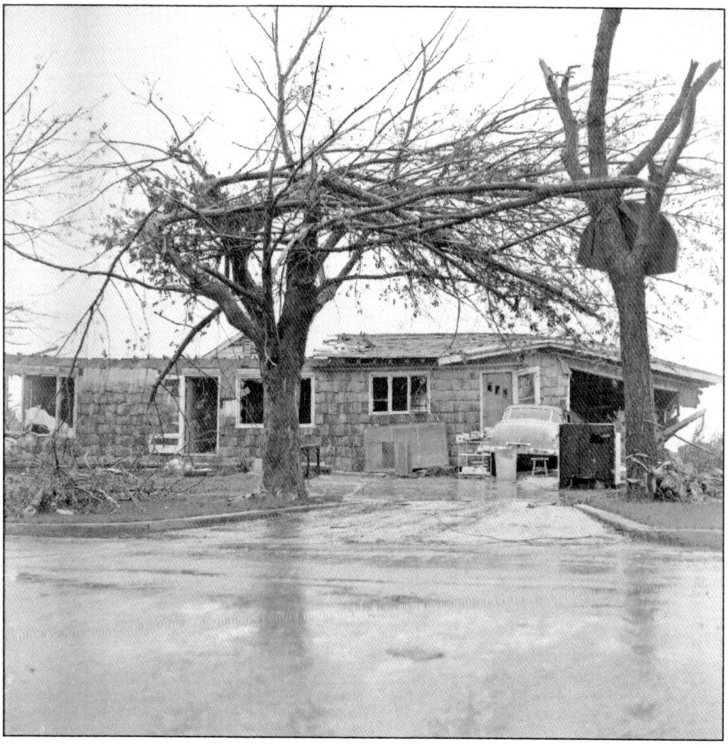

Col. Homer G. Goebel, the chief of staff of the headquarters group of the North Dakota Air National Guard, was not home when the tornado hit. However, his wife, Mildred, and four young sons were home at the time. A basketball backboard flew into the branches of the tree at right.

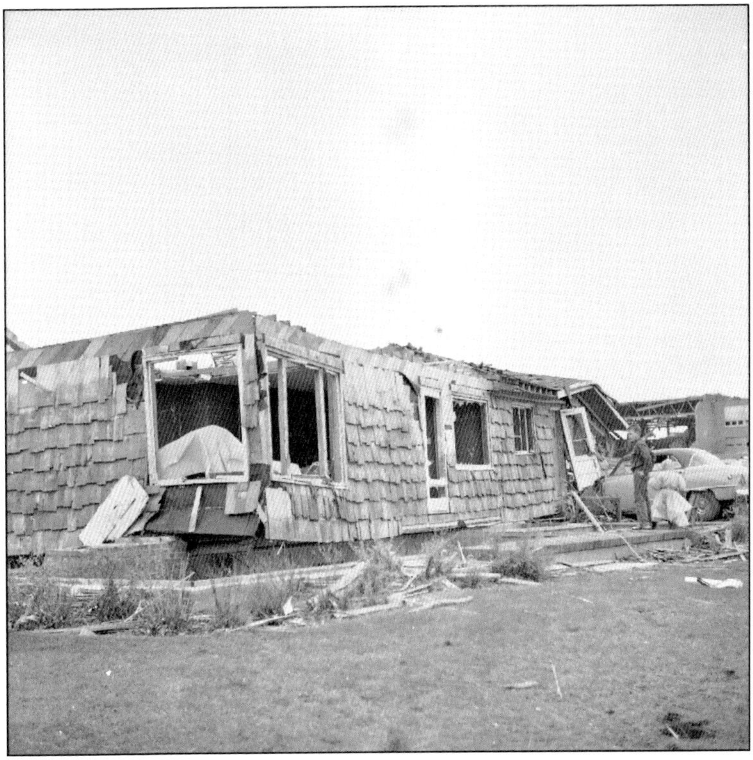

From another angle, the damage to Homer Goebel's home is much more apparent. The roof is completely missing, and the entire house was shifted off its foundation. The house stood at 819 Thirteenth Avenue North. Two children, possibly Goebel's sons, stand in front of the house. Unable to repair, the family built a new two-story home on the same lot.

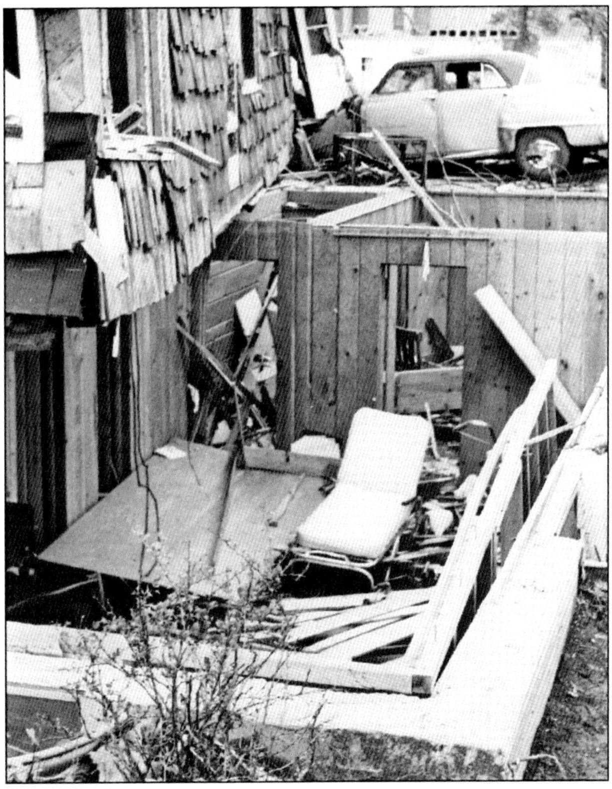

Mildred Goebel and her sons, 12-year-old Homer Junior, nine-year-old Jonathan, and seven-year-old twins Bruce and Brian, were home when the tornado hit. They were pummeled by rubble and trapped in the home. According to the *Fargo Forum*, Brian proclaimed, "Mommy, are we dead yet?" Fortunately, they all survived and were not severely hurt.

The home of Carl O. Uthus, at 818 Thirteenth Avenue North, lost its roof, which lies in the yard. A man stands in front of another destroyed roof to the left. Missing roofs were common along the tornado's path. The Goebel family, whose story was detailed in the previous three images, lived directly across the street.

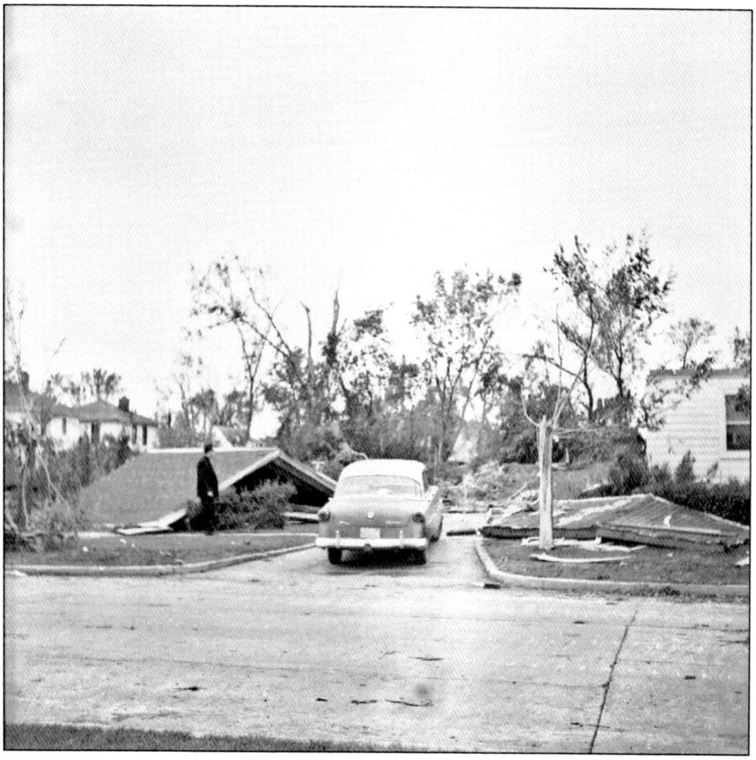

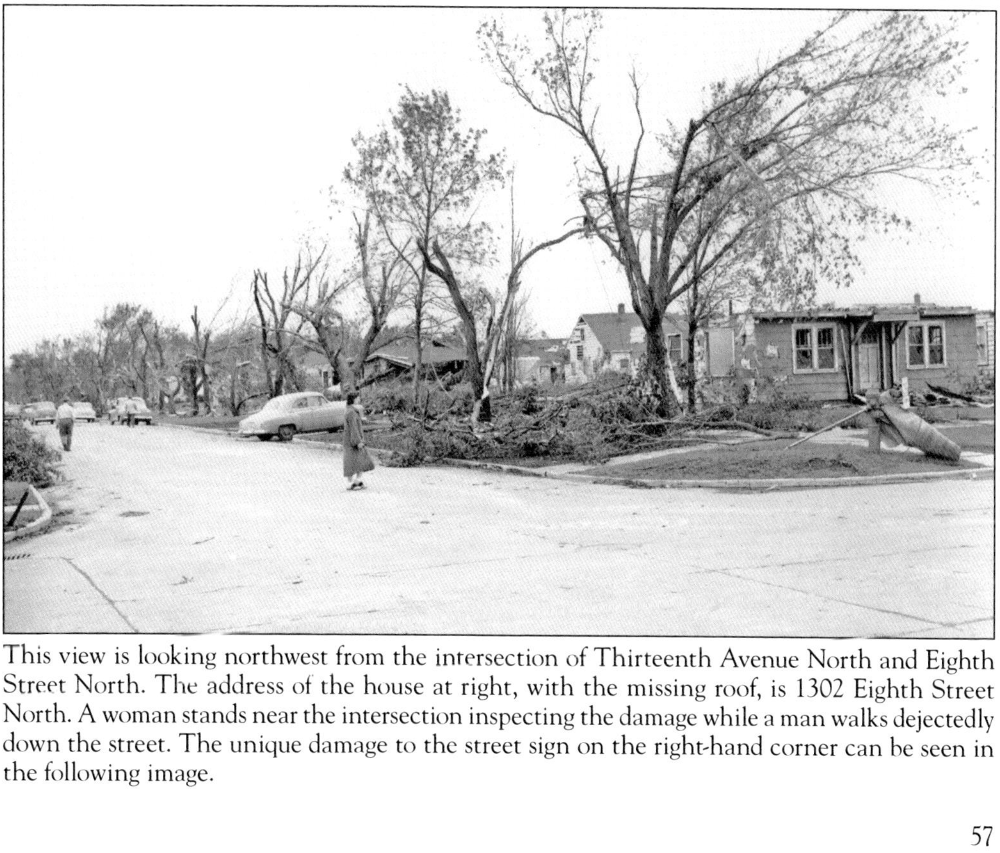

This view is looking northwest from the intersection of Thirteenth Avenue North and Eighth Street North. The address of the house at right, with the missing roof, is 1302 Eighth Street North. A woman stands near the intersection inspecting the damage while a man walks dejectedly down the street. The unique damage to the street sign on the right-hand corner can be seen in the following image.

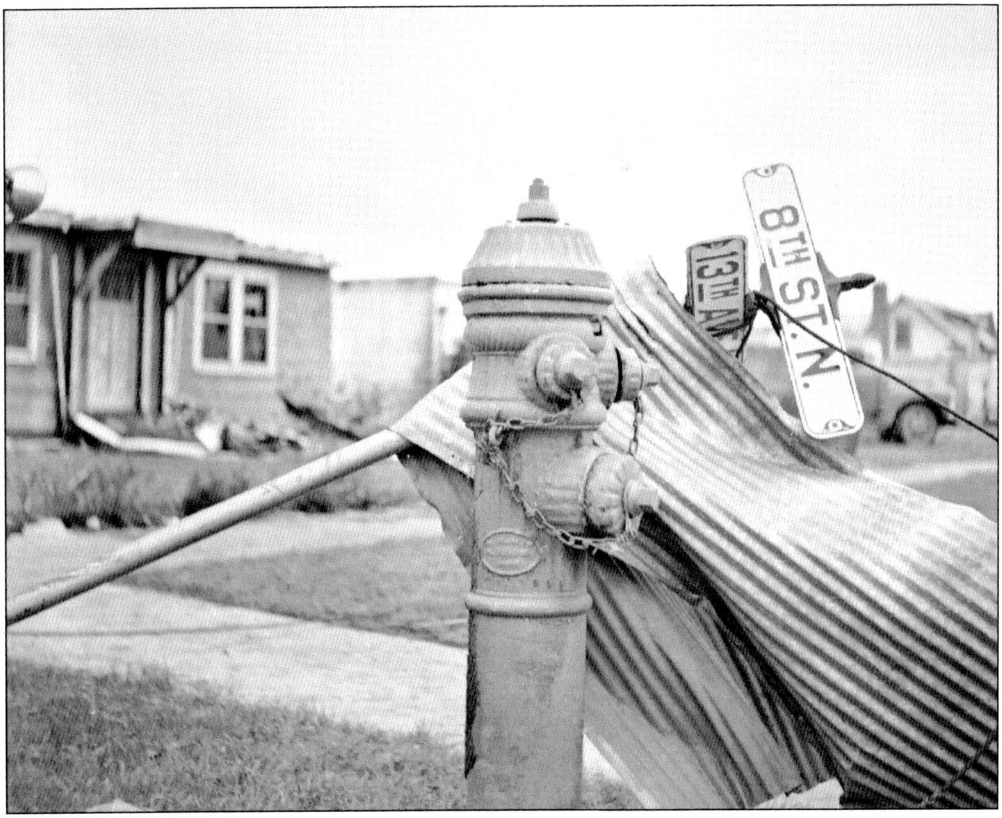

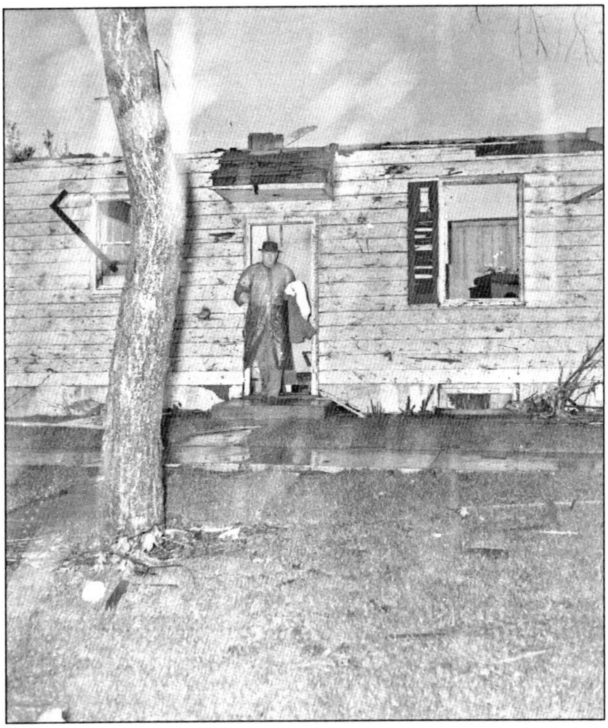

A flying piece of corrugated sheet metal bent over a street sign at the intersection of Eighth Street North and Thirteenth Avenue South, illustrating the incredible force of the tornado. This image shows the danger of being without shelter when a tornado strikes. Flying debris causes most deaths and injuries during tornadoes, according to the Centers for Disease Control.

Stanford Oksness stands in front of his destroyed home at 1302 Ninth Street North after gathering his few remaining belongings. This photograph was likely taken shortly after the tornado, due to the dark sky and rain drops. Part of the frame of a shutter hangs awkwardly from the left window, and the right window only has one damaged shutter left.

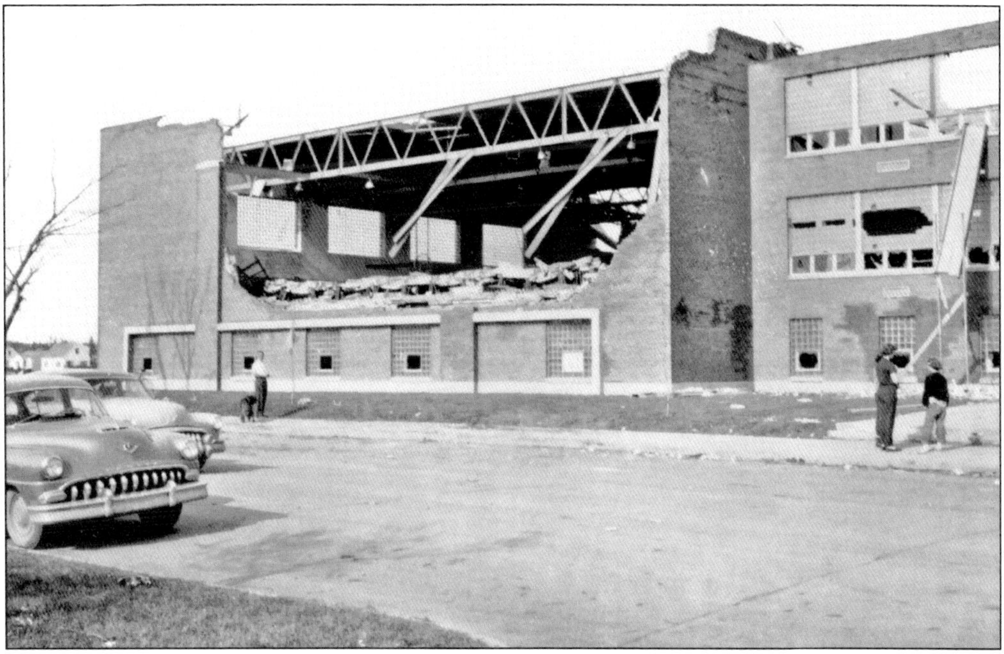

In 1950, Sacred Heart Academy, a Catholic high school, moved to a brand new building at 705 Thirteenth Avenue North. The school was renamed after Bishop John Shanley, the first bishop of the Diocese of Fargo. Shanley High School was severely damaged by the tornado. However, the school was quickly rebuilt. The school moved to a new building in south Fargo in 2002.

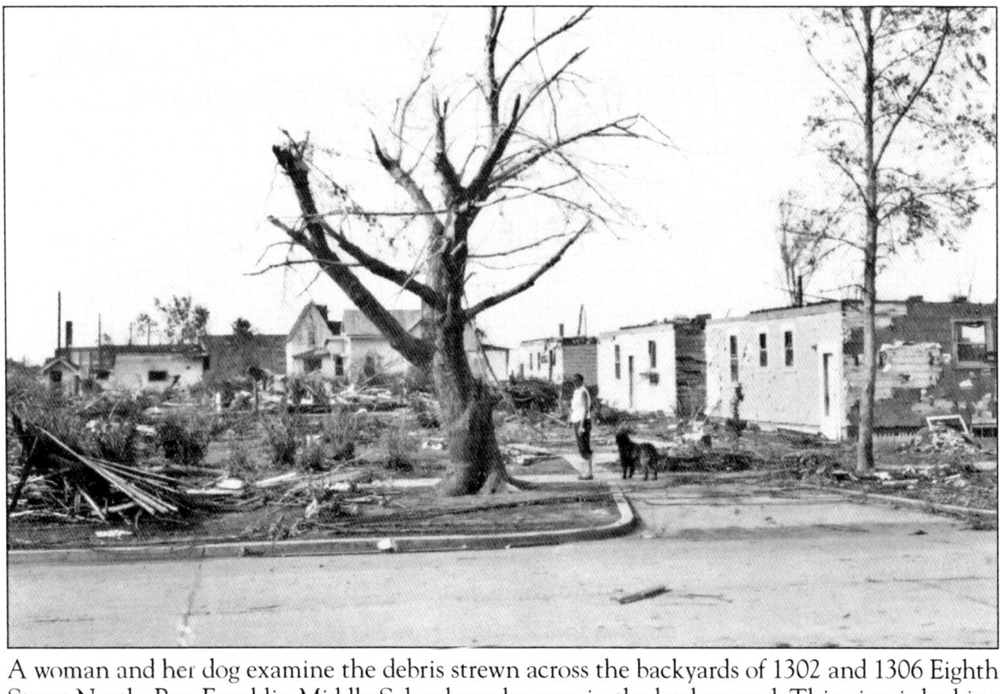

A woman and her dog examine the debris strewn across the backyards of 1302 and 1306 Eighth Street North. Ben Franklin Middle School can be seen in the background. This view is looking north. Shanley High School is directly east of where the houses are facing. Dr. G. Wilson Hunter took this photograph, and the woman is most likely his wife, Phyllis.

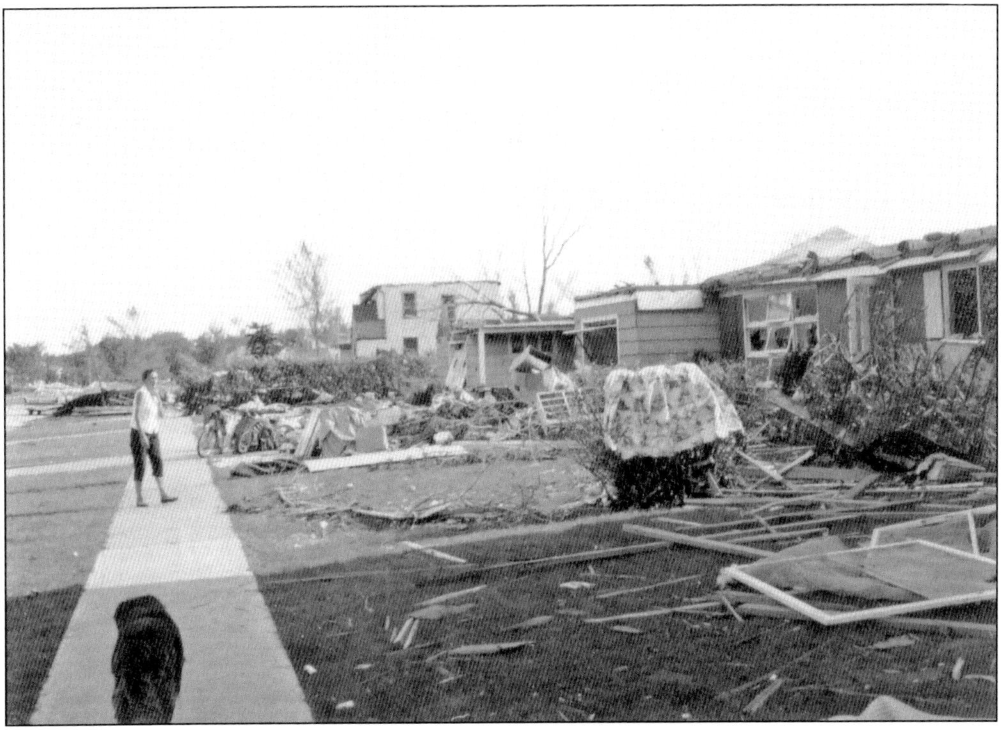

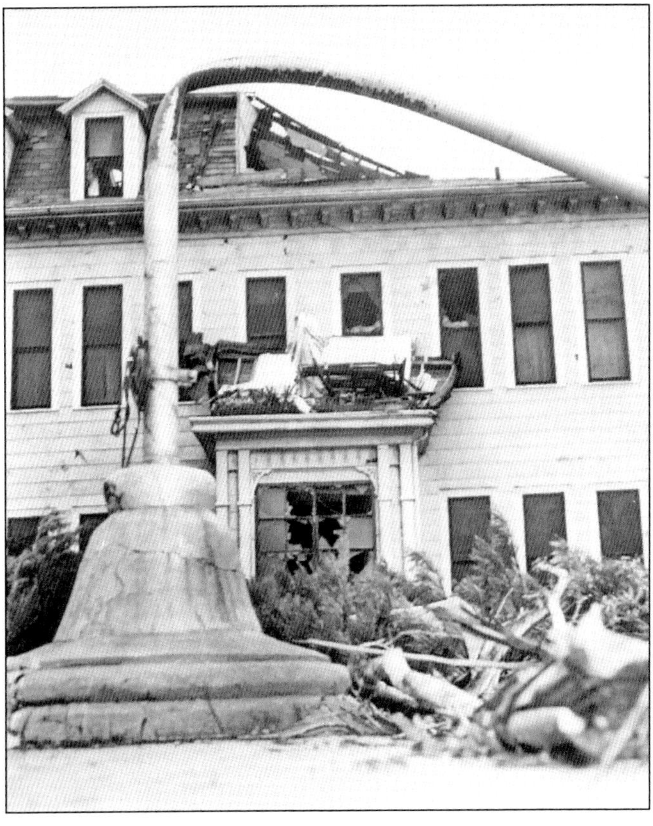

Phyllis Hunter and her dog continue their walk to look at the damage throughout their neighborhood. After crossing Broadway, they head south along Fifth Street North. Broken window panes and household belongings litter the front yards of these homes. Oddly, a blanket gracefully covers a bush.

The Sacred Heart Convent at 1310 Broadway was heavily damaged by the tornado. The flagpole is completely bent over and is surrounded by destroyed trees. Fortunately, only one of the approximately 75 nuns who lived at the convent was slightly injured. While most of the nuns made it to the basement before the tornado hit, some had to hide in closets and stairwells on the upper floors.

The Sisters of the Presentation of the Blessed Virgin Mary were not able to hold their annual tea on June 30 at the Sacred Heart Convent as planned. A tree had crashed through the tea room's window. From left to right are Mother M. St. Kevin Brennan, Sister Genevieve Murphy, and Sister Antonine Foy.

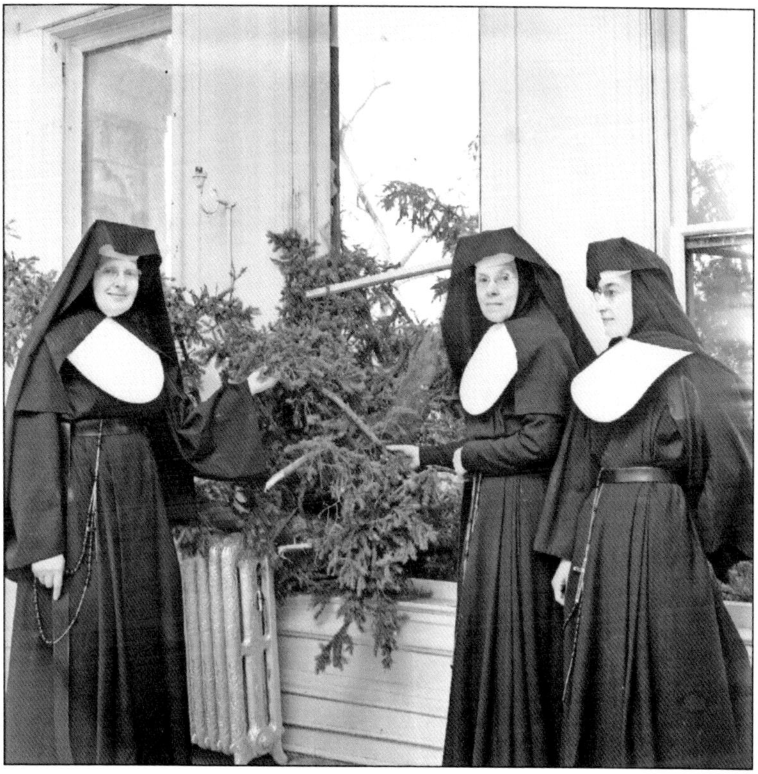

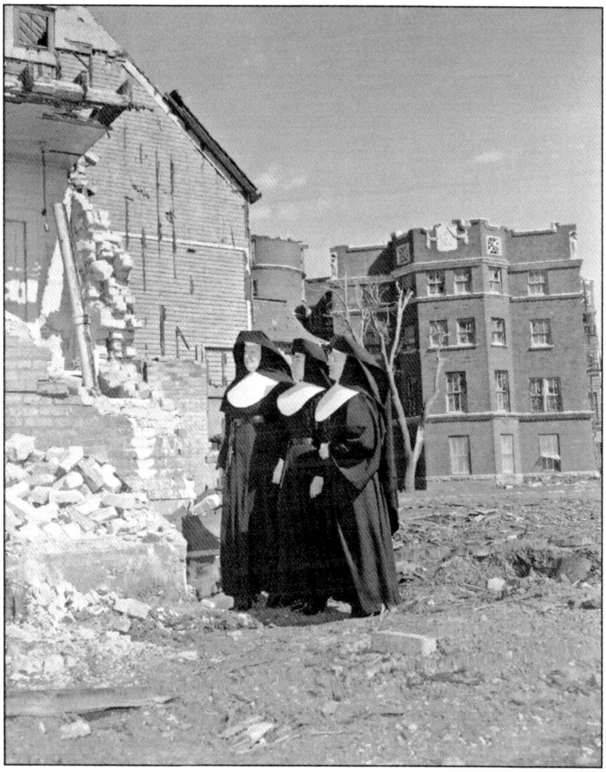

From left to right, Mother M. St. Kevin Brennan, Sister Antonine Foy, and Sister Scholastica Marquart examine the convent's ruins. The convent was so heavily damaged, the nuns decided to build a new convent in south Fargo, where they still live to this day. The new convent opened in 1961. The nuns lived in the undamaged parts of the old convent until they could move.

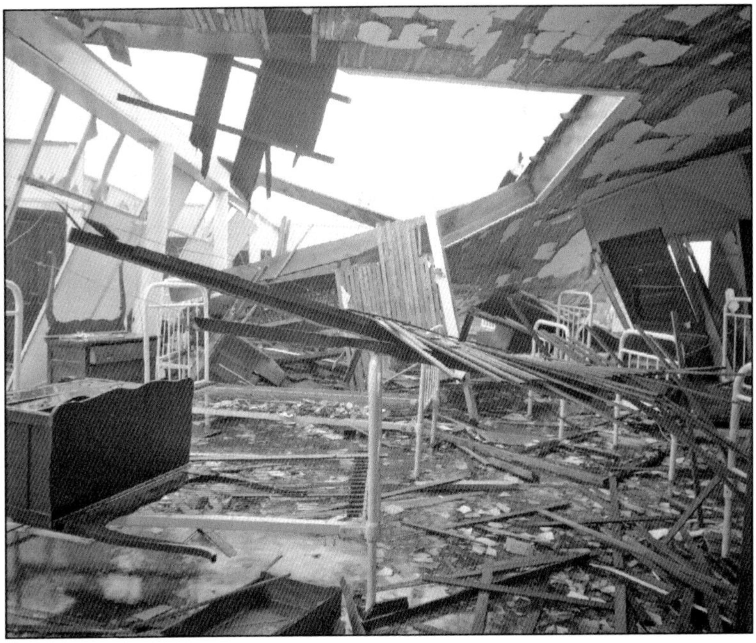

The dormitory of Sacred Heart Convent offers evidence of the severity of damage. The nuns were forced to stay at private homes or St. John's Orphanage the night following the tornado. Volunteers helped the nuns gather their belongings and stored them at the Holy Spirit School and St. John's Orphanage.

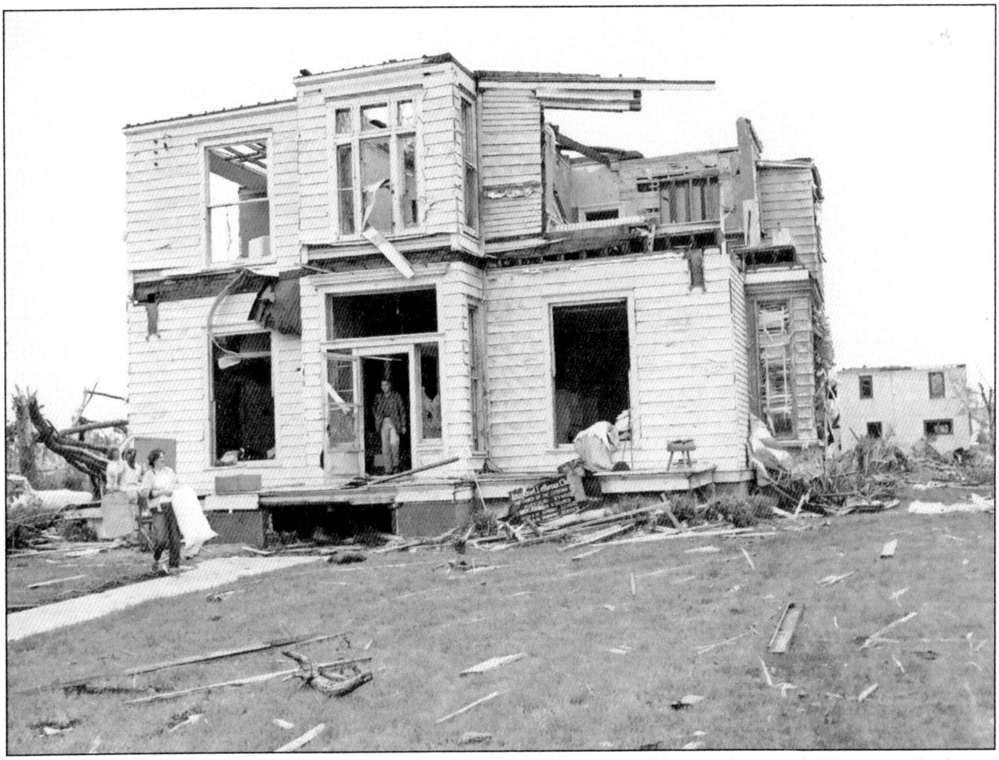

The Colonial Apartments building at 1317 Broadway was owned by Arthur and Margaret Fosburg. Margaret and four tenants ran to the basement when the tornado hit, but when Arthur did not come down, Margaret went up to find him. The tornado struck, and she was unable to open the door to the basement. All survived with few injuries. The sign for Immanuel Lutheran Church blew into the front yard.

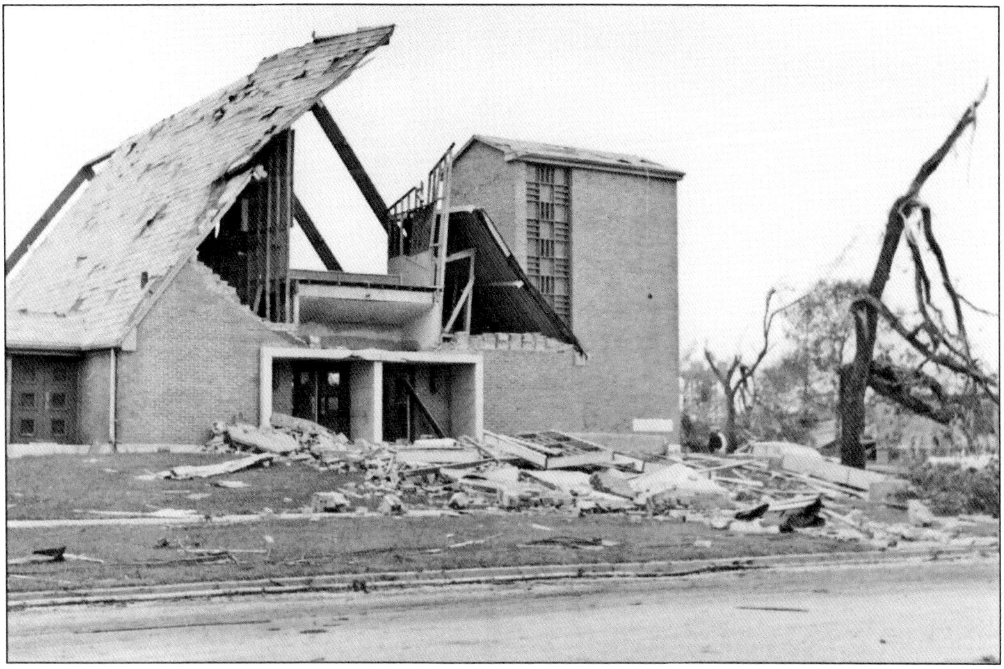

Looking west from North Broadway, Immanuel Lutheran Church is shown with a destroyed roof and damage to the front lawn and surrounding trees. At the time of the tornado, a group of Sunday school teachers was meeting at the church and took refuge in the basement. The preliminary estimate of damage to the church by the Red Cross was $225,000.

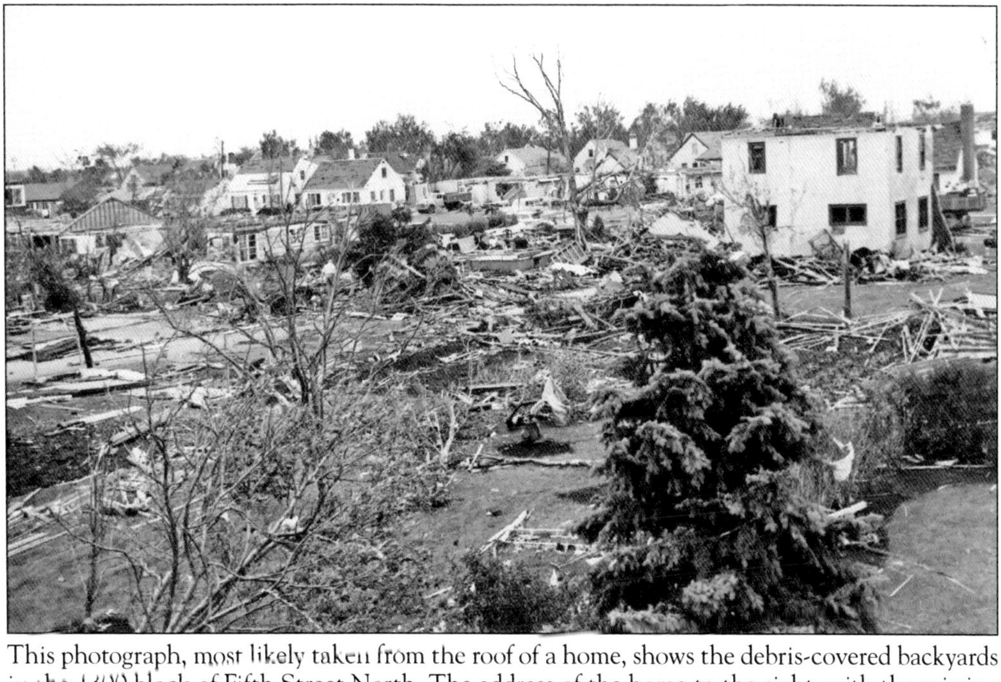

This photograph, most likely taken from the roof of a home, shows the debris-covered backyards in the 1300 block of Fifth Street North. The address of the home to the right, with the missing roof, was 1316 Fifth Street North. The tornado stripped the trees of their leaves, although the pine tree fared a bit better.

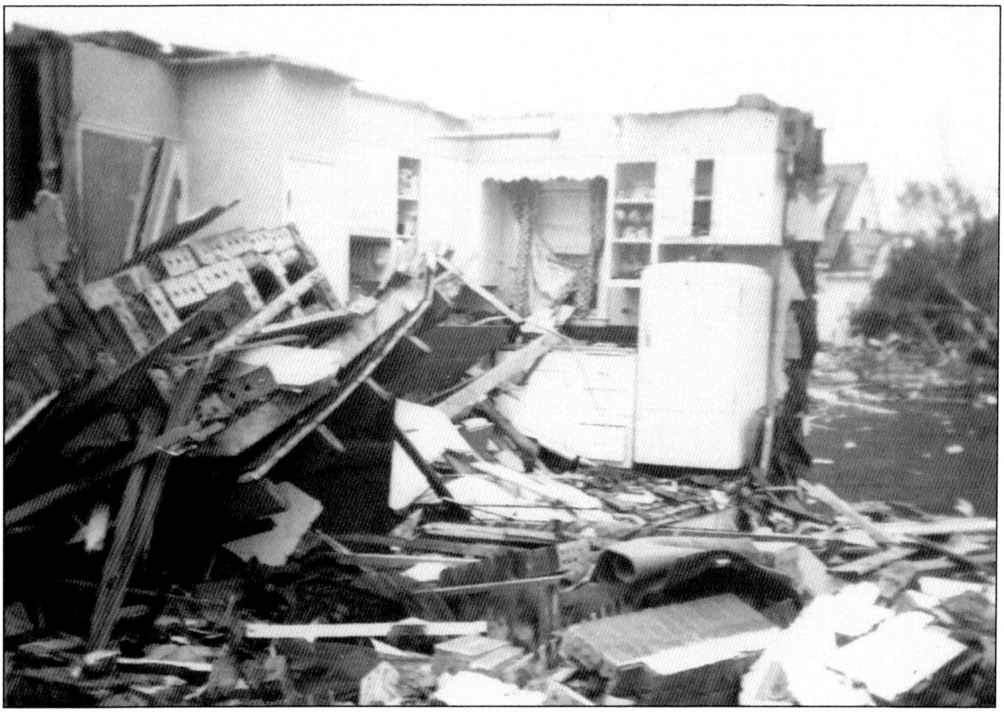

Bricks from a fallen chimney at Arthur W. Rohde's home at 1309 Fifth Street North are on the ground. A kitchen is visible at center with the curtains still hanging over the sink. Dishes appear to be unharmed in the cabinet to the left of the refrigerator.

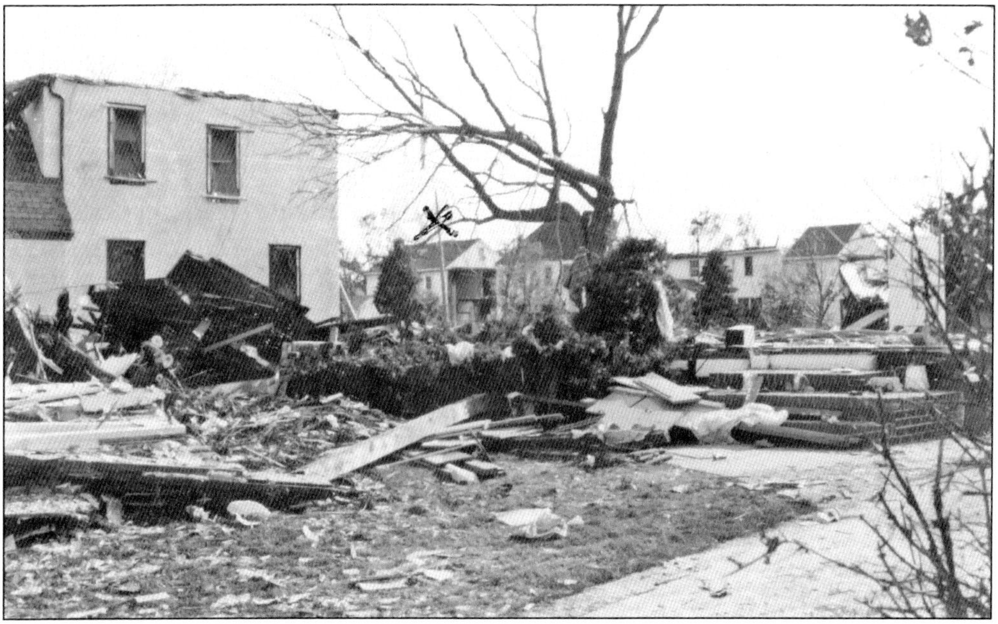

On Fifth Street North, a tree stands between a heavily damaged home and another that was completely destroyed with nothing but its foundation left. The Plath family lived in the damaged home to the left, and the Haslerud family lived in the home that was destroyed. In the background are damaged homes in the 1300 block of Broadway.

This view of the 1300 block of Fifth Street North is looking west. A building or house has been destroyed on the corner. Wood debris is scattered around the lawn and into the street. The Fosburgs' Colonial Apartments is the white building in the background, and far in the background on the right is the Sacred Heart Convent.

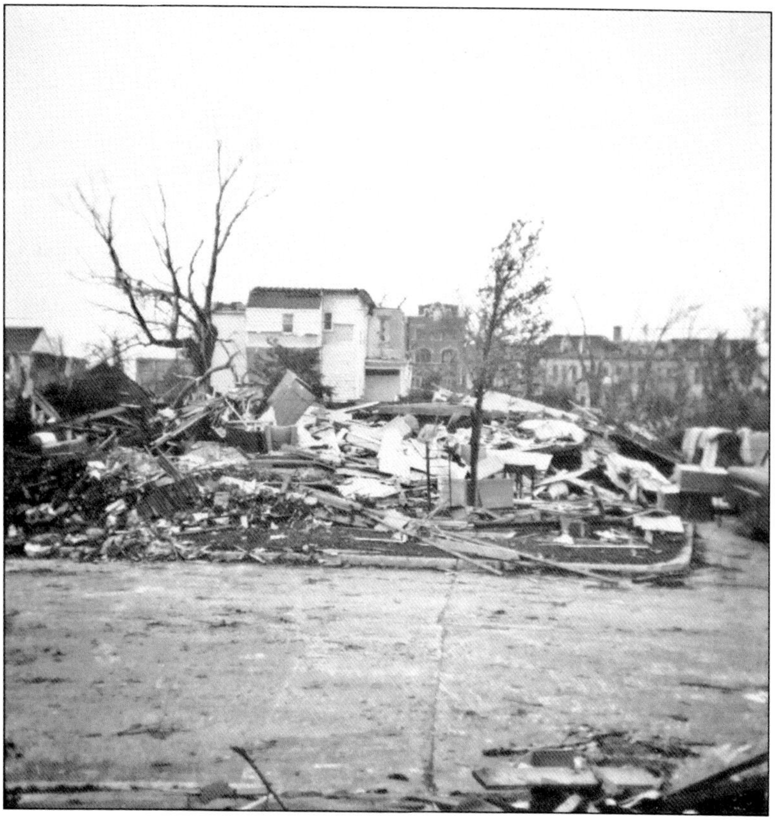

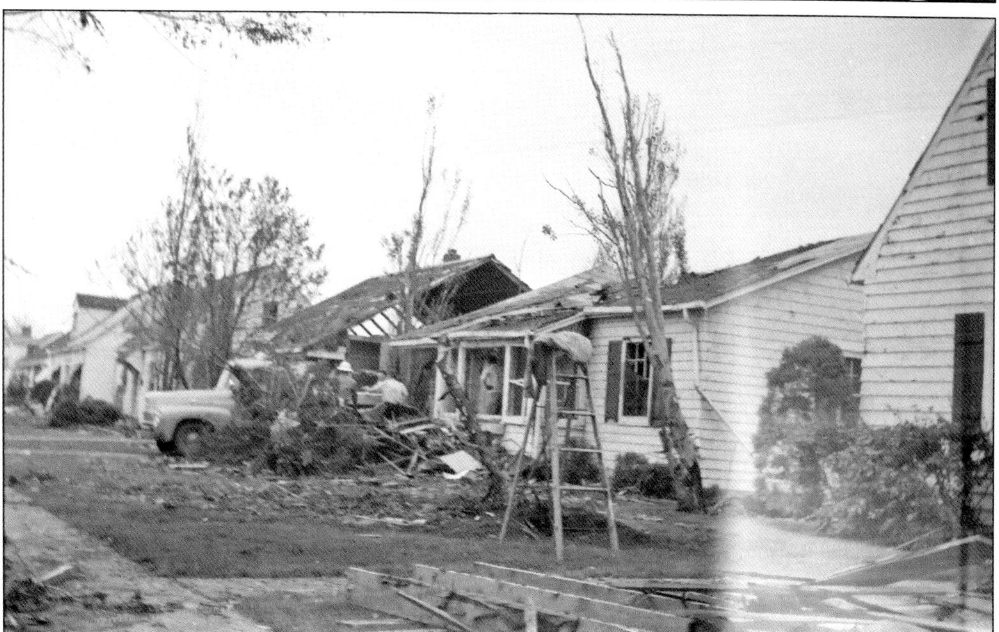

This view is looking north on the east side of the 1300 block of Second Street North. The first full house is 1317 Second Street North. The roof on the second house appears to have extensive damage. A truck with workers can be seen at center, and debris is visible in the foreground.

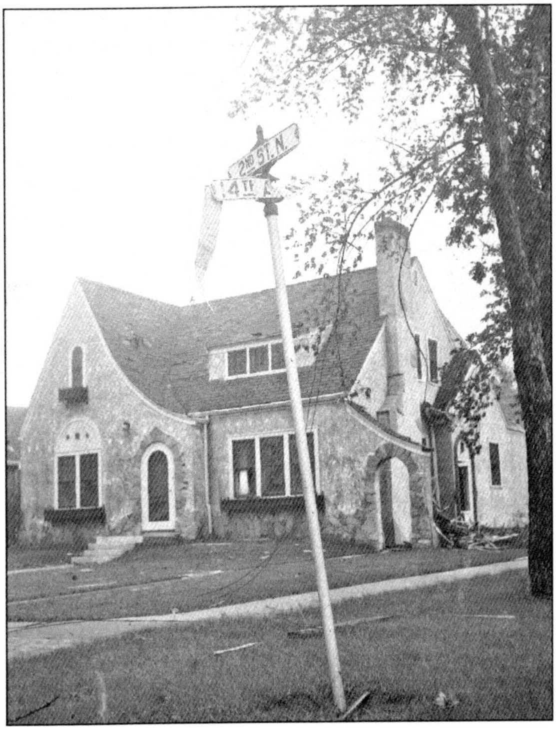

Fargo Forum editor John D. Paulson's house sat at 1362 Second Street North. Paulson, his wife Zoe, and their four children took shelter in the basement. Paulson reported to the *Forum* that while their house had minimal damage, their two-car garage disappeared and part of a chimney landed on their car. Afterwards, Paulson went directly to work, then returned to his home to survey the damage to the neighborhood.

Warren B. Diederich's home was less than a block south of the El Zagal Bowl at 1321 First Street North. Diederich's wife, Irene, and children Michael, Laura, and Don were unharmed but trapped in the home. Fortunately, neighbors led by Jack Charbonneau freed the family. Oddly, the dining room table is still surrounded by its chairs, even though the rest of the furniture in the room is strewn about.

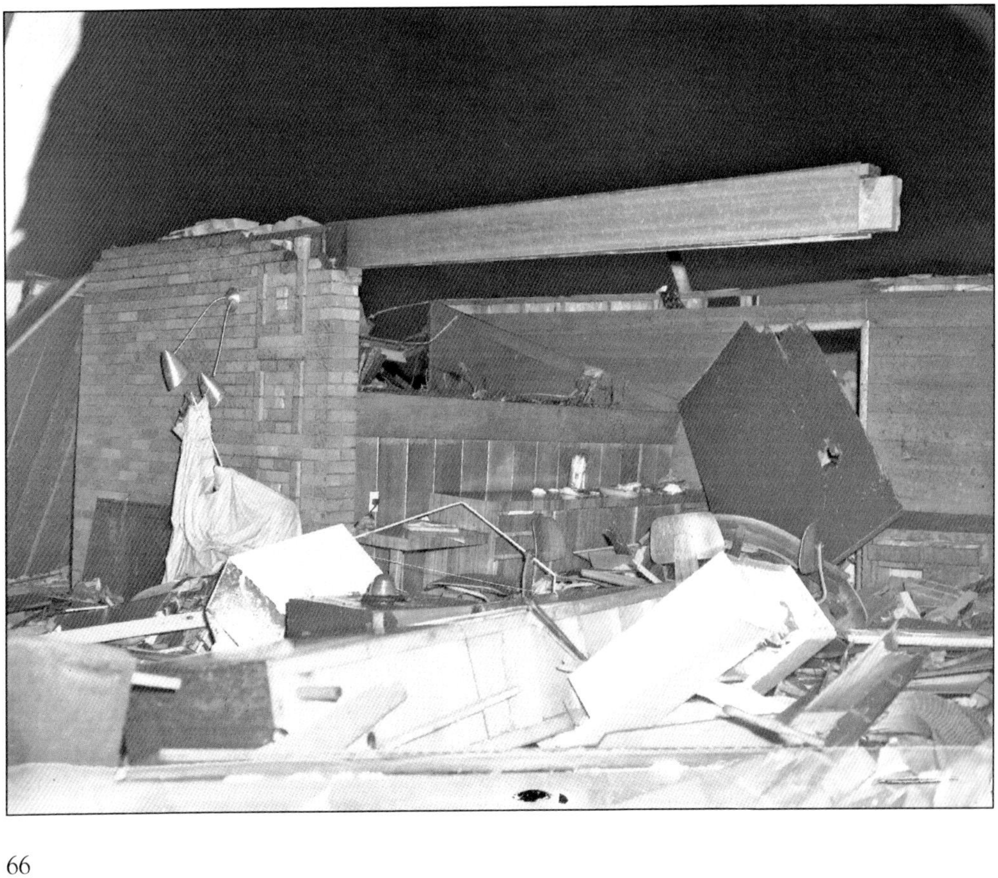

Here is another view of the Diederich family home. The roof and some walls are missing or have fallen over, and it is unclear what the home originally looked like or where it stood. To the right of the building is a cement foundation. A Diederich son appears to be standing to the right of the house.

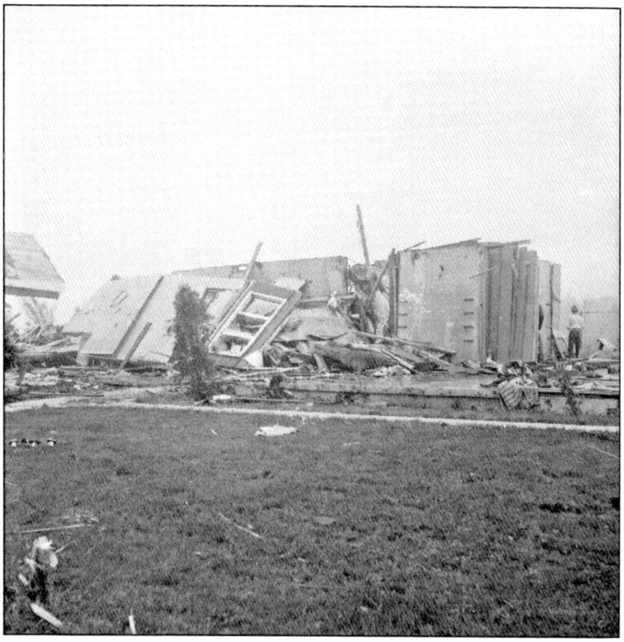

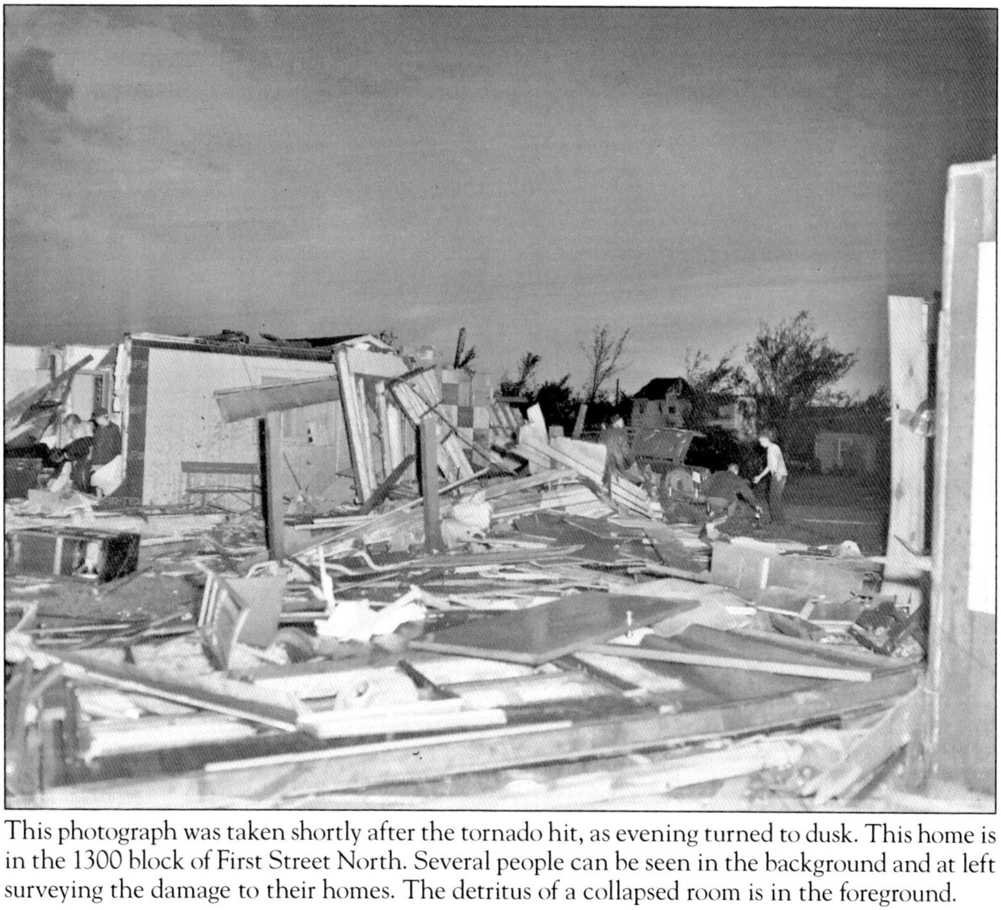

This photograph was taken shortly after the tornado hit, as evening turned to dusk. This home is in the 1300 block of First Street North. Several people can be seen in the background and at left surveying the damage to their homes. The detritus of a collapsed room is in the foreground.

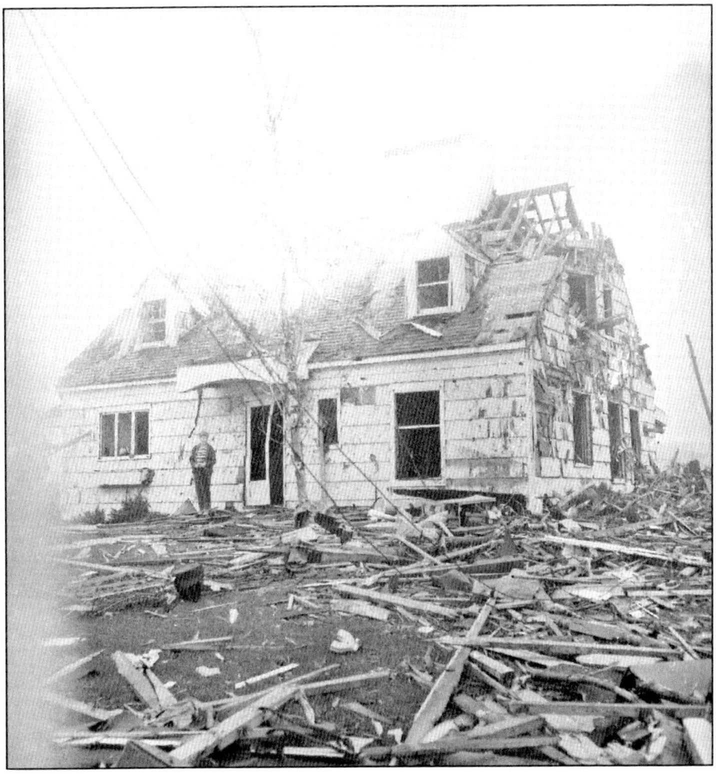

This one-and-a-half-story wood frame house was heavily damaged by the tornado, with part of the roof and shingles missing and debris scattered all over the yard and the roof. A person is standing by a twisted front door. This home is located at 1325 First Street North and, according to the *Fargo Forum*, belonged to Dr. Hugh Hawn.

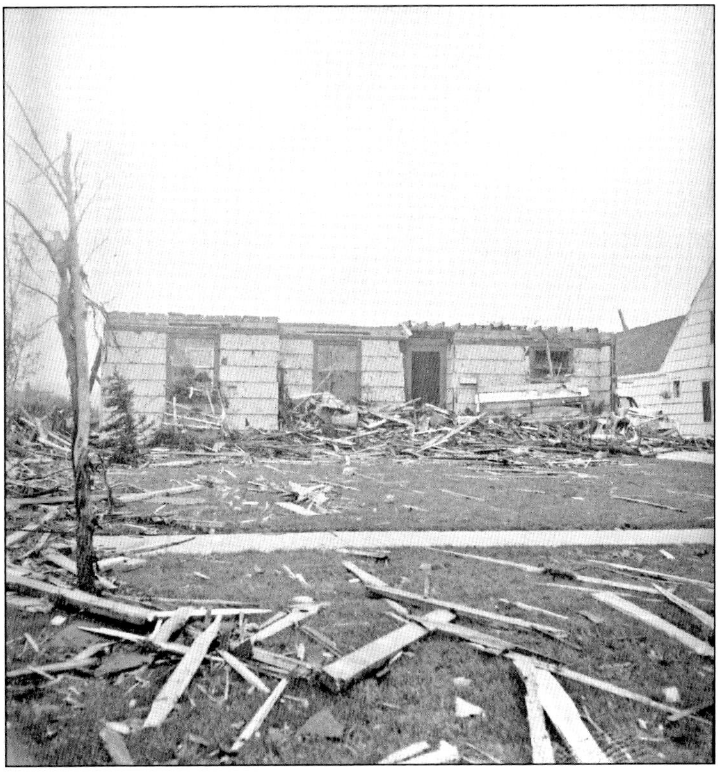

Victor H. Leeby Jr.'s home at 1329 First Street North had a missing roof and debris littering the yard and curbside in the front. In the foreground at left, only the trunk and a few branches remain of a tree. The house next door, at right, appears to still have its roof.

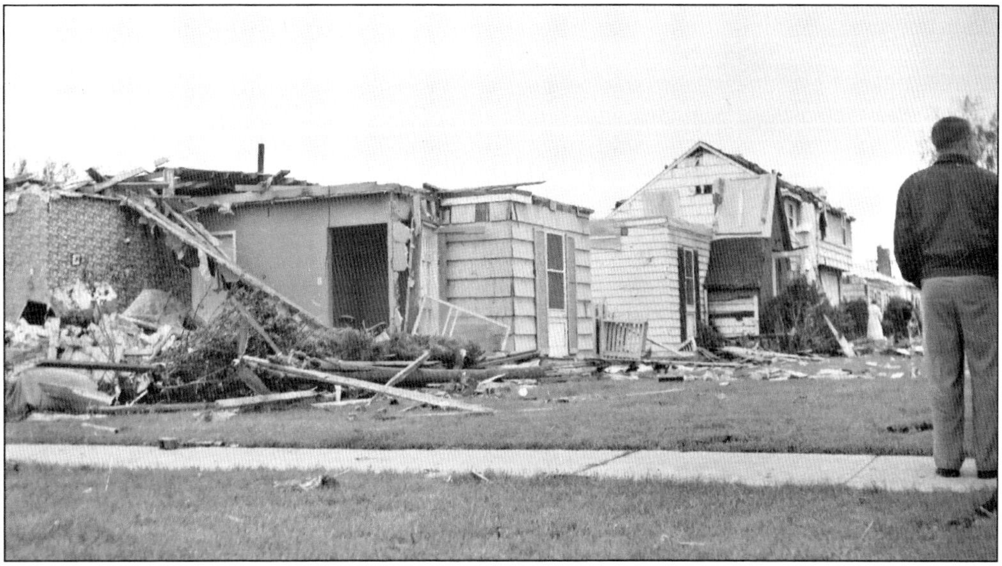

Looking north at the west side of the 1300 block of First Street North, the home in the foreground, 1302 First Street North, is missing a roof and some walls, exposing the interior. Wallpaper on the interior walls of an exposed room can be seen at left.

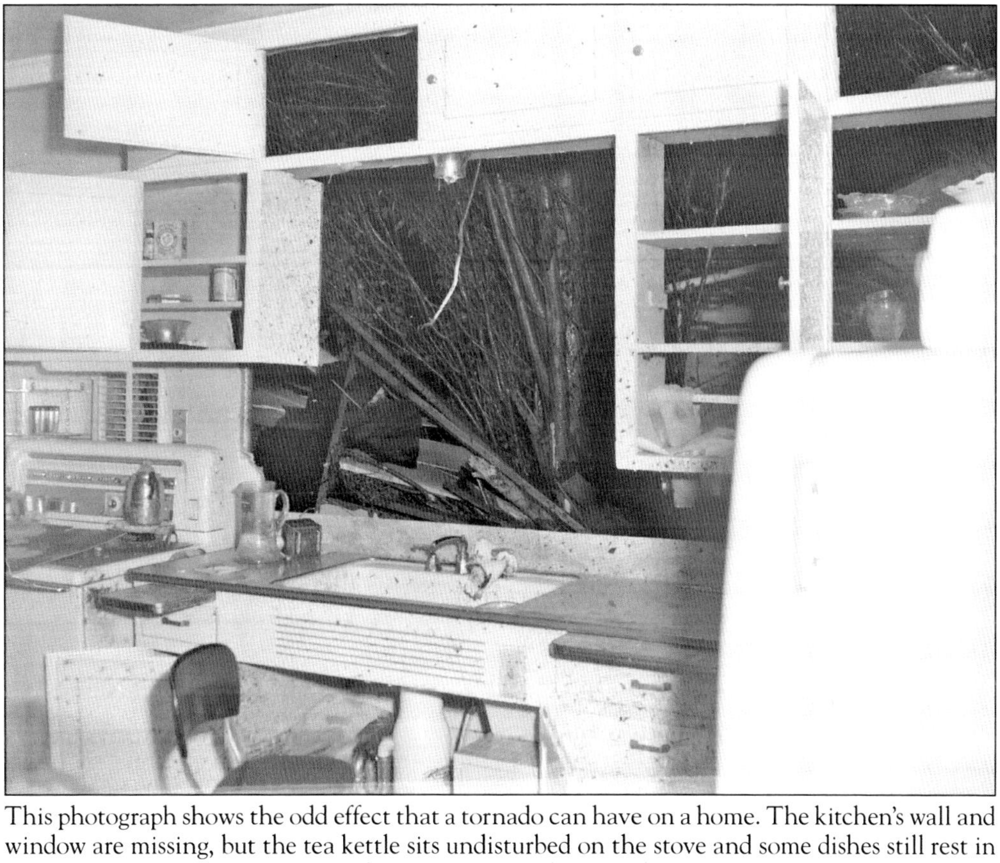

This photograph shows the odd effect that a tornado can have on a home. The kitchen's wall and window are missing, but the tea kettle sits undisturbed on the stove and some dishes still rest in the cabinets. Debris and trees can be seen through the hole that was once a window.

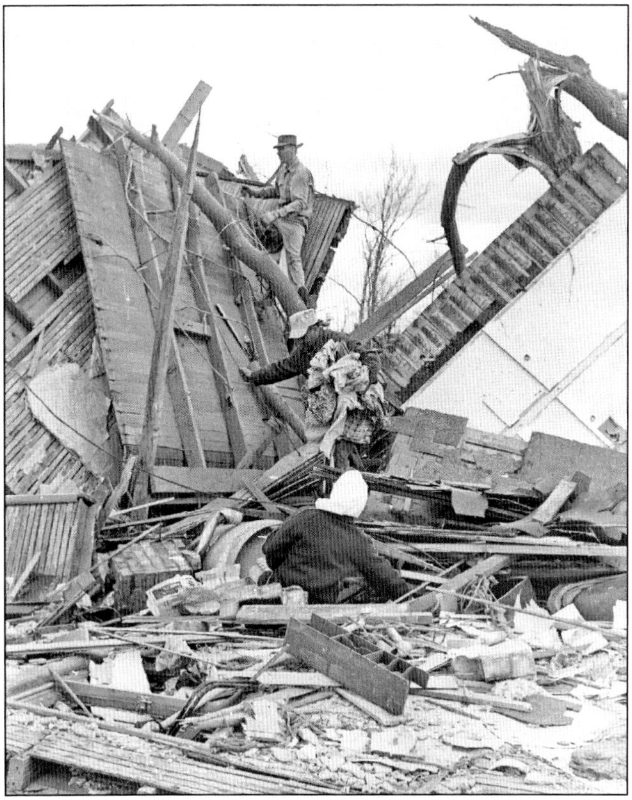

At an unknown location are the remains of a house with three people surveying the damage. There appears to be part of a chimney to the left of the person on the ground as well as other debris littered around. The person in the middle seems to be carrying some kind of fabric.

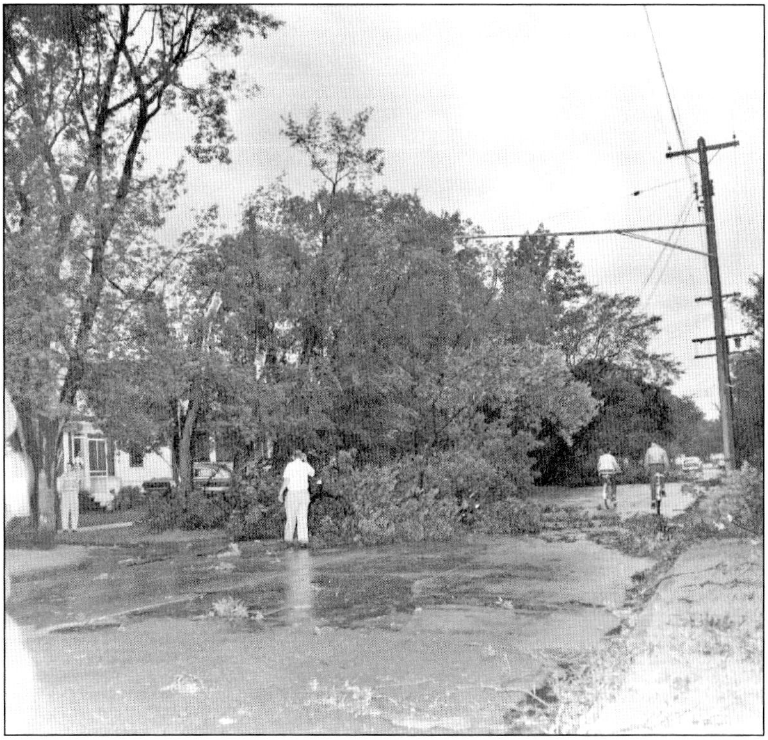

Immediately following the tornado, many residents had to walk or ride bicycles in order to get around before downed trees could be removed by city workers or volunteers. Fortunately, this tree did not topple onto a home, and the power lines did not come down, which would have made travel more dangerous.

Four

RECOVERY

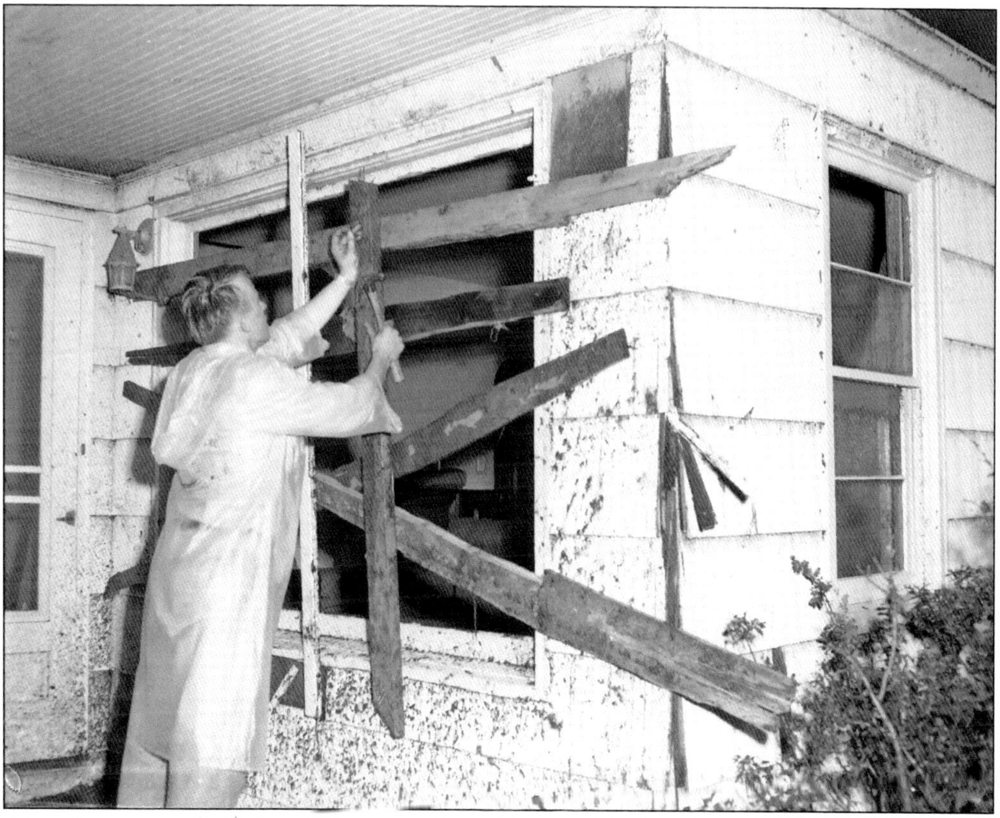

After the storm subsided, residents moved quickly and did what they could with any available materials to protect their damaged homes and belongings from further destruction and looting. Here, John Lunday works in the rain at the home of his mother, Belva Lunday, at 1345 First Street North. In addition to broken windows, this home also suffered damage to its siding.

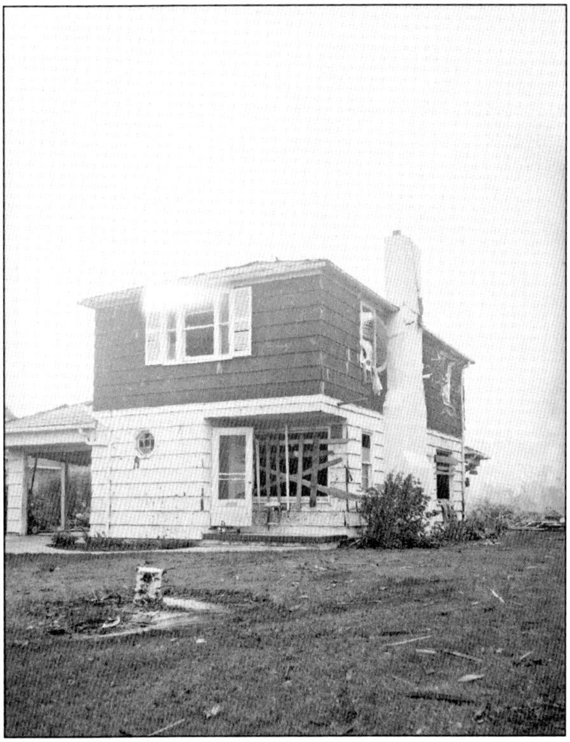

Another view of the tornado-damaged house owned by Belva Lunday is seen here. In the daylight, the true damage to the home is visible. The two-story lap-sided house has multiple broken windows, and debris is visible on the right. The window boarded up by John Lunday in the previous image can be seen.

Looking south from the 900 block of College Street, a truckload of men, identified by the *Fargo Forum* as traveling from Galesburg, North Dakota, stand in the back of a Chevrolet pickup truck. These men are returning from work at the south end of the North Dakota Agricultural College campus, now North Dakota State University. The address of the house at far right is 910 College Street.

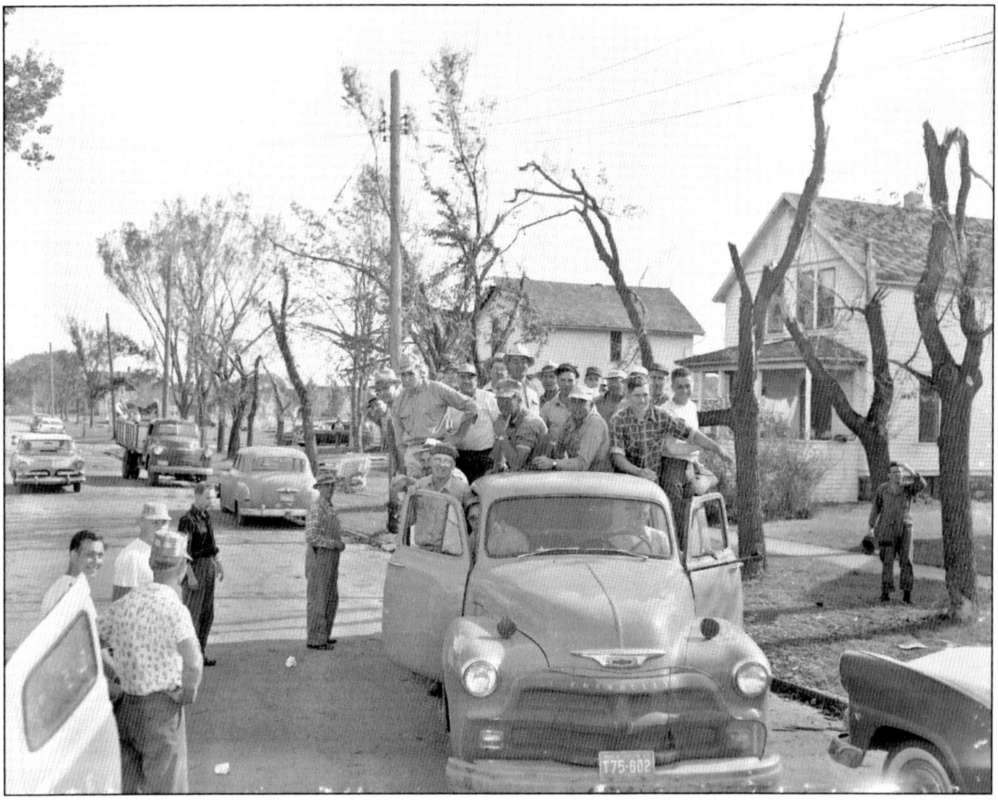

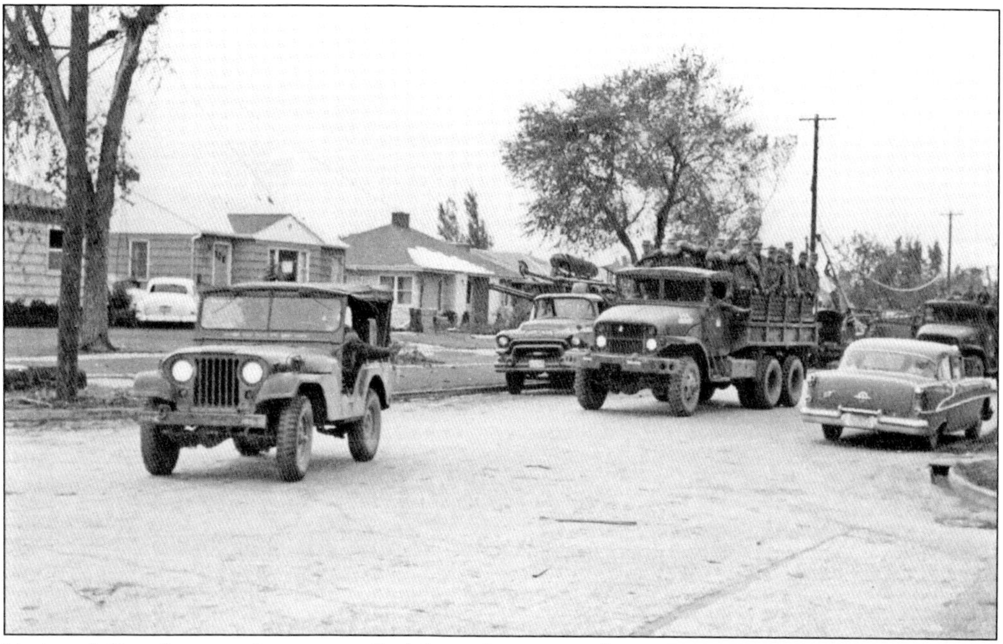

National Guardsmen, who were pulled from their annual encampment at Camp Grafton near Devils Lake, North Dakota, poured into Fargo to assist with the recovery and cleanup efforts. Looking north from Fourteenth Avenue North, a caravan of National Guard vehicles, led by a single Jeep, travels down Broadway. Numerous men stand in the truck beds, and downed power lines are visible at left.

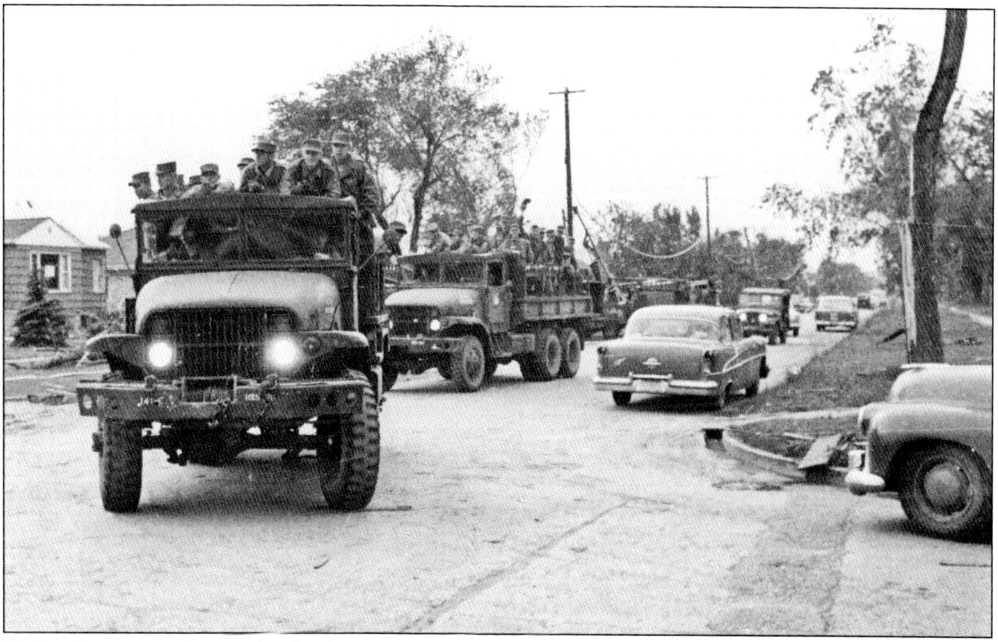

Multiple National Guard vehicles continue to drive south on Broadway in an attempt to survey the initial damage caused by the tornado. The two midsize trucks have numerous men in National Guard uniforms standing in them, while other vehicles follow behind in the caravan. The arrival of the National Guard was a welcome sight for residents who were in need of assistance.

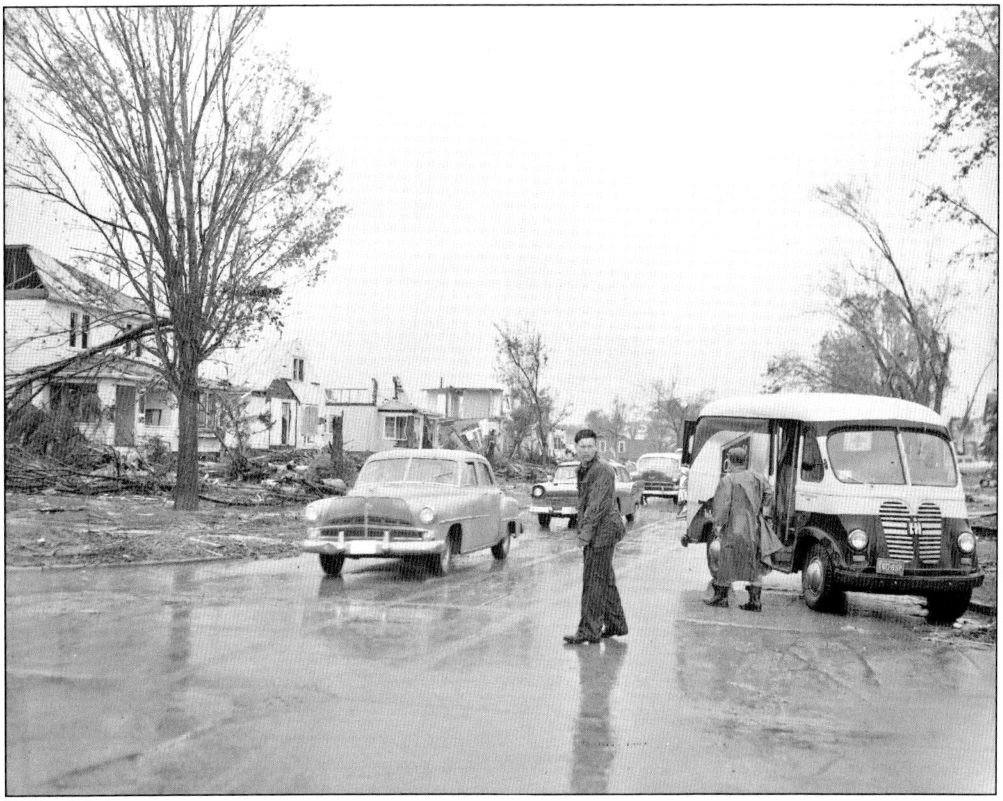

Heavy rain followed the storm and hampered recovery efforts, causing additional damage to structures impacted by the tornado. The man at center was identified by the *Fargo Forum* as Air National Guardsman Dan McCreadie, from Grandin, North Dakota. The truck at right was used to transport residents and cleanup workers to Plymouth Congregational Church for meals at its food station.

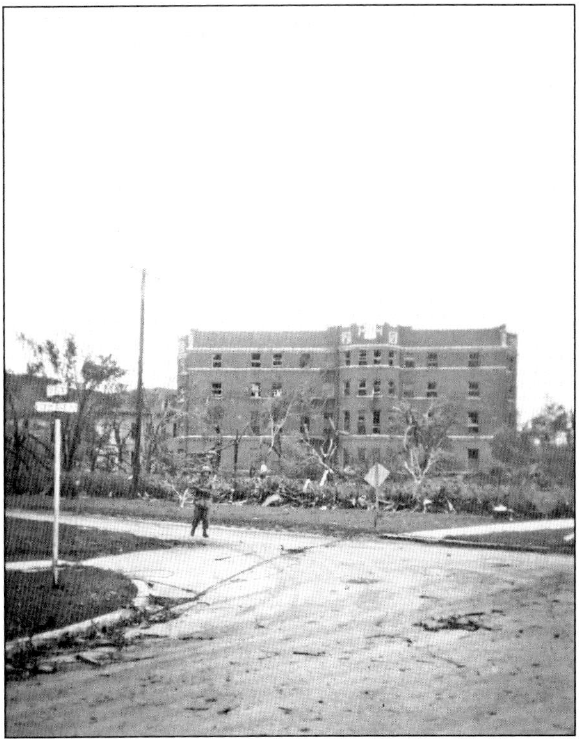

Abandoned streets were common after the tornado struck. Looking northeast, an unidentified National Guardsman patrols near the intersection of Thirteenth Avenue North and Seventh Street North while holding something close to the right side of his body. The damaged Sacred Heart Convent stands behind him. As in other locations, broken trees and debris litter the ground and street.

Safe road travel was especially important in tornado-damaged neighborhoods. Looking southeast, an unidentified National Guardsman, with a weapon on his hip, directs traffic at the intersection of Thirteenth Street North, now University Drive, and Twelfth Avenue North. Severely damaged houses and buildings as well as debris are visible. St. Paul's Newman Center, located at this intersection, was also damaged by the tornado.

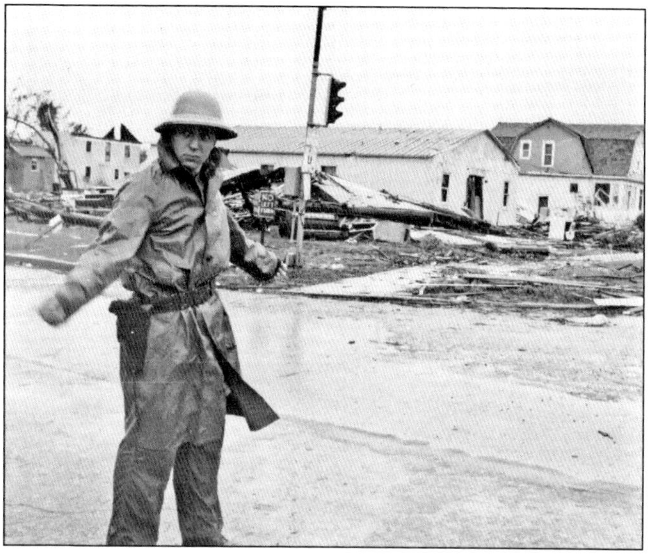

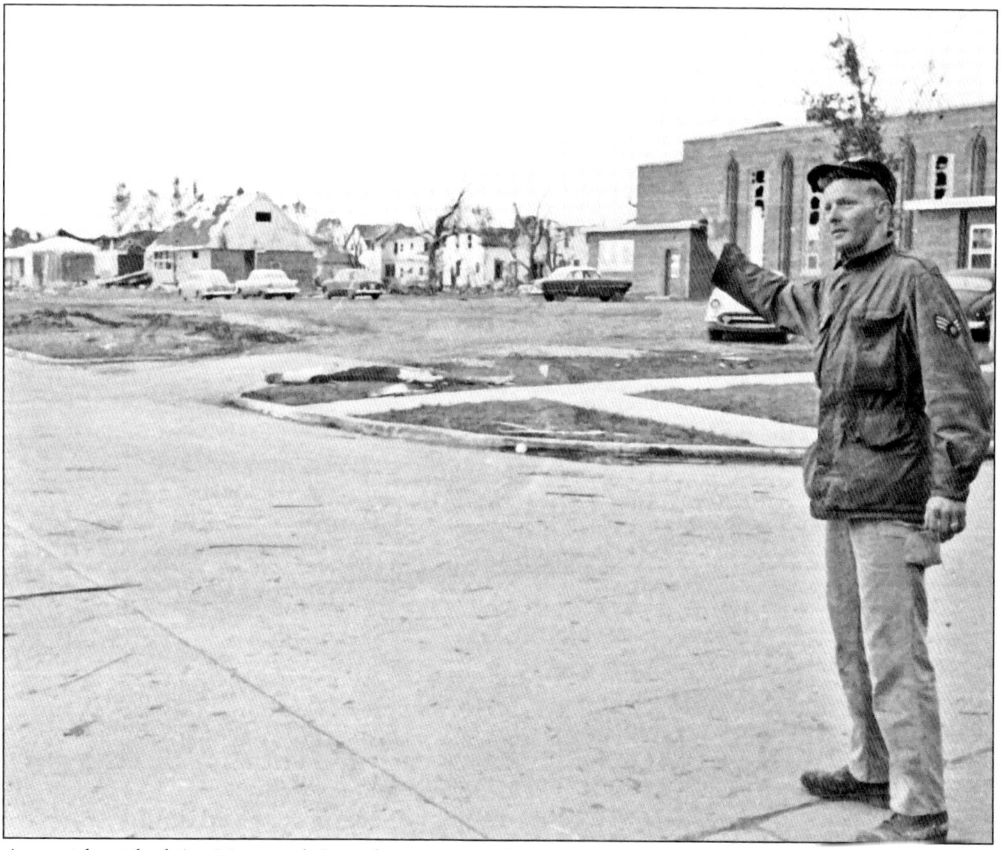

An unidentified Air National Guardsman contributes to the recovery process by directing traffic at the intersection of Twelfth Avenue North and Eleventh Street North. The 957th Field Artillery Battalion of the North Dakota National Guard relieved the Air National Guardsmen after they arrived in Fargo. Directly behind this man is the damaged American Lutheran Church, currently Peace Lutheran Church. Other damaged homes and buildings are visible in the distance.

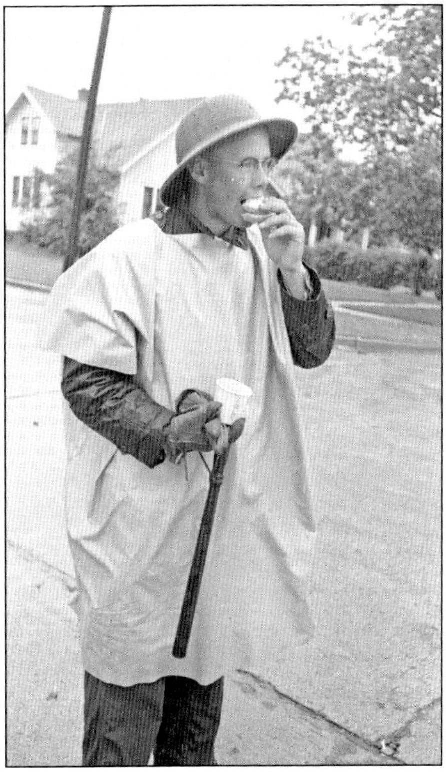

Norton Berg, an 18-year-old Air National Guardsman, stands at the intersection of Twelfth Avenue North and Second Street North taking a short break from his official duties to eat a sandwich and drink a cup of coffee. The address of the home in the background is 1145 Second Street North.

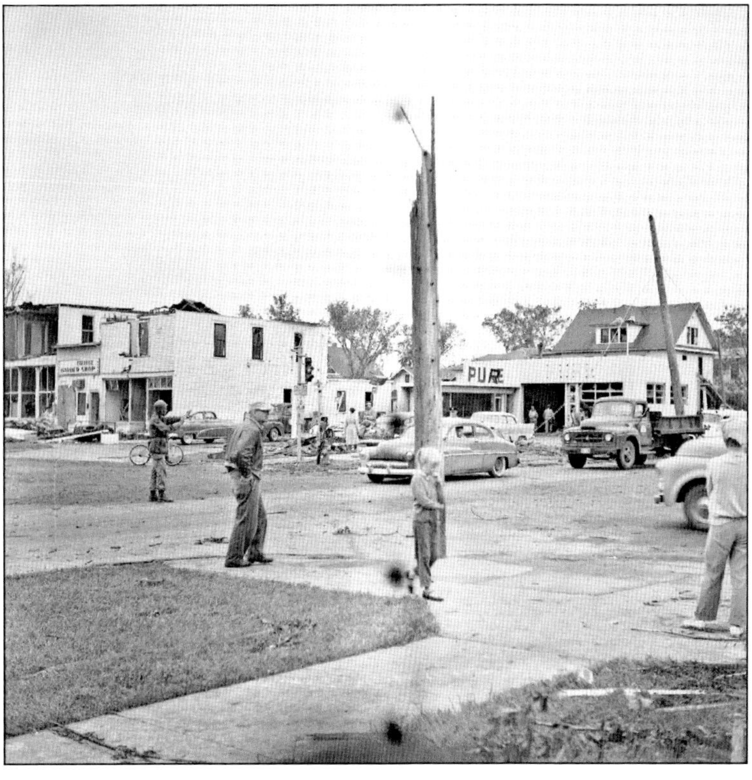

Looking southwest across Thirteenth Street North, now University Drive, and Twelfth Avenue North, buildings with various degrees of damage are visible, including the College Pure Oil gas station, College Grocery, College Barber Shop, and College Inn restaurant. Several vehicles, pedestrians, and a National Guardsman directing traffic are also visible. The utility pole in the foreground has been snapped in half.

Controlling traffic in and out of damaged neighborhoods was an important duty for National Guardsmen after the tornado. Here, an unidentified guardsman gestures with a baton and speaks with a driver on First Street North. The house directly behind the vehicle, located at 1301 First Street North, has a damaged roof and boarded-up windows.

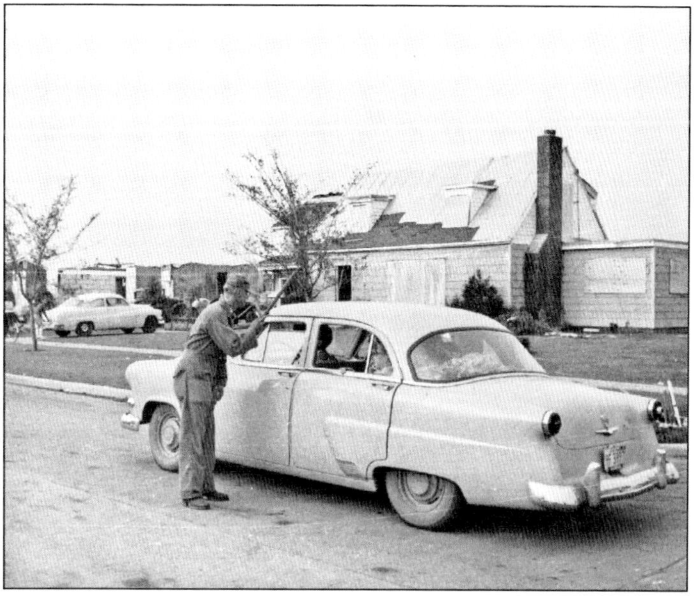

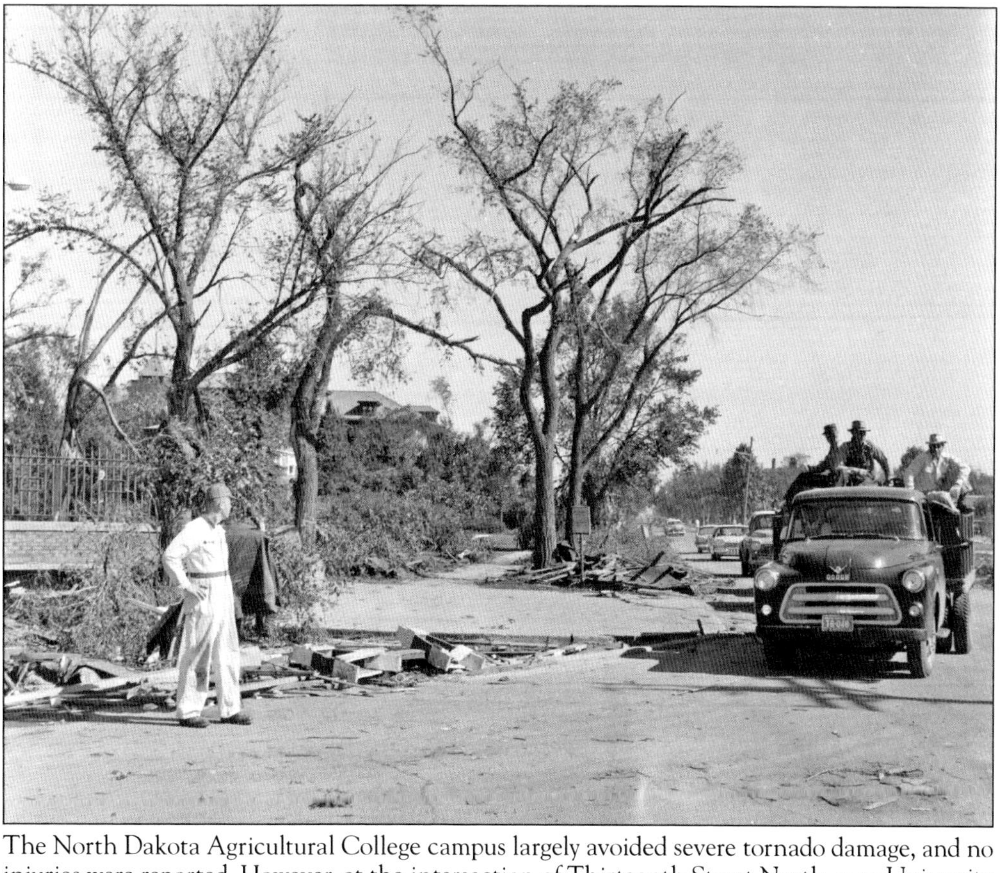

The North Dakota Agricultural College campus largely avoided severe tornado damage, and no injuries were reported. However, at the intersection of Thirteenth Street North, now University Drive, and Twelfth Avenue North, the destroyed campus gates are seen. The old President's House and Ceres Hall are in the background. Volunteers arrive in a truck to begin repairs.

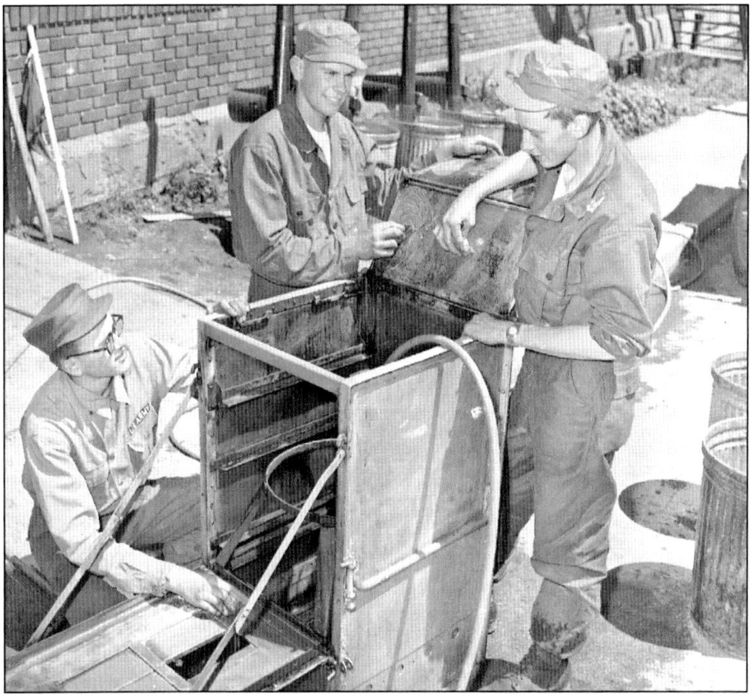

Tornado recovery efforts took many different forms for North Dakota National Guardsmen, including equipment maintenance and cleaning. On the sidewalk outside the Fargo Armory at Broadway and First Avenue South, three unidentified guardsmen clean a piece of equipment during their tireless recovery assistance.

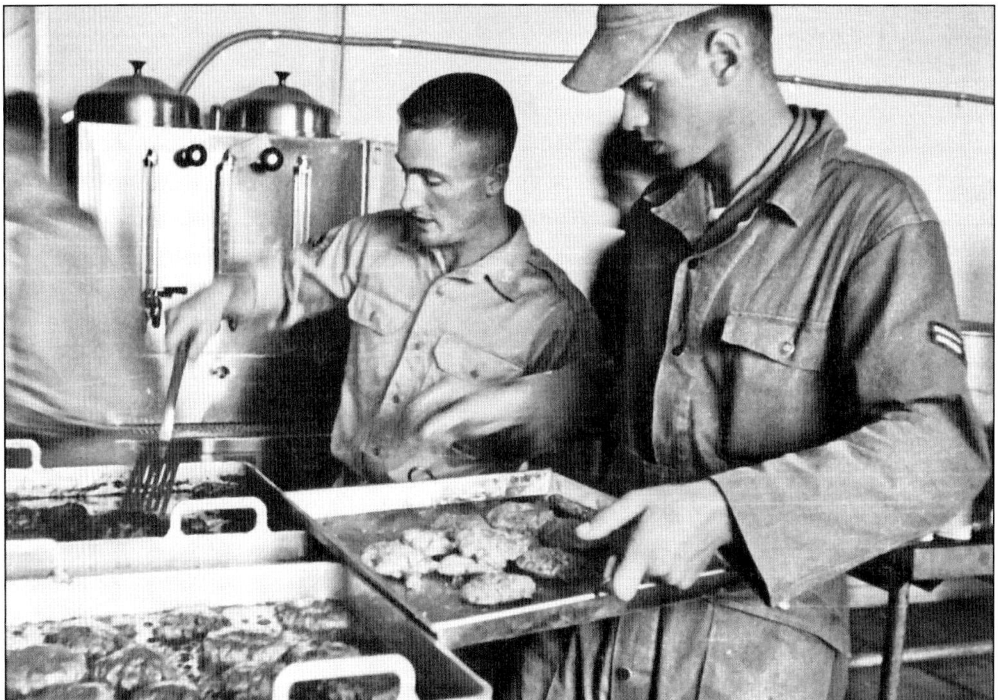

National Guardsmen not only assisted with recovery efforts, some, such as these two men, also served their fellow guardsmen by cooking meals. The meal appeared to be some type of meat patty. These guardsmen shared the cooking and serving duties, and the amount of food visible attests to the large number of guardsmen who served in Fargo following the tornado.

While serving the tornado-ravaged neighborhoods, the National Guardsmen took a well-deserved break to refuel. The large pots suggest some type of soup or stew. The men appear to be dressed in official but more relaxed National Guard attire during a hard day's work.

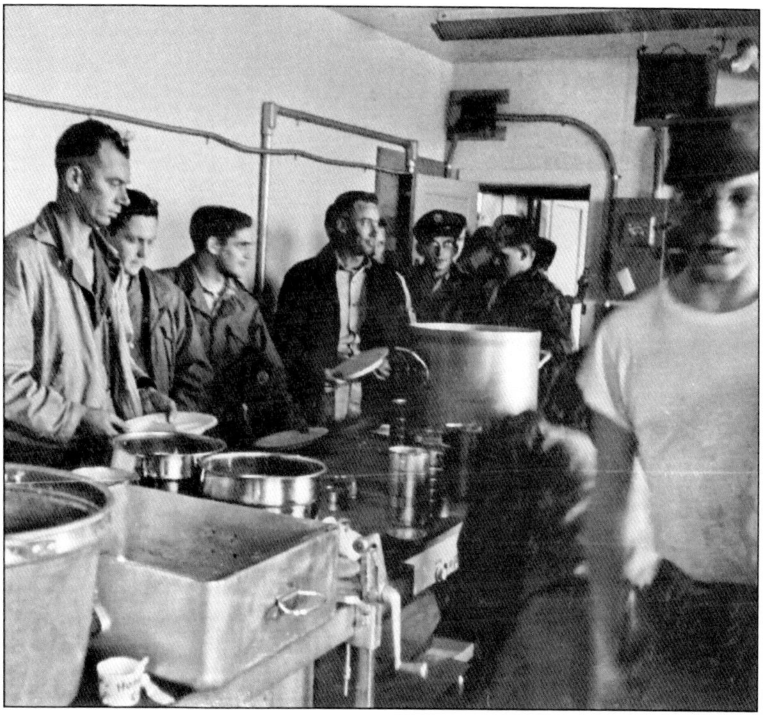

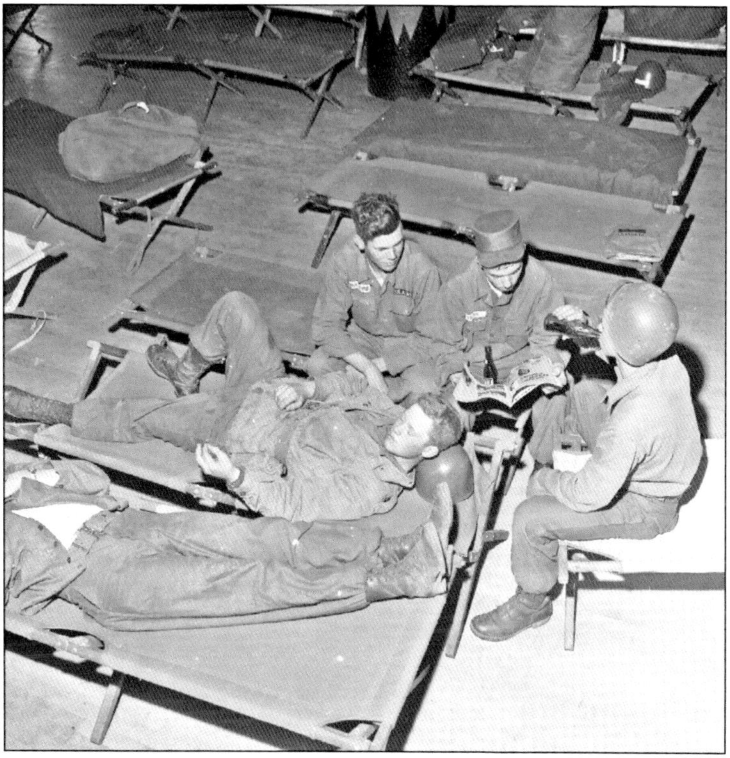

Members of Battery A, 957th Field Artillery Battalion rest from tornado recovery efforts in the Crystal Ballroom of the Fargo Armory, located at Broadway and First Avenue South. From left to right are Pfc. James Buttke, of Lucca, North Dakota (face not shown); Robert Silvernail, of Milnor, North Dakota; Bernard McRitchie, of Sheldon, North Dakota; and Lyle Otteson and Jerome Jankowski, both of Enderlin, North Dakota.

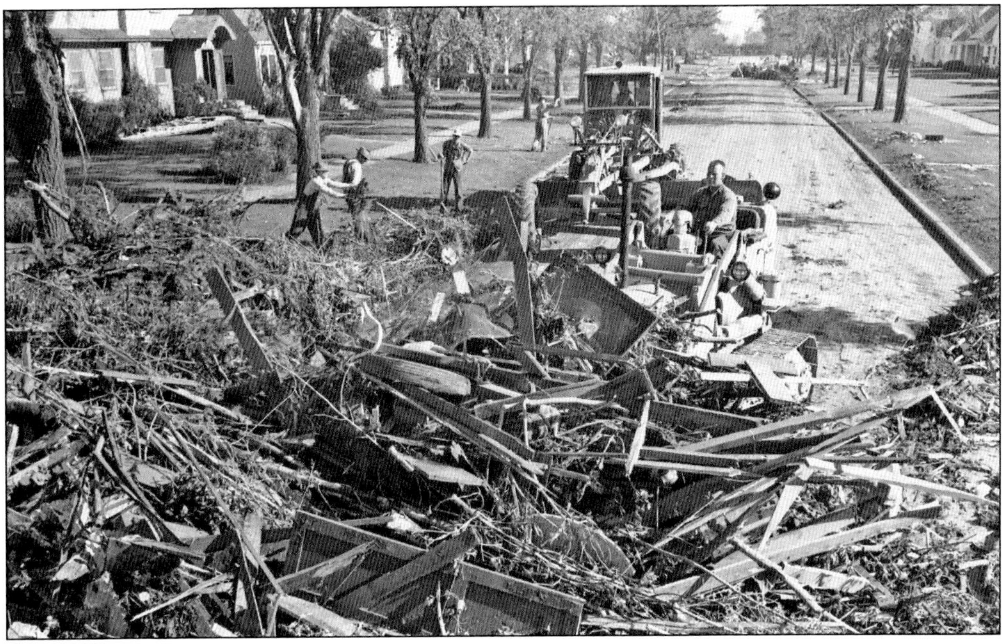

The tornado left large amounts of debris and wreckage in the city streets, making them impassable and recovery almost impossible. Looking north in the 1300 block of Third Street North, a bulldozer and loader work to remove large tree branches and other debris from the street to make it passable. This debris likely came from damaged houses and buildings nearby. At left, several people are assisting with the substantial cleanup. At least one person appears to be holding a shovel. Houses are partially visible on both sides of the street, and another pile of rubble is visible in the distance.

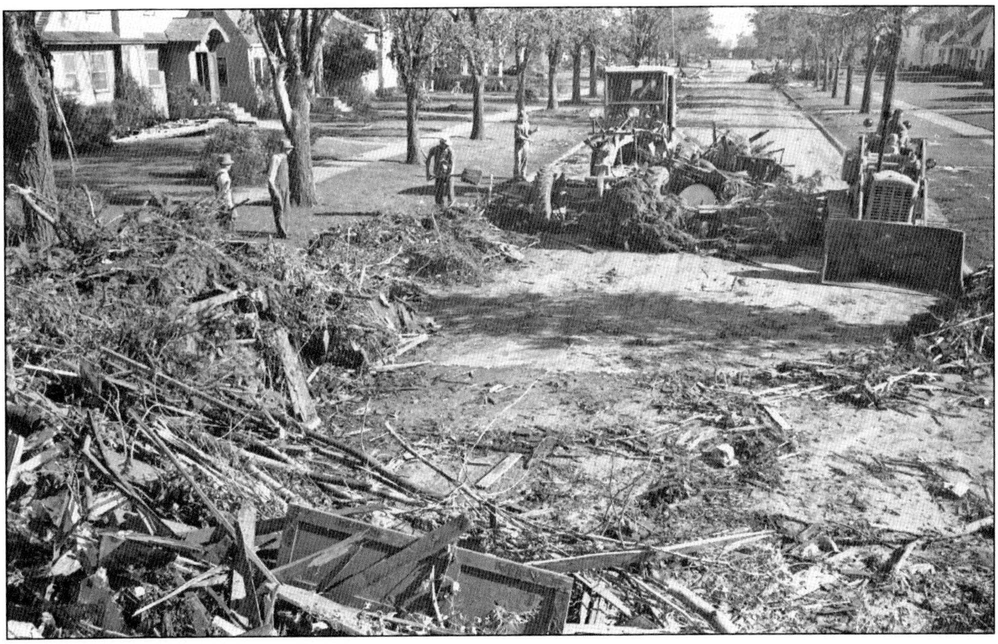

In heavily damaged areas, tornado debris was burned, as the cost to transport it away would have been too high. Here, a large pile of rubble and wreckage composed of mainly wood and pieces from tornado-damaged homes burns in the Golden Ridge neighborhood. A severely damaged house is visible in the background, and additional burn piles are seen throughout the area.

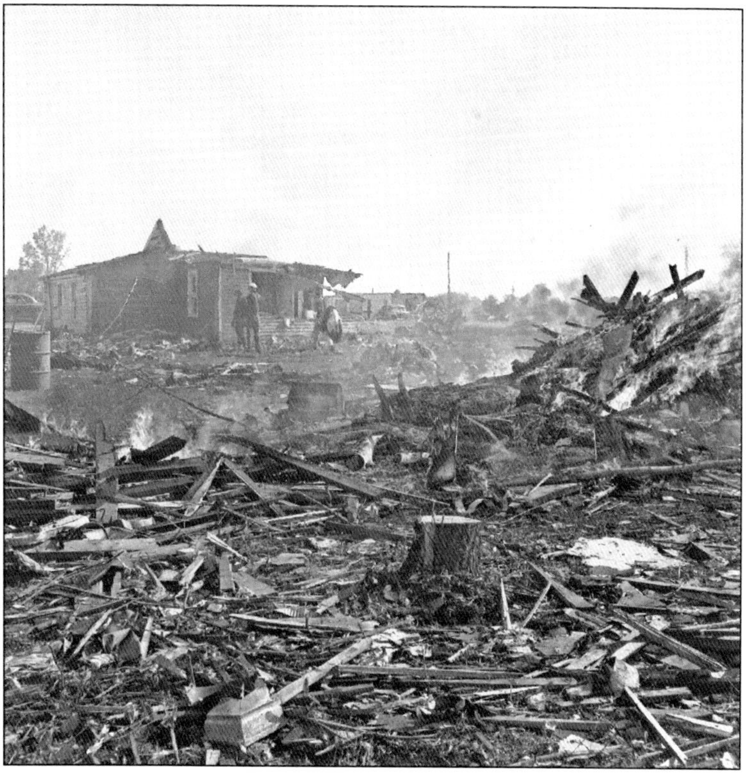

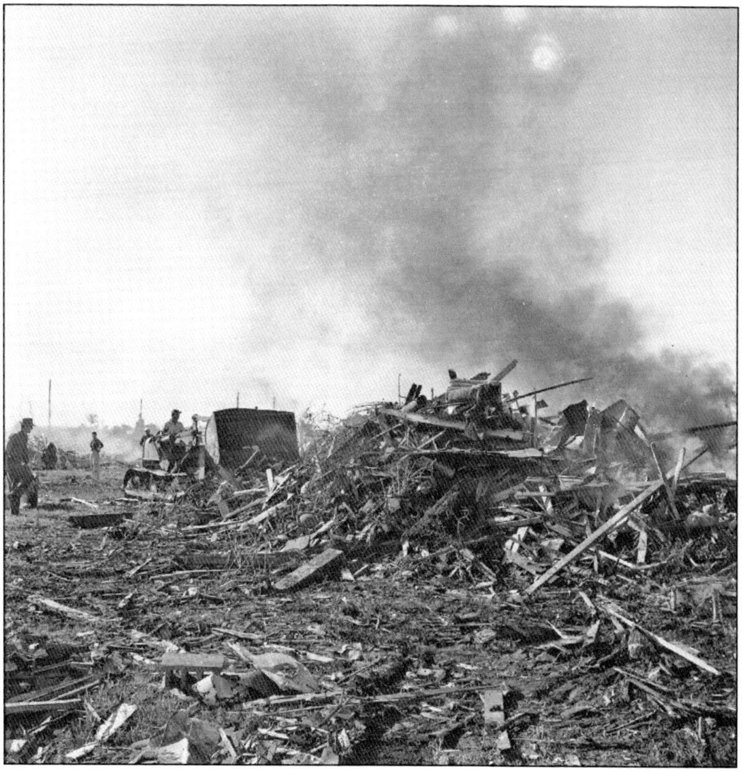

The Golden Ridge neighborhood suffered severe tornado damage. One hundred twenty-one homes were totally destroyed, 15 partially damaged, and six suffered minor damage. Here, a bulldozer pushes debris into a large pile of burning rubble. Smoke plumes indicate additional burn piles elsewhere in the neighborhood. Several people are visible to the left of, as well as behind, the bulldozer.

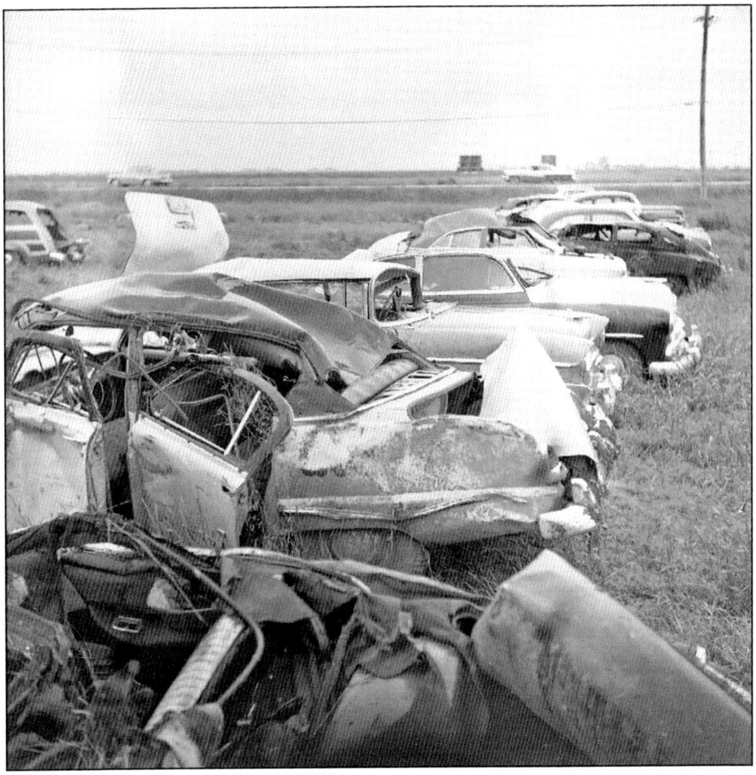

After the tornado struck, many locations were repurposed to assist with the cleanup efforts. The Red River Valley Fairgrounds, between Seventeenth Avenue North, Nineteenth Avenue North, and Thirteenth Street North, now North University Drive, stored about 75 vehicles damaged by the tornado. Multiple vehicles are visible with varying types and severity of damage; these vehicles are parked near what is now University Village.

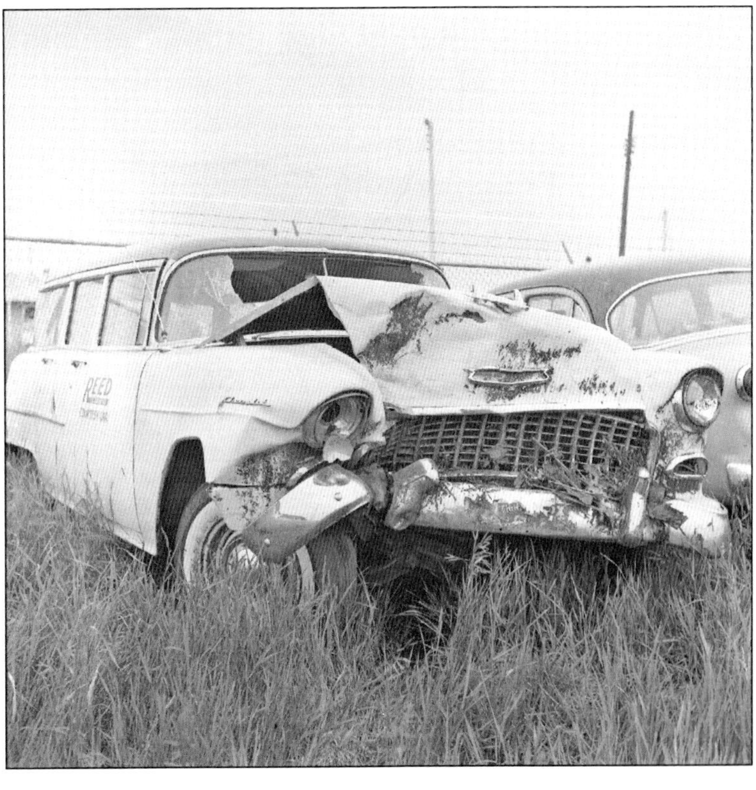

A tornado-damaged Chevrolet station wagon is parked at the Red River Valley Fairgrounds. "Reed Cleaners" is painted on the passenger door. Reed Cleaners was located near the Hasty Tasty on Thirteenth Street North, now University Drive. The front windshield is largely missing, and the remaining fragments are shattered, while the hood and entire front of the vehicle is crushed.

The damage suffered by this vehicle was severe; the entire roof and front windshield are missing and the interior, front panel, and seats are also in poor condition. The Red Cross estimated that 200 vehicles were destroyed and 300 were damaged. These damaged vehicles were only one example of the losses suffered by tornado survivors.

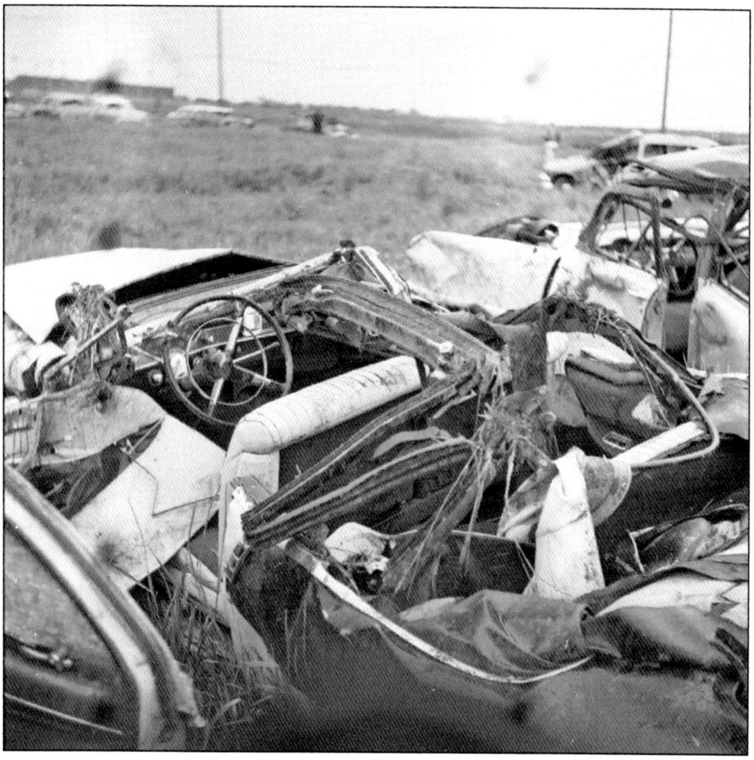

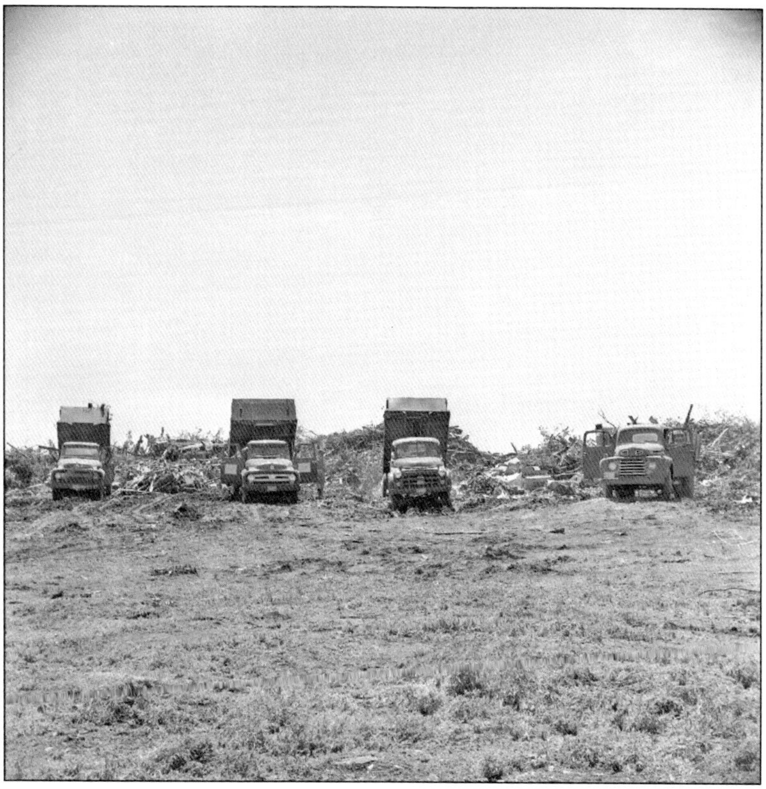

After the tornado, the cleanup of debris and rubble was an immediate priority to make neighborhoods and streets safe. Here, four dump trucks unload the debris they collected from across the city at the Fargo landfill. Dump trucks arrived at the rate of two per minute the Monday after the tornado to ensure timely cleanup of debris.

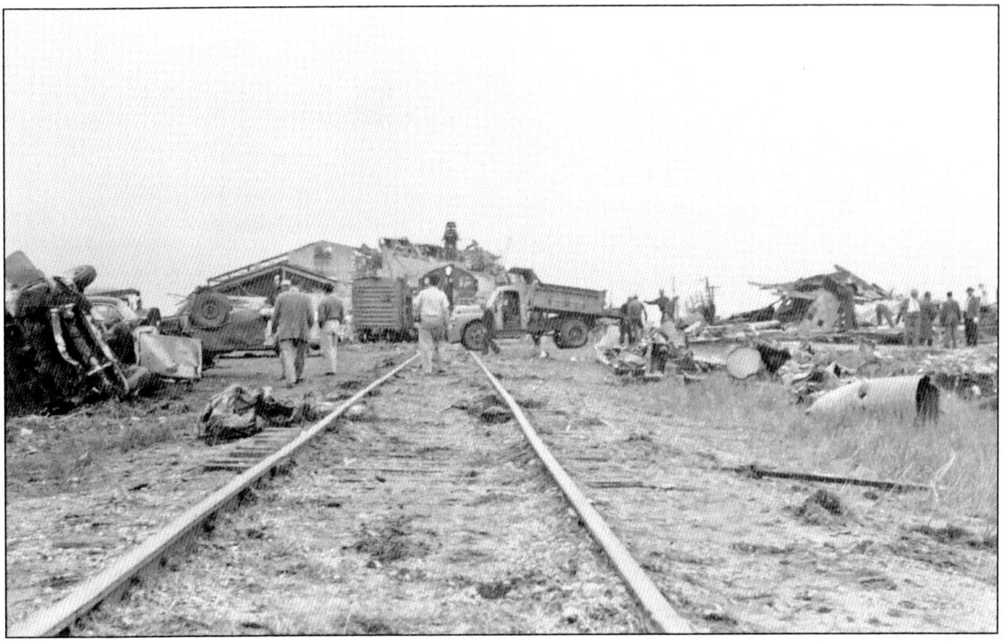

The power of the Fargo tornado was a sight to behold. The force of the winds overturned cars and distributed rubble across the Great Northern Railroad tracks in Fargo. Individuals are shown surveying the damage. The Peavey Fertilizer plant is in the background.

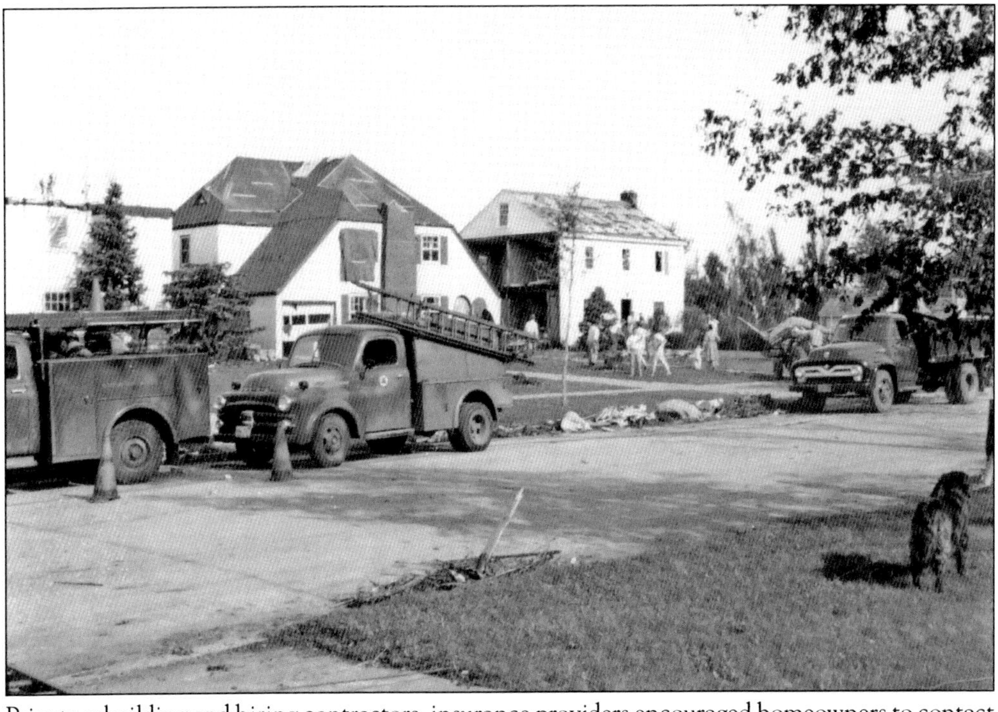

Prior to rebuilding and hiring contractors, insurance providers encouraged homeowners to contact them to ensure that all regulations were followed and that reputable contractors were used, as swindlers tried to take advantage of survivors. Here, the reconstruction of two houses at 1305 and 1301 Broadway starts as the trucks of numerous contractors are parked on the street.

In the light of day, the tornado's destruction and the persistence required to recover would have seemed overwhelming. At 802 Twenty-ninth Street North, Helen Loberg stands in the foreground and watches several unnamed men as they assess the damage and start picking up debris at the site of her tornado-damaged home.

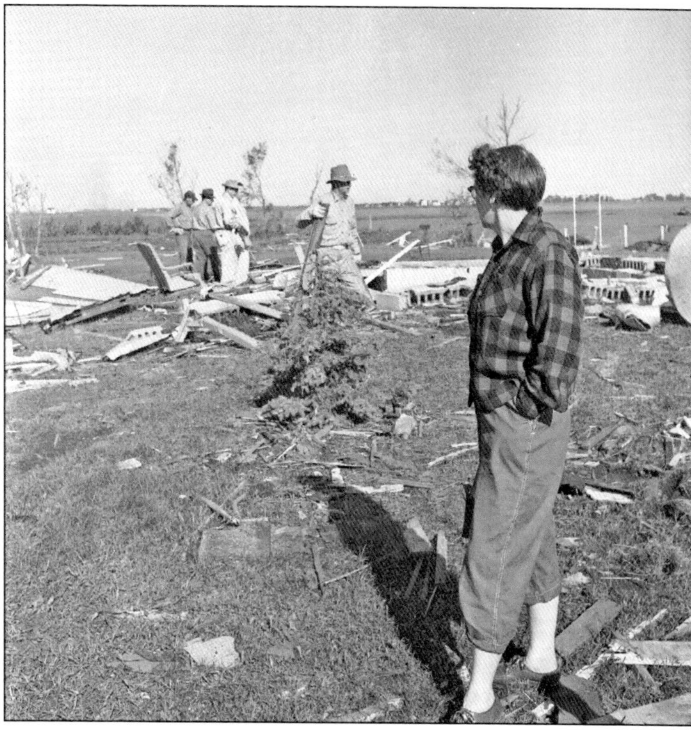

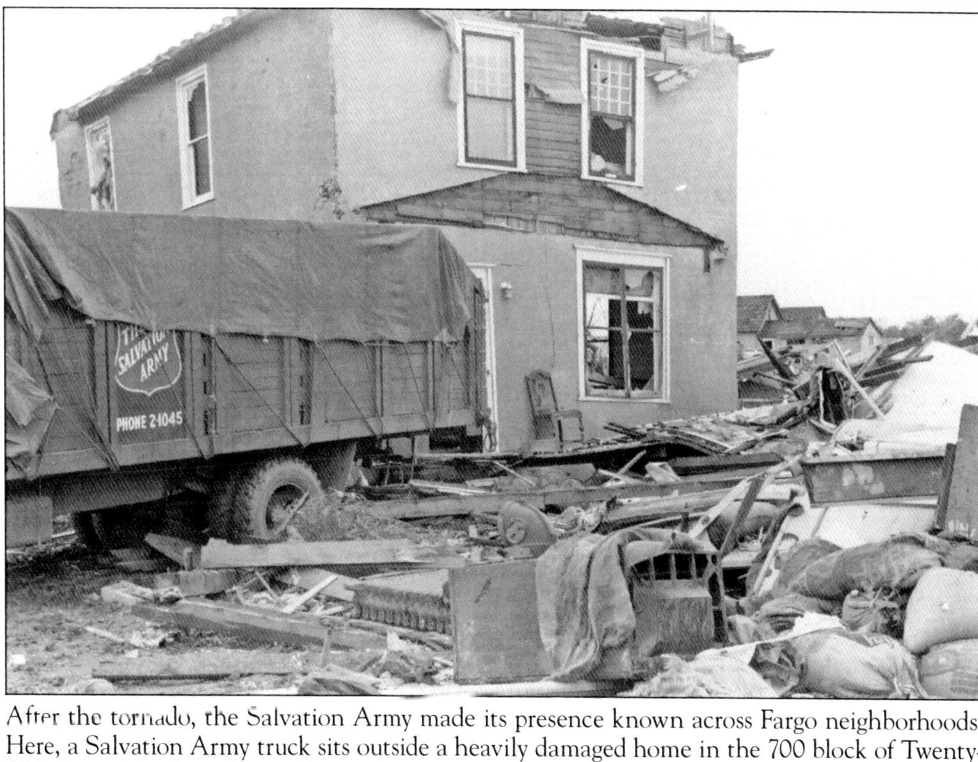

After the tornado, the Salvation Army made its presence known across Fargo neighborhoods. Here, a Salvation Army truck sits outside a heavily damaged home in the 700 block of Twenty-fifth Street North in the Golden Ridge neighborhood. Debris is visible in the foreground and at right, while other tornado-damaged homes can be seen in the distance.

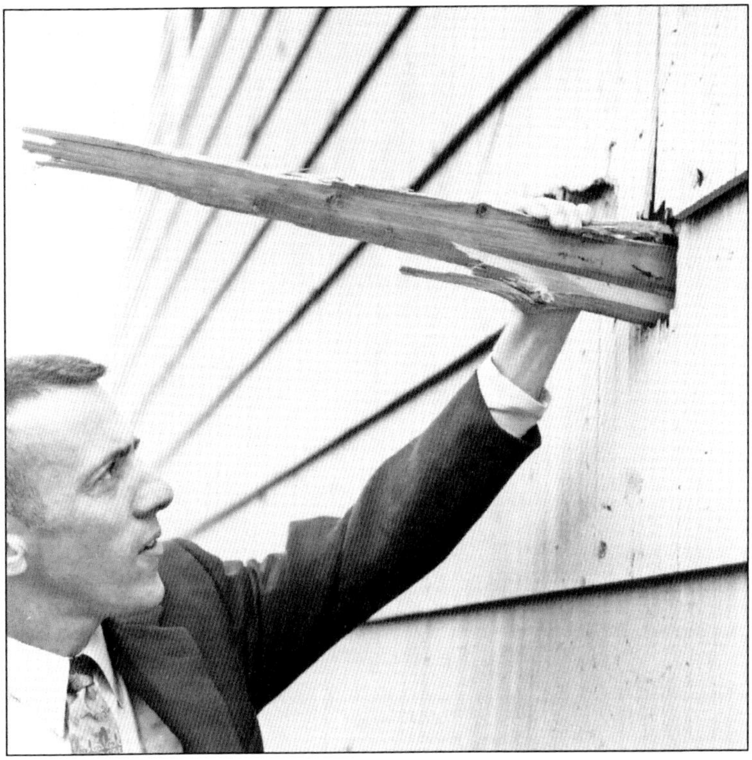

A man inspects a long wooden spike, probably from a tree, fence, or utility pole, protruding from the side of a home. The strong winds resulting from the tornado turned debris into flying shrapnel that could penetrate walls. Recovery took a lot of different forms, from completely rebuilding to removing debris from homes and yards.

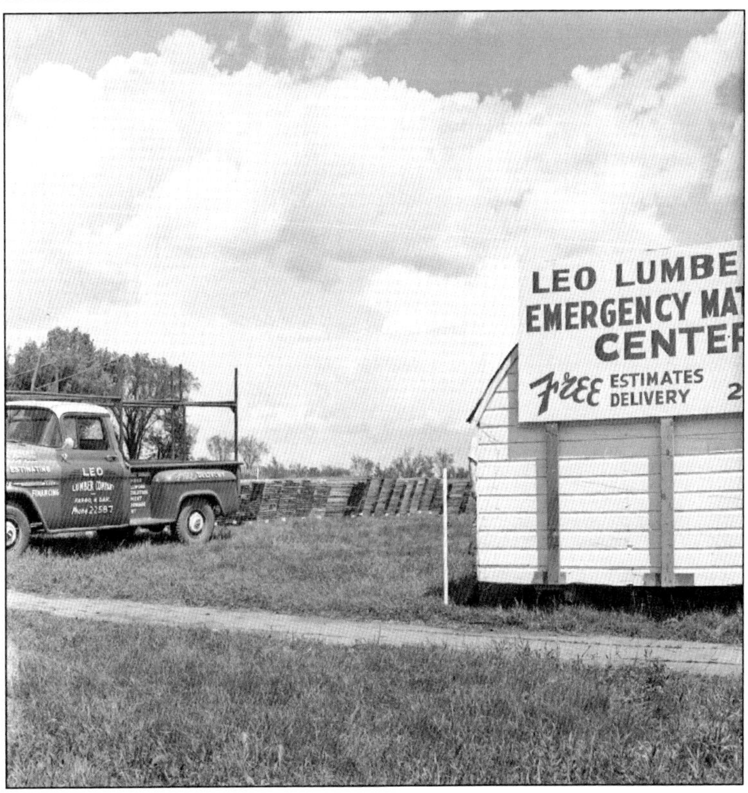

Emergency building supplies offered by the Leo Lumber Company after the tornado are pictured at 3300 Main Avenue. A Leo Lumber Company truck is at left, with stacks of lumber in the background. Lumber companies around the country made Fargo tornado survivors a priority when filling orders.

After the tornado, companies outside of Fargo offered their assistance and support to residents. Here, A.J. Larson, owner of A.J. Larson Construction Company of Minneapolis, oversees the reconstruction of Hart Motor Express at Seventeenth Street North and Seventh Avenue North 10 days after the tornado. Building supplies and lumber can be seen, and other tornado-damaged buildings are visible in the distance.

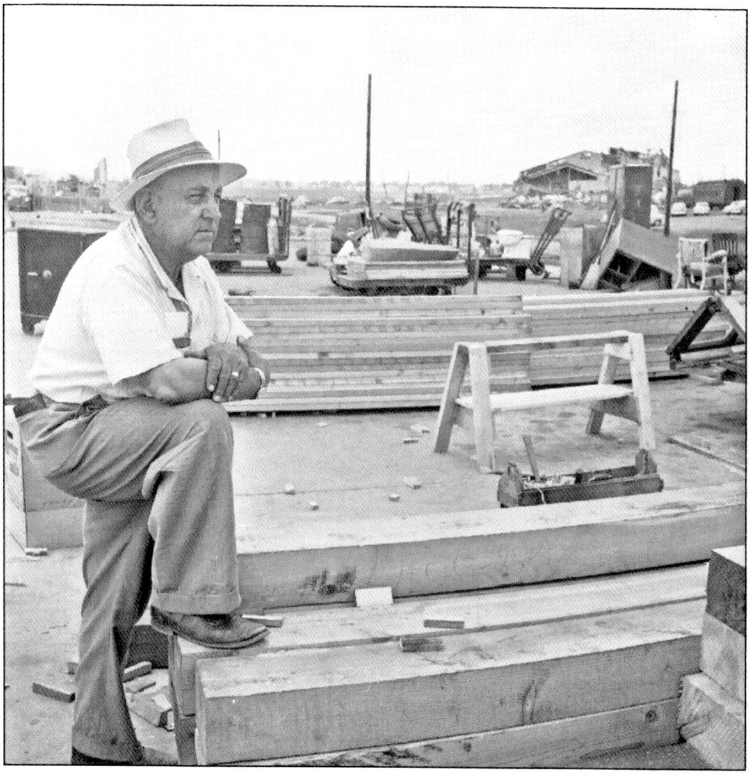

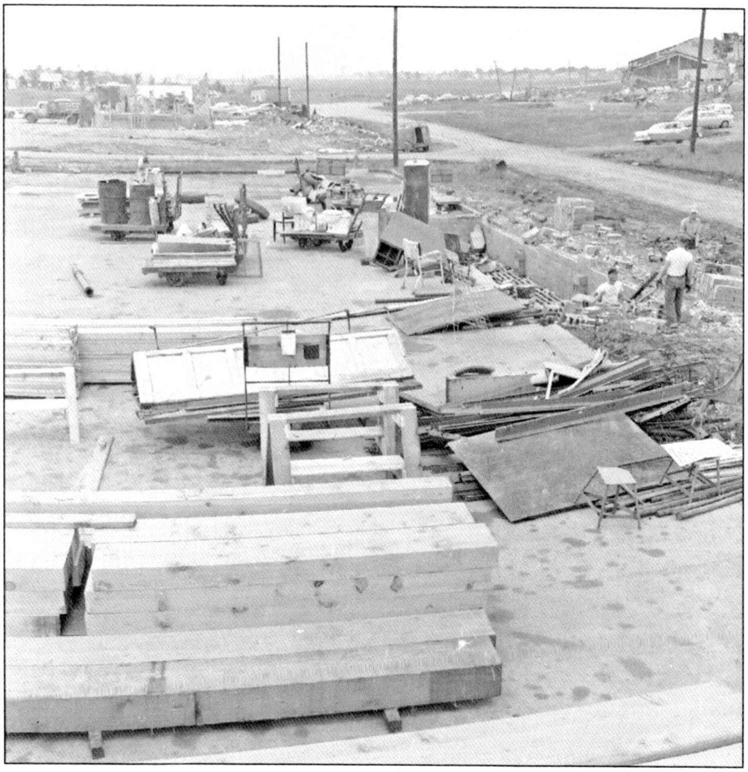

At first, recovery and reconstruction might have seemed daunting, but any progress brought hope to the community. Here is an elevated view of the rebuilding process of Hart Motor Express. Three men construct a cement cinder block foundation at right, and other building supplies and damaged structures are visible throughout the area.

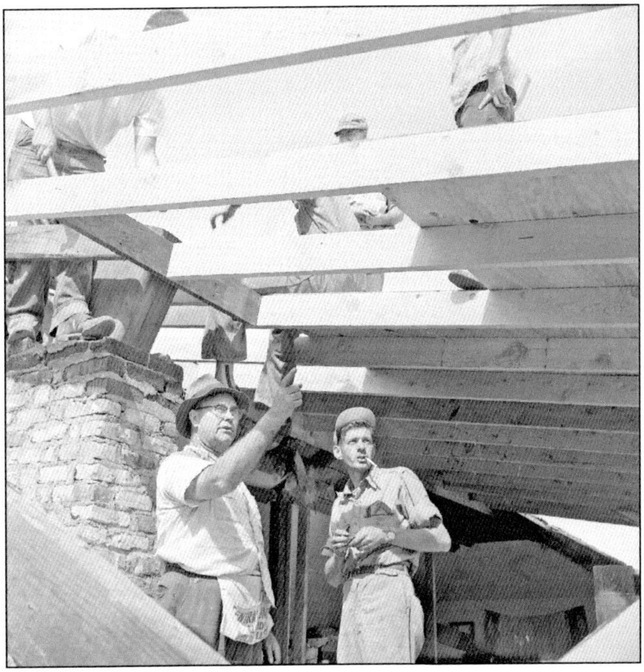

Two men stand by a brick chimney and under the beams of a new roof as construction takes place overhead at 1122 College Street. The man smoking a cigarette at right is O.H. "Buck" Shirk, who owns the home. Shirk worked in the engineering division of the Northern Pacific Railroad and was in Jamestown, North Dakota, when the tornado hit.

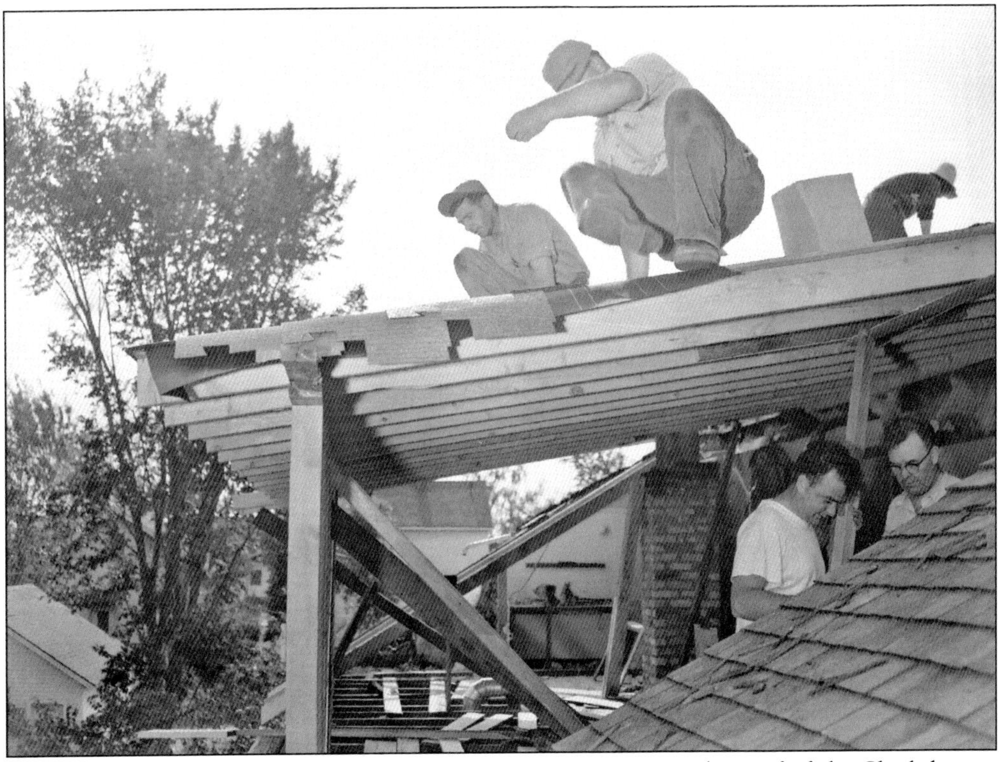

Approximately five men are visible as they work to reconstruct the roof of the Shirk home. According to the *Fargo Forum*, Buck and Pat Shirk had recently remodeled the attic bedroom that belonged to their sons. They had to start over after the tornado hit but were happy to add a dormer, which they had previously wanted anyway for their sons' room.

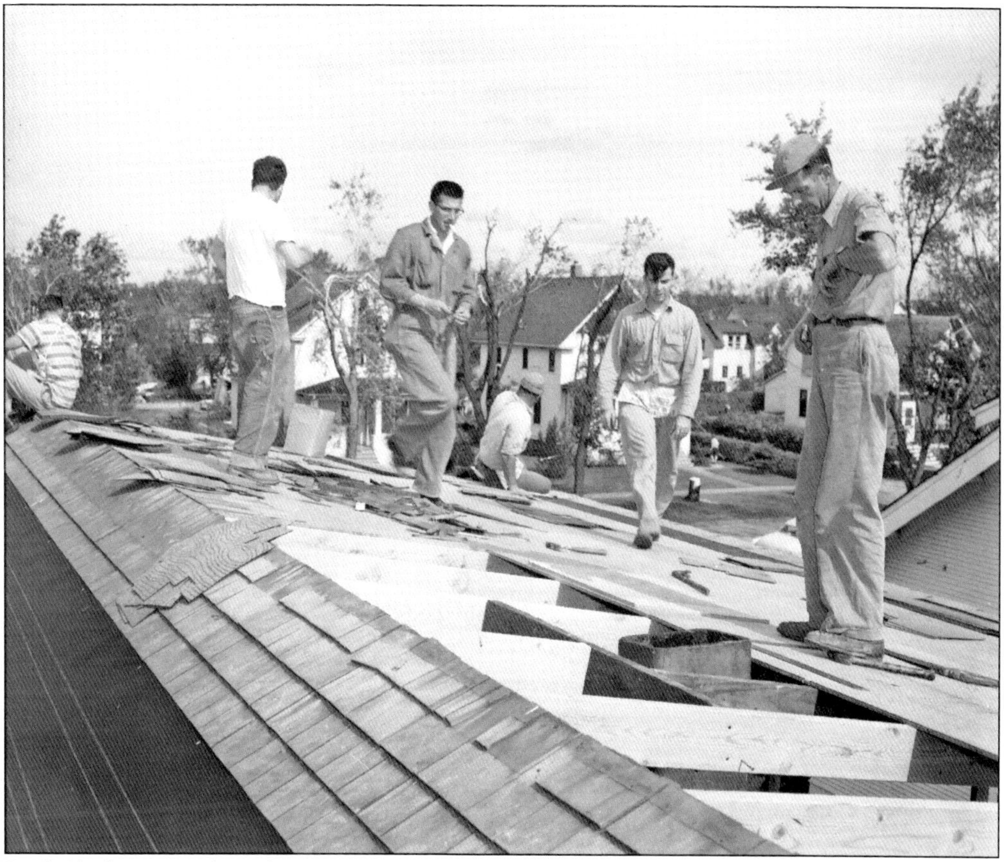

Buck Shirk, seen at far right, works with five other men to repair his roof. Shirk's colleagues from the railroad and family members assisted with repairs. The workers put in 134 hours total by the Sunday following the tornado to complete the work. Repair following the tornado was a necessity to protect homes against other summer storms.

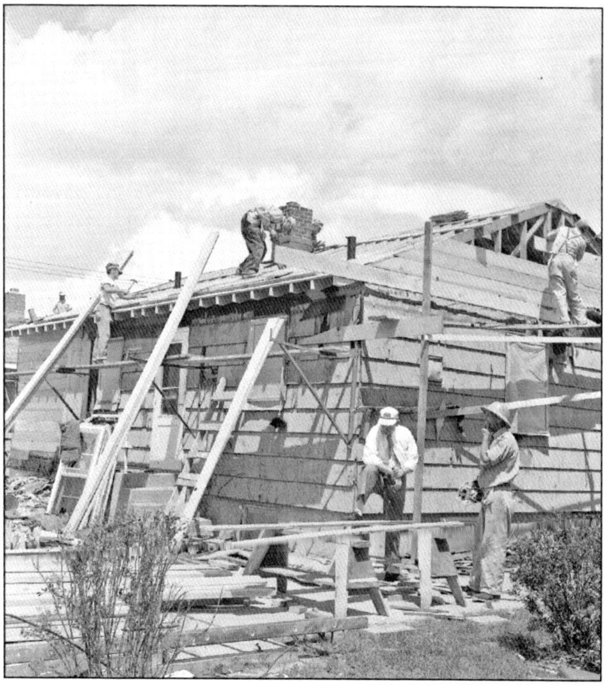

Ten days after the tornado, men work to reconstruct the home of Erwin Steinbrook at 1252 Ninth Street North. The work was done by the Lund and Leonard Construction Company of Fargo and included re-siding as well as repairing the roof. Four construction workers are visible working on the roof, while two individuals are seen on the ground.

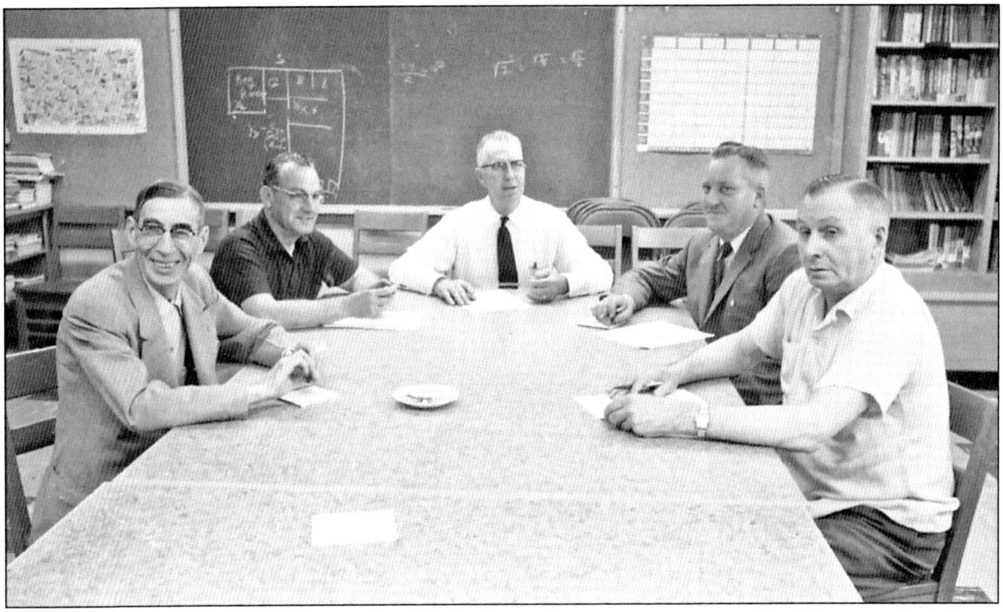

Community members, from left to right, E.J. McCannel, city commissioner; Earl Singiser, Red Cross building advisor; Fred Saefke, fire chief and committee chairman; E.C. Billigmeier, employment service; and W.W. Murrey, president of the North Dakota Federation of Labor, banded together to form the Tornado Manpower Recovery Committee. Meetings like this were likely held at Emerson H. Smith School at 211 Eleventh Street South.

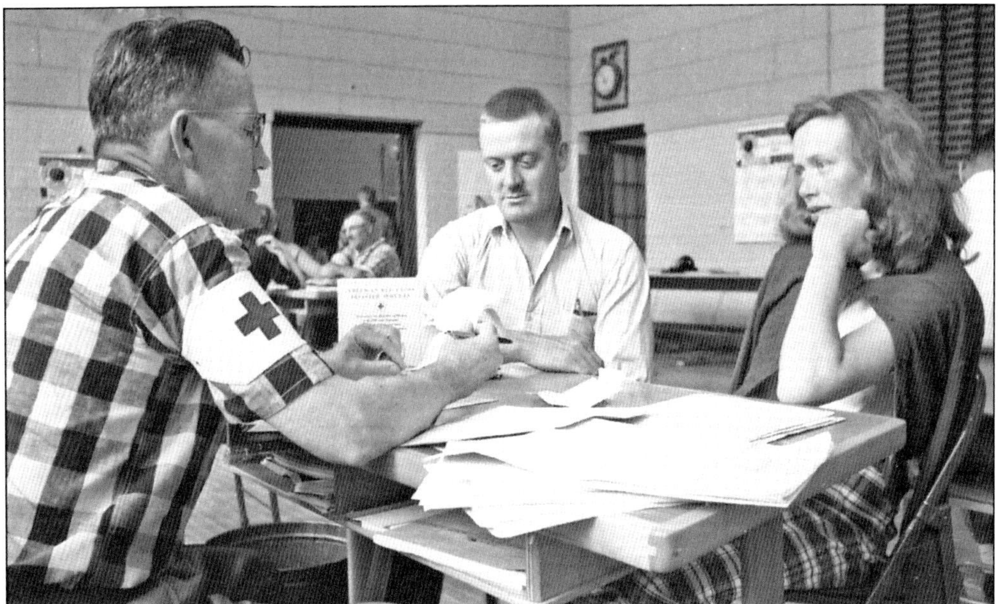

A man and woman consult with a Red Cross worker. The Cass County Red Cross Chapter was instrumental in helping affected families recover. The Red Cross helped find shelter for the 656 people left homeless, and organized and distributed donations of supplies and clothing. Additionally, national Red Cross disaster specialists came to Fargo and set up their offices in the gymnasium of Emerson H. Smith School.

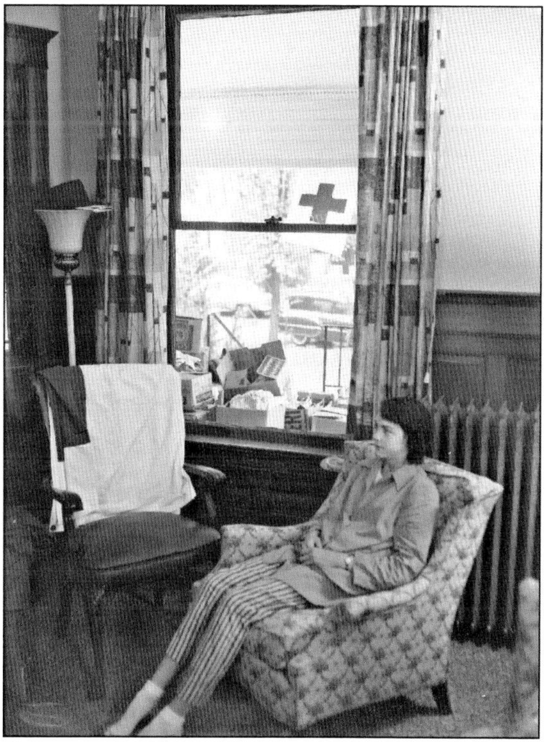

Red Cross headquarters, at 1102 Third Avenue South, served as a starting point for many tornado survivors. This image shows a young woman, identified as Barbara Linow, seated in one of two chairs while a Red Cross flag flies outside the window. The *Fargo Forum* reported that the Linow family visited the Red Cross to seek information on emergency housing.

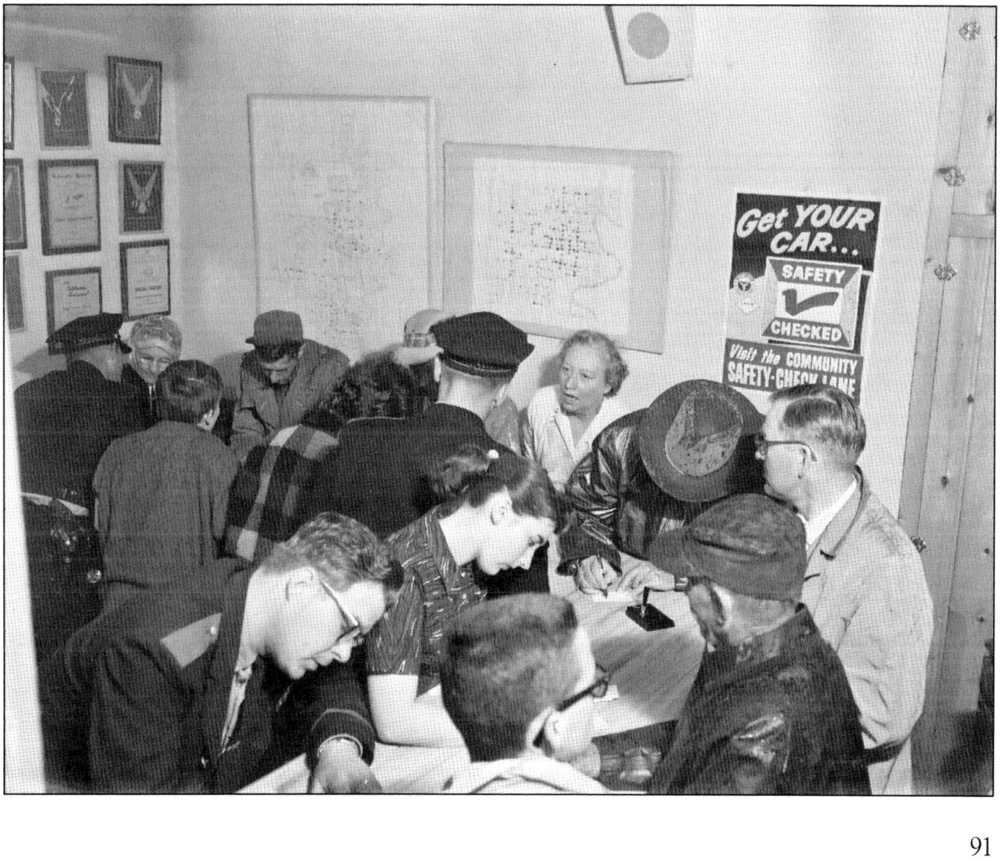

After the tornado, severely damaged neighborhoods were deemed potential safety and looting hazards and only authorized individuals, such as those who had lived there, were allowed in. The Fargo Police Department served as the location where survivors filled out identification cards confirming their authorization. This image shows police officers assisting survivors during this process.

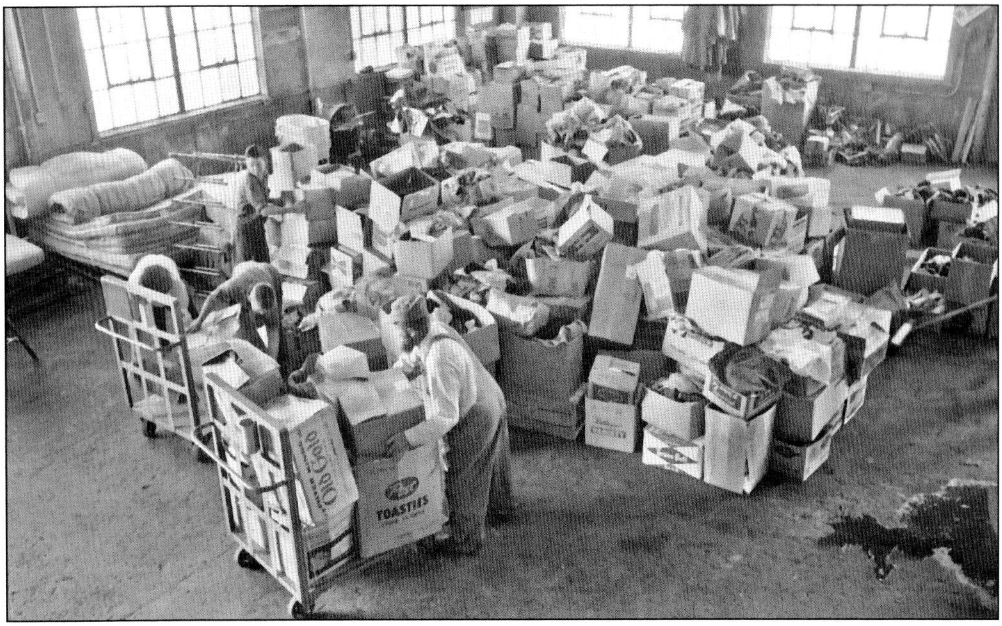

This elevated view shows the warehouse at Thirteenth Street North, now University Drive, and Seventh Avenue North that served as the Red Cross clothing depot. Four individuals unload numerous boxes of donated items onto the floor. What appears to be donated mattresses are visible at left. According to the *Fargo Forum*, these items were donated by people in Minot, North Dakota.

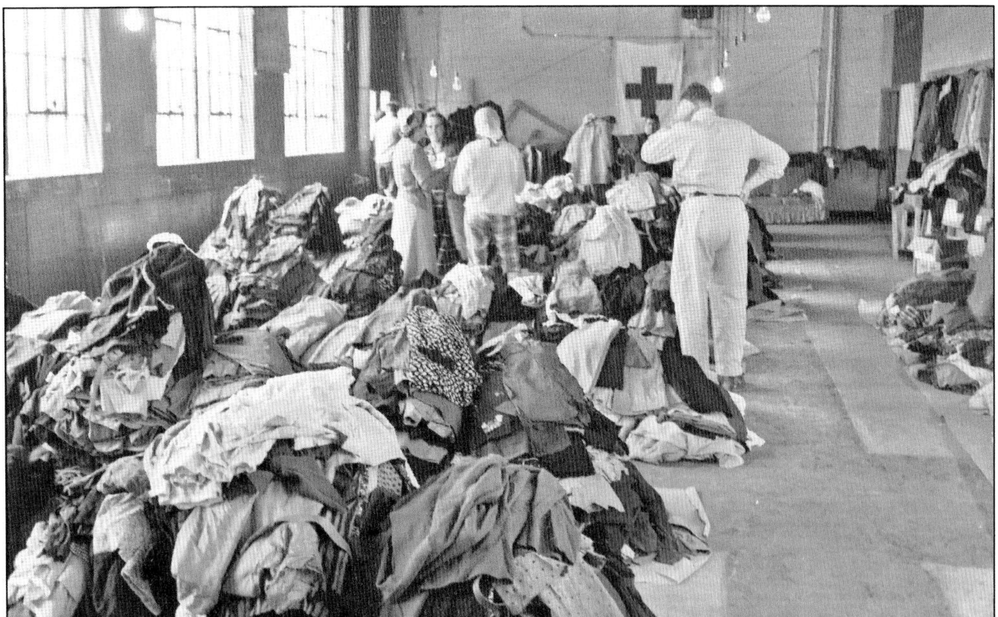

Numerous volunteers sort through and begin to organize stacks of recently delivered clothing at the Red Cross clothing depot. According to the *Fargo Forum*, the clothing was delivered, along with food and furniture, in two trucks soon after word of the tornado reached other communities. This location currently houses the Fargo Brewing Company.

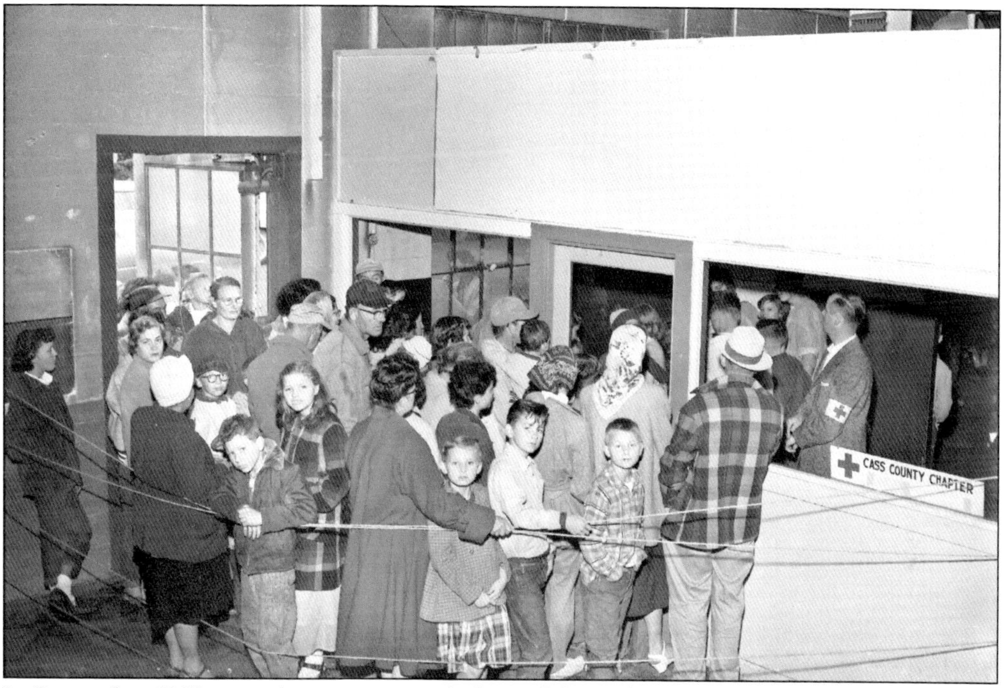

In September 1957, tornado survivors, including adults and children, stand in line at the Red Cross clothing depot to get outfitted for winter. The clothing depot continued to fulfill the needs of tornado survivors months after the disaster as the seasons changed. The man with the Red Cross armband is Richard Hall, Red Cross disaster committee chairman.

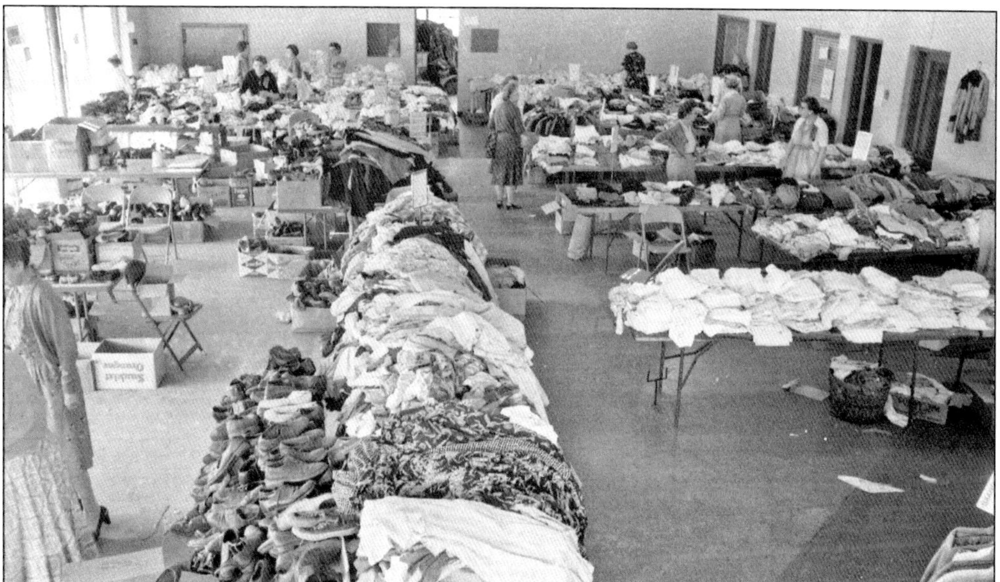

An elevated view of the Red Cross clothing depot shows the dedication of volunteers to organize donated items to make them easily accessible. Individuals throughout North Dakota and the United States donated over 100 tons of clothing and bedding to the Red Cross. Clean clothing, although seemingly small compared to other needs, helped bring a sense of normalcy back to the day-to-day lives of survivors.

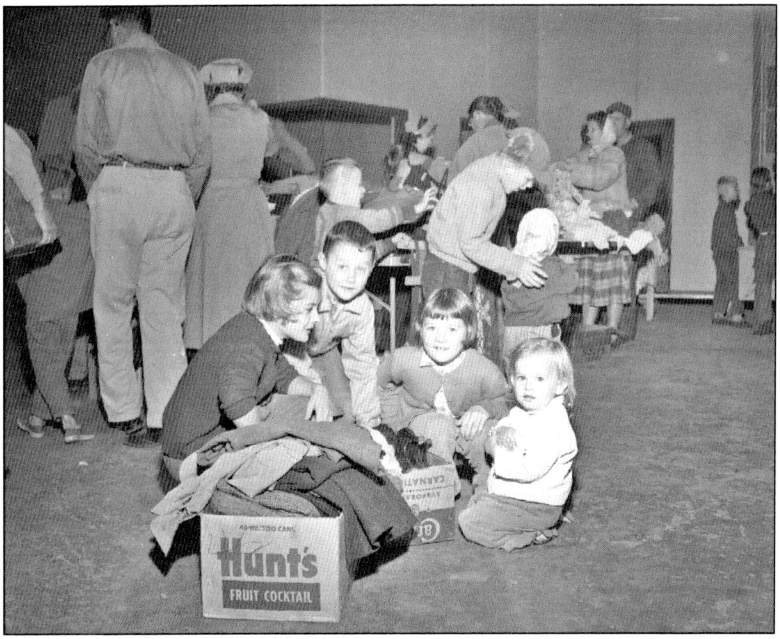

Even the youngest tornado survivors spent time at the Red Cross clothing depot. Here, four children of various ages gather around and investigate boxes of clothing and shoes. As their parents and other adults seek out new clothing for their families, the children try to find their own ways to stay entertained.

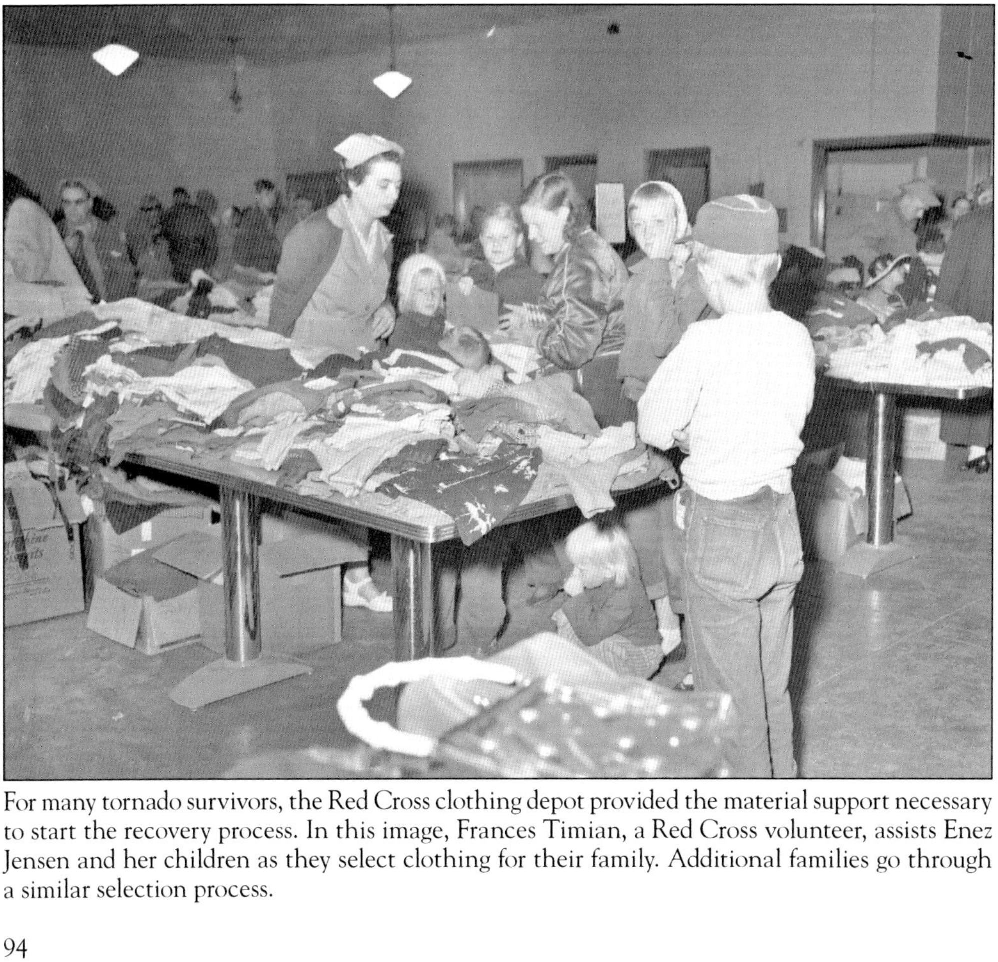

For many tornado survivors, the Red Cross clothing depot provided the material support necessary to start the recovery process. In this image, Frances Timian, a Red Cross volunteer, assists Enez Jensen and her children as they select clothing for their family. Additional families go through a similar selection process.

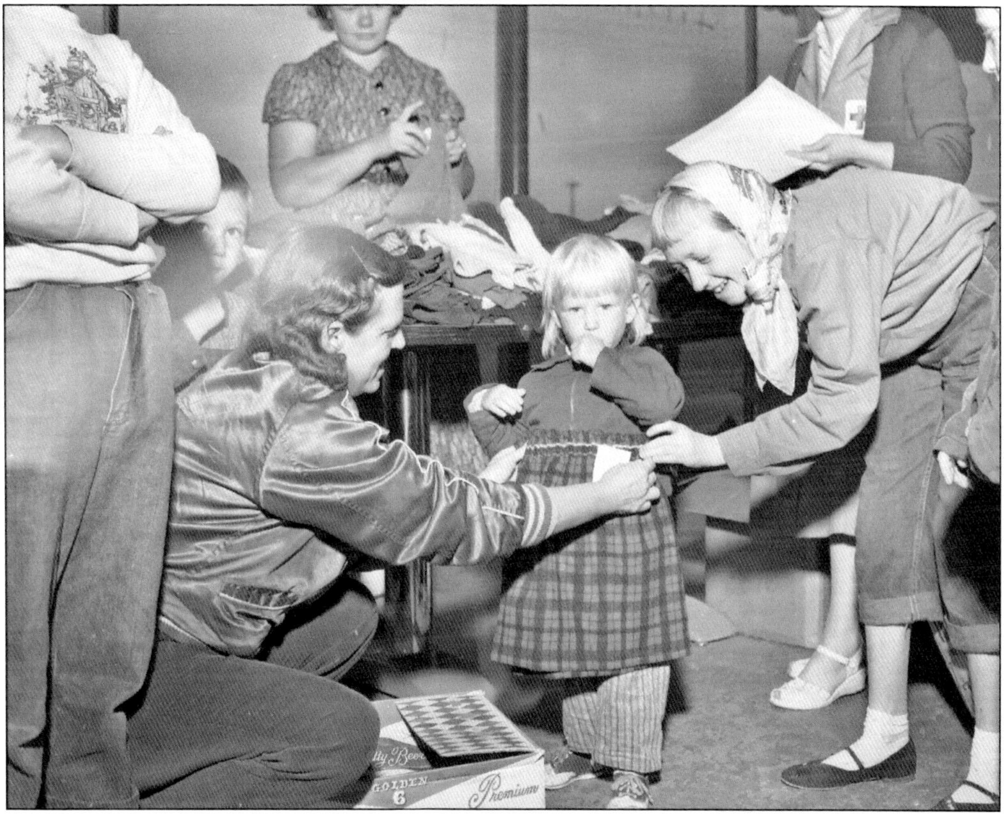

Enez Jensen holds a skirt up to young Betty Jensen to check the size at the Red Cross clothing depot. Carolyn Jensen stands behind Betty Jensen and helps hold the skirt. Two other children and three adults, including one who is wearing a shirt with the Red Cross symbol, look on.

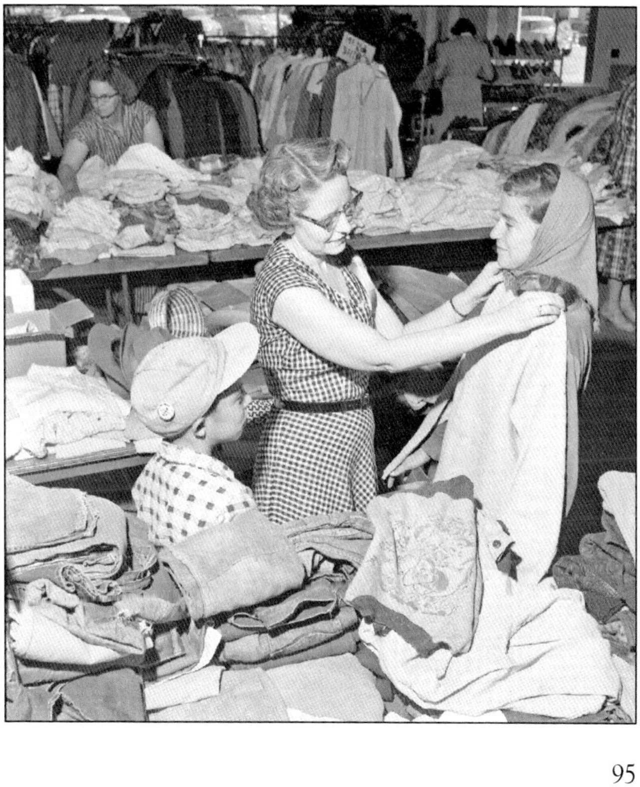

In the Red Cross clothing depot, a volunteer holds a long-sleeved shirt up to a girl to check the size while a boy looks on. Donations from residents of Fargo as well as donations from across the state of North Dakota and the entire country ensured that those who lost everything could recoup a small but important part of their daily lives.

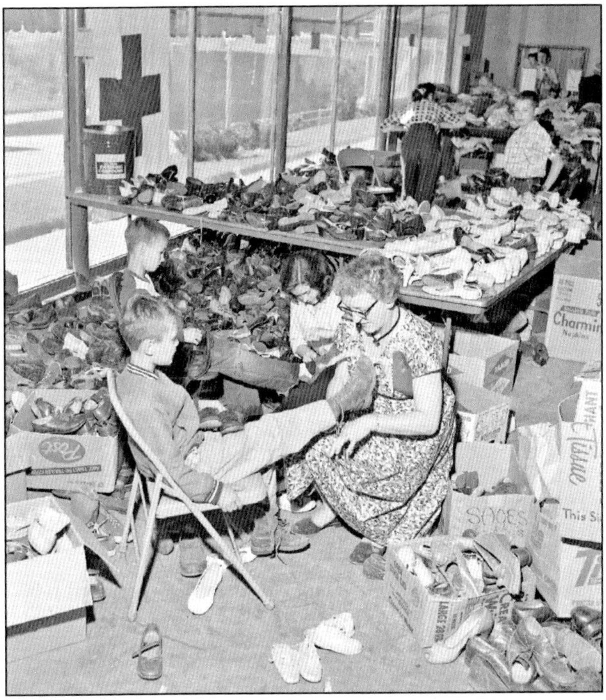

At the Red Cross clothing depot, Tillie Forseth helps 10-year-old Thomas Conner find a new pair of shoes, while behind them, Judy Jensen assists 10-year-old Gary Morris. Volunteers and family members may have spent many hours going through donated clothing and shoes to find the correct sizes for themselves and family members.

Two individuals, identified by the *Fargo Forum* as Ervin and Clara Weeks (first row), leave St. Mary's Cathedral, located at 619 Seventh Street North, after retrieving clothing for themselves and their six children. The Weeks's home, at 714 Twenty-seventh Street North, was flattened. Here, they are assisted by Desmo Anderson and another unidentified man holding the door.

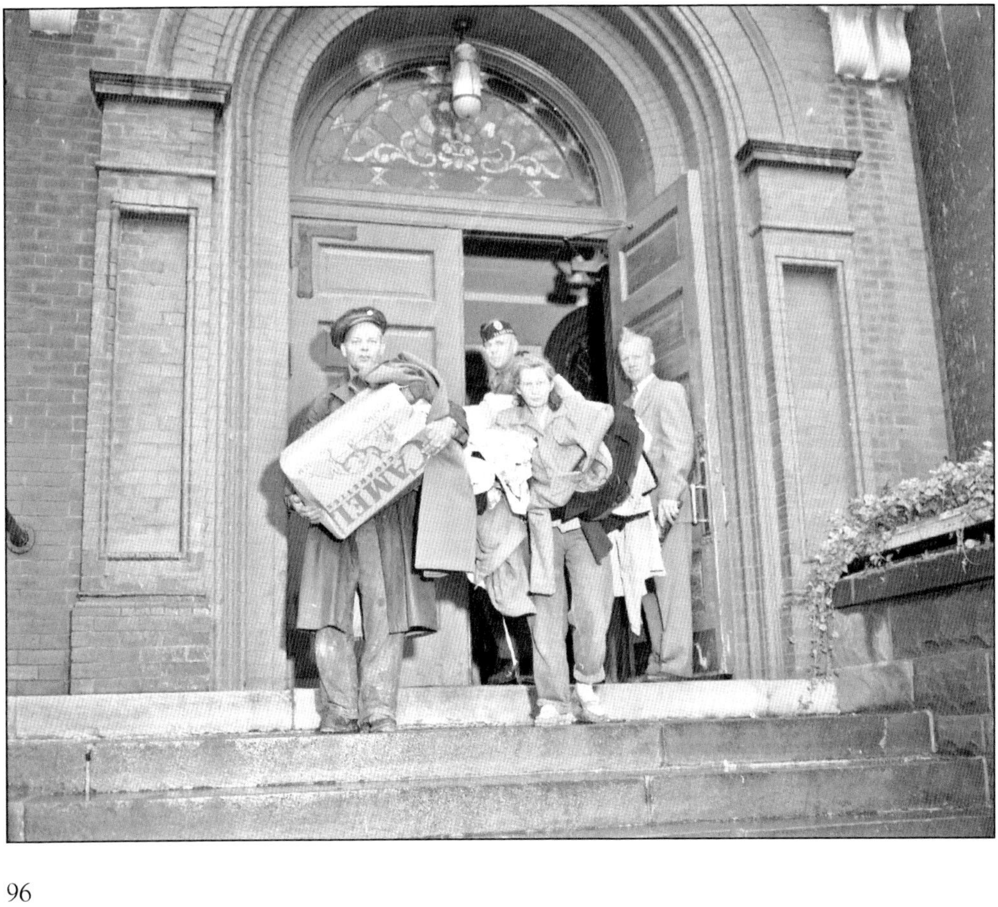

The arrival of an American Red Cross vehicle in the 2800 block of Eighth Avenue North made a group of young children take notice. Surrounded by their heavily damaged Golden Ridge neighborhood, these children set out on an exploration to see what the vehicle would bring. A damaged but still standing house is seen in the distance.

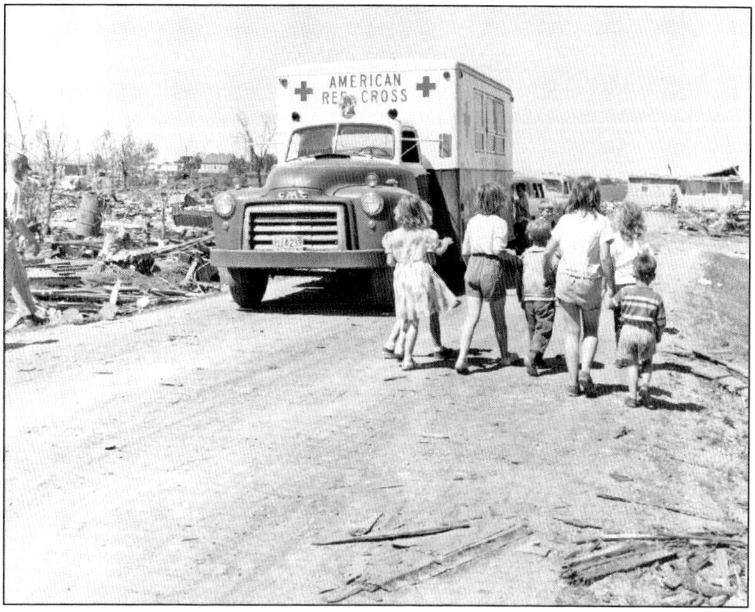

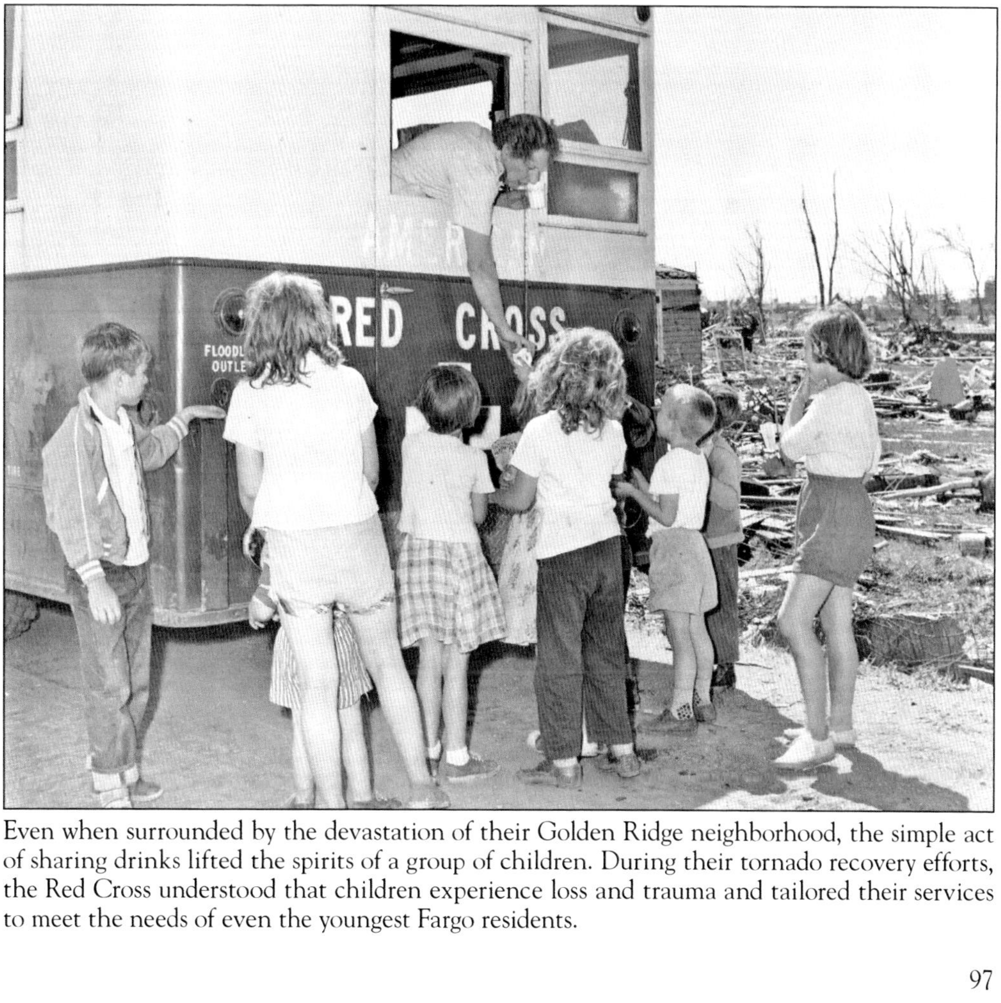

Even when surrounded by the devastation of their Golden Ridge neighborhood, the simple act of sharing drinks lifted the spirits of a group of children. During their tornado recovery efforts, the Red Cross understood that children experience loss and trauma and tailored their services to meet the needs of even the youngest Fargo residents.

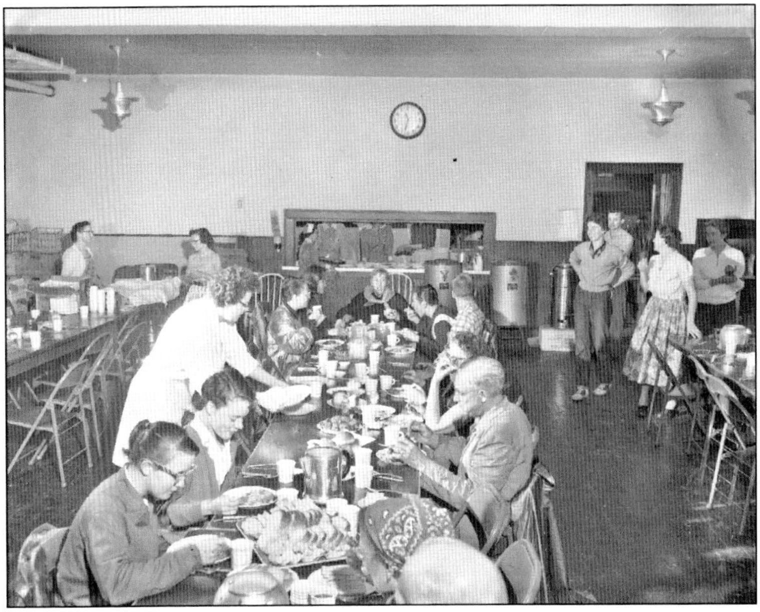

After the tornado, a meal would have been difficult to come by if it were not for the efforts of local organizations, such as Plymouth Congregational Church, located at 901 Broadway North. At approximately 11:30 a.m., tornado survivors of all ages gathered to share a meal prepared by volunteers in the basement of the church.

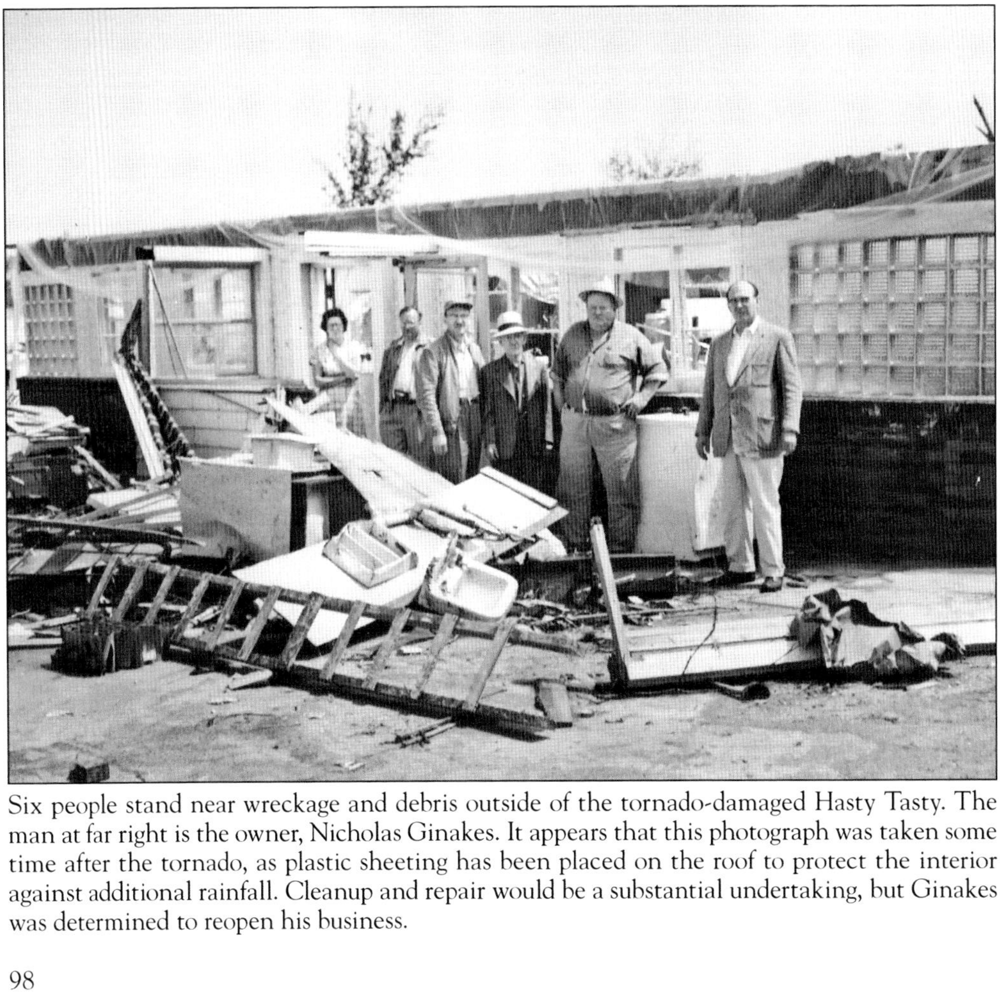

Six people stand near wreckage and debris outside of the tornado-damaged Hasty Tasty. The man at far right is the owner, Nicholas Ginakes. It appears that this photograph was taken some time after the tornado, as plastic sheeting has been placed on the roof to protect the interior against additional rainfall. Cleanup and repair would be a substantial undertaking, but Ginakes was determined to reopen his business.

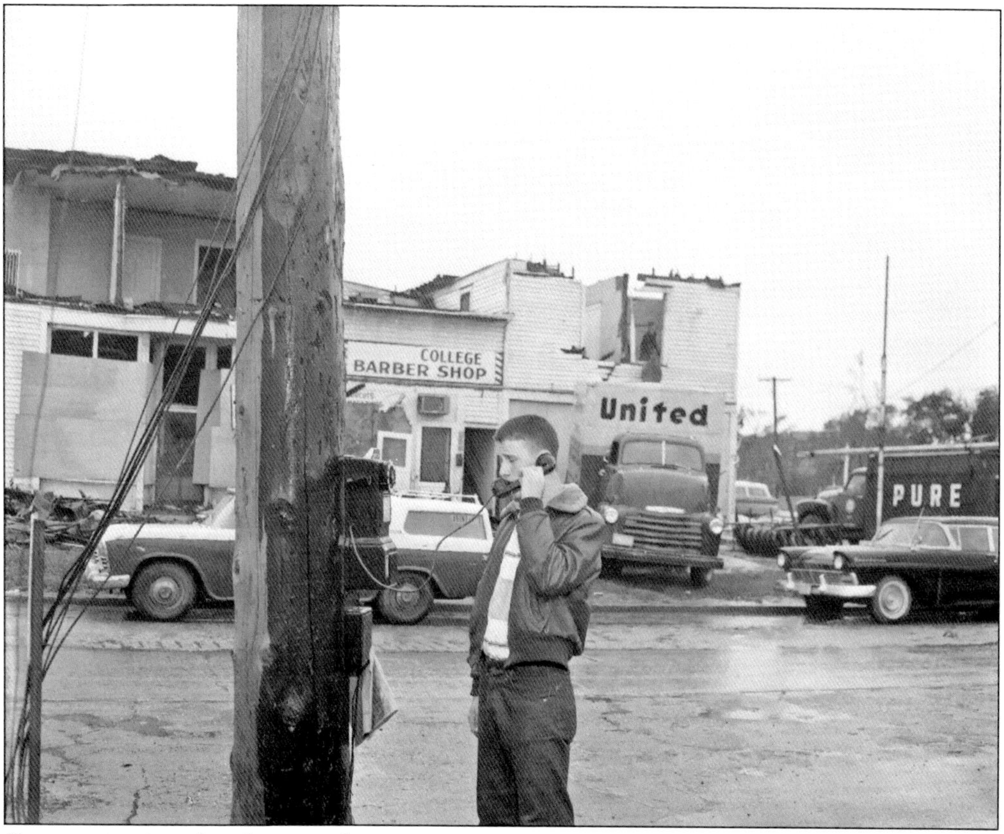

Communication after the tornado was a necessity but also a struggle as the high winds and flying debris damaged many of the city's telephone booths and telephone lines. Here, Mike O'Leary uses a temporary telephone attached to a utility pole at Thirteenth Street North (now University Drive) and Thirteenth Avenue North. The *Fargo Forum* reported that the original telephone booth at this location was blown a half block away by the tornado.

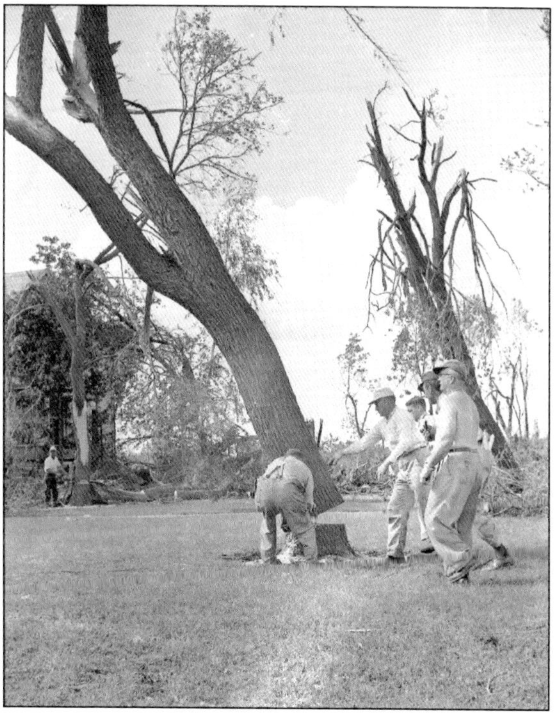

The speed of the tornado winds damaged numerous trees in Fargo. If these damaged trees were to fall, it was likely that they would cause additional injuries or structural damage. Residents and cleanup crews worked diligently to remove these hazards. Here, a group of men cut down a heavily damaged tree outside the Sacred Heart Convent. The tree in the background looks like it will go next.

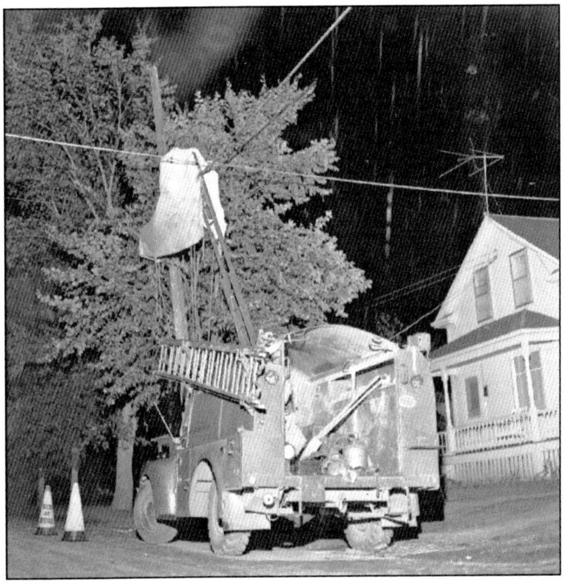

After the tornado, workers from Northwestern Bell Telephone Company set to work repairing the downed telephone lines and poles in Fargo. Workers fixed the poles under canvas enclosures on the evenings of June 24 and 25. Due to the high winds, many telephone poles and wires were damaged. The house in the background appears to have weathered the tornado without harm.

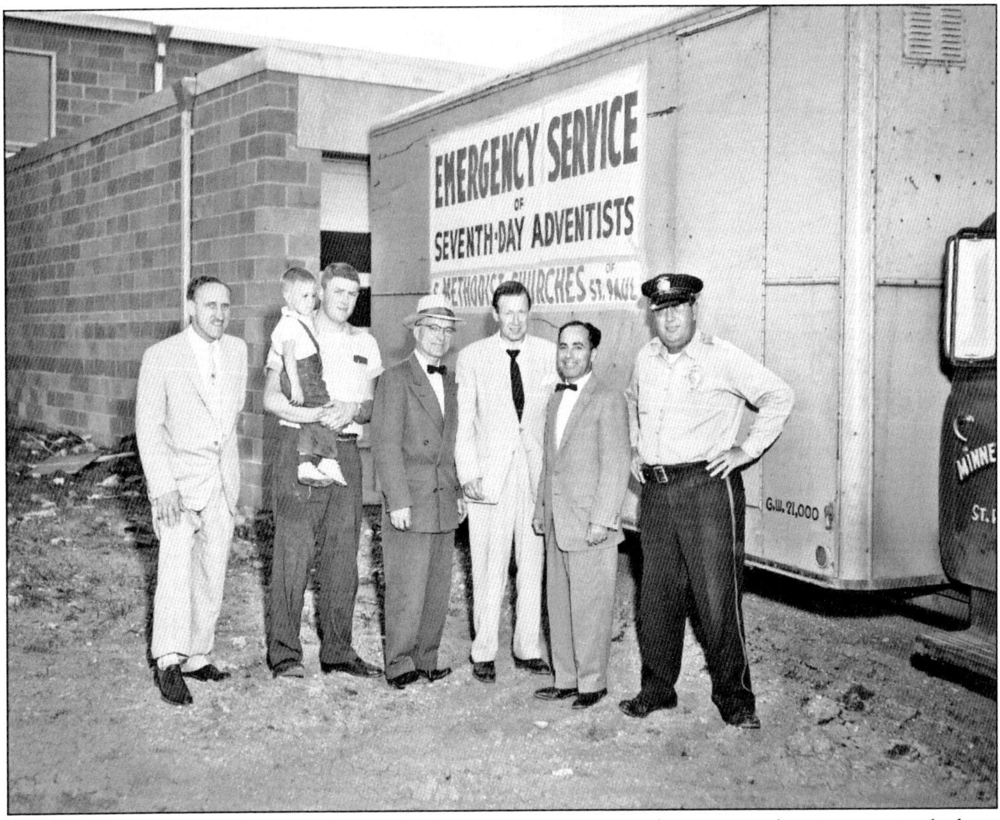

Many church groups donated food, clothing, and other goods to tornado victims, including supplies delivered in this six-ton truck from the Methodist and Seventh-day Adventist churches of Minneapolis and St. Paul. From left to right are Rev. H.R. Cullen, truck driver Don Cantrell holding a child, R.D. Steinke, Fargo mayor Herschel Lashkowitz, Rev. A.M. Matar, and Fargo patrolman Ervin Korsgaden.

Among the many companies that donated money for survivor relief was the Joseph Schlitz Brewing Company of Milwaukee. Here, Mayor Herschel Lashkowitz receives a $5,000 check from Schlitz northern division manager J.R. Moriarity with gratitude. From left to right are Fargo city commissioner Earl McCannel, Schlitz wholesaler Arne Bergseth, Lashkowitz, Moriarity, and Federal Civil Defense Administration safety officer Kenneth A. Lake.

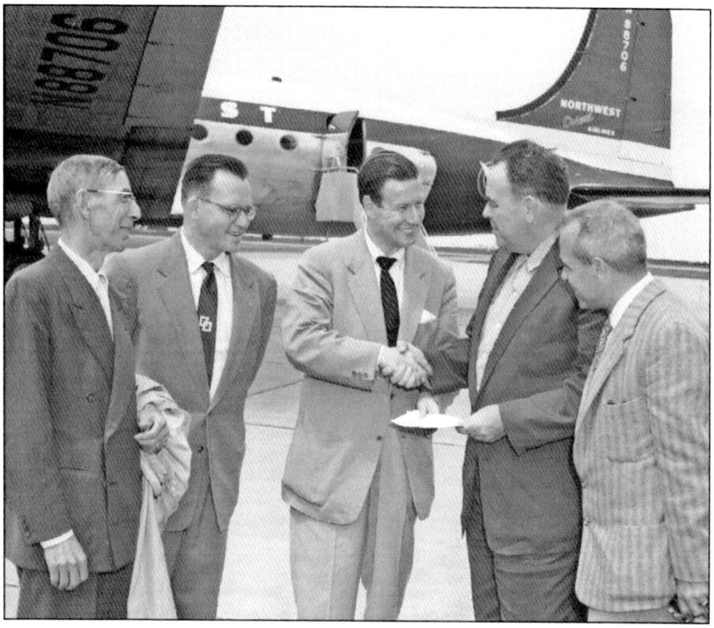

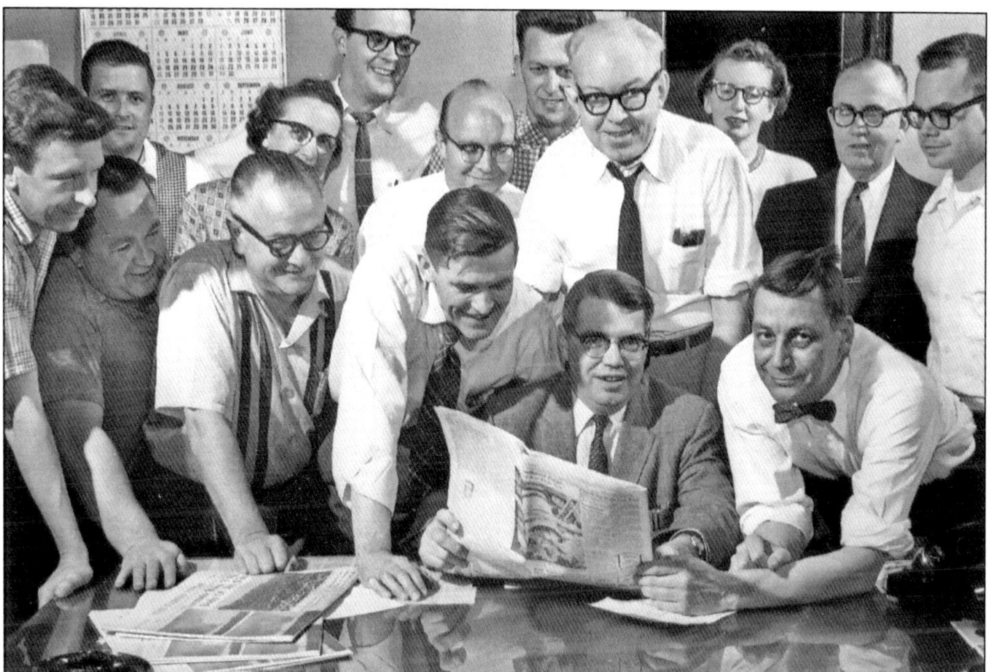

The *Fargo Forum* staff who won the 1958 Pulitzer Prize are, from left to right, (first row) Chet Gebert, Alf T. Olsen, Gifford Herron, Wallace Lindell, John D. Paulson, and Ross Phipps; (second row) Ruth Fairbanks, Tom Lucier, James C. Acton, Roy P. Johnson, and Tom Lundquist; (third row) Del Johnson, Cal Olson, Gerry Rafftery, and Doris Eastman. Not pictured are Phil Penas, Eugene Fitzgerald, Ed Kolpack, Alden McLachlan, Ed Eastman, and John Lohman.

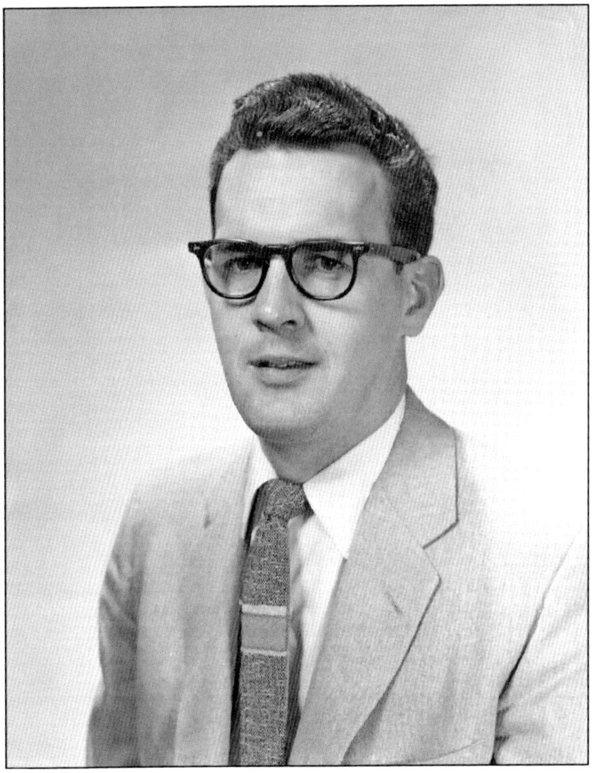

Fargo Forum photojournalist Cal Olson took the majority of the photographs in this book. He worked for the *Forum* from 1950 to 1978. In 1978, he became the editor of the *Sioux City Journal* in Iowa, and in 1990, the *Journal* was nominated for a Pulitzer Prize for its coverage of the 1989 crash of United Airlines Flight 232.

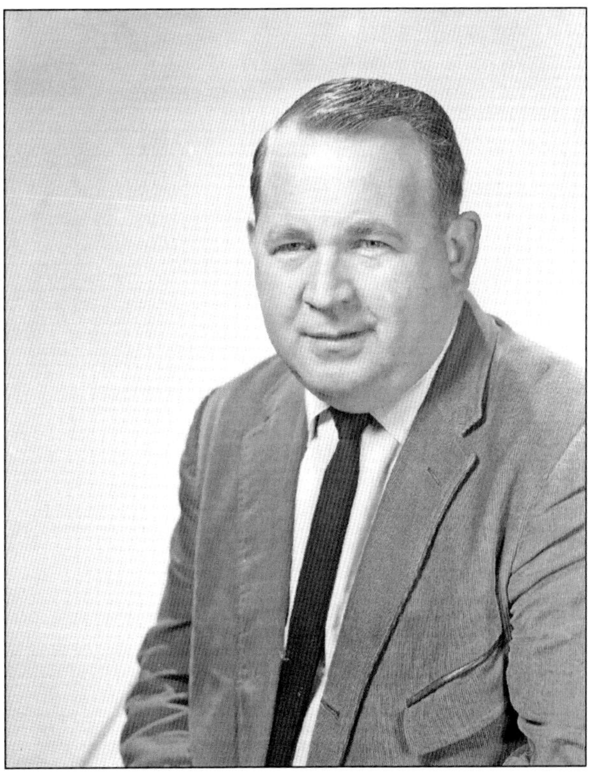

Fargo Forum photojournalist and editor Alf T. Olsen captured the infamous tornado photograph that included his and his neighbors' children seen on page 10. His wife, Charlotte, had been on vacation, so he was responsible for looking after the children. After taking the photograph, he gathered his children into his car and drove away from the tornado. Olsen worked at the *Forum* from 1953 until his death in 1970.

When the tornado hit, *Fargo Forum* photojournalist Chester "Chet" Gebert made sure his wife, Violet, and daughters Valerie and Kimberly were safe in their basement, then headed out to take photographs. He had started working at the *Forum* two years previously, and would work at the paper for 37 years. His photography not only earned him a Pulitzer Prize, but he also won the Graflex Grand Prize for his tornado photography.

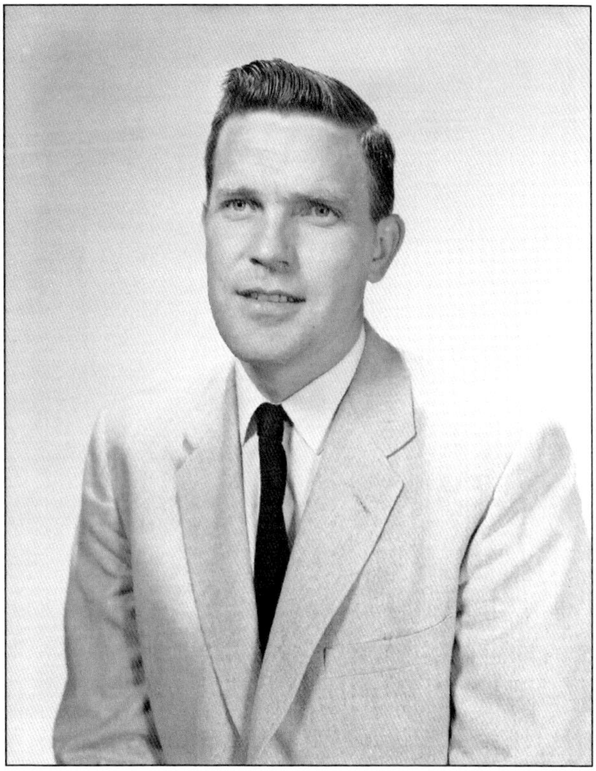

The entire *Fargo Forum* 20-member staff all reported to work, unasked, after the tornado hit. At 1:09 a.m., 5 hours and 29 minutes after the tornado struck, a special edition of the *Forum* went to press, containing 24 columns of print and many photographs. The Pulitzer Prize was the fruit of their incredible dedication.

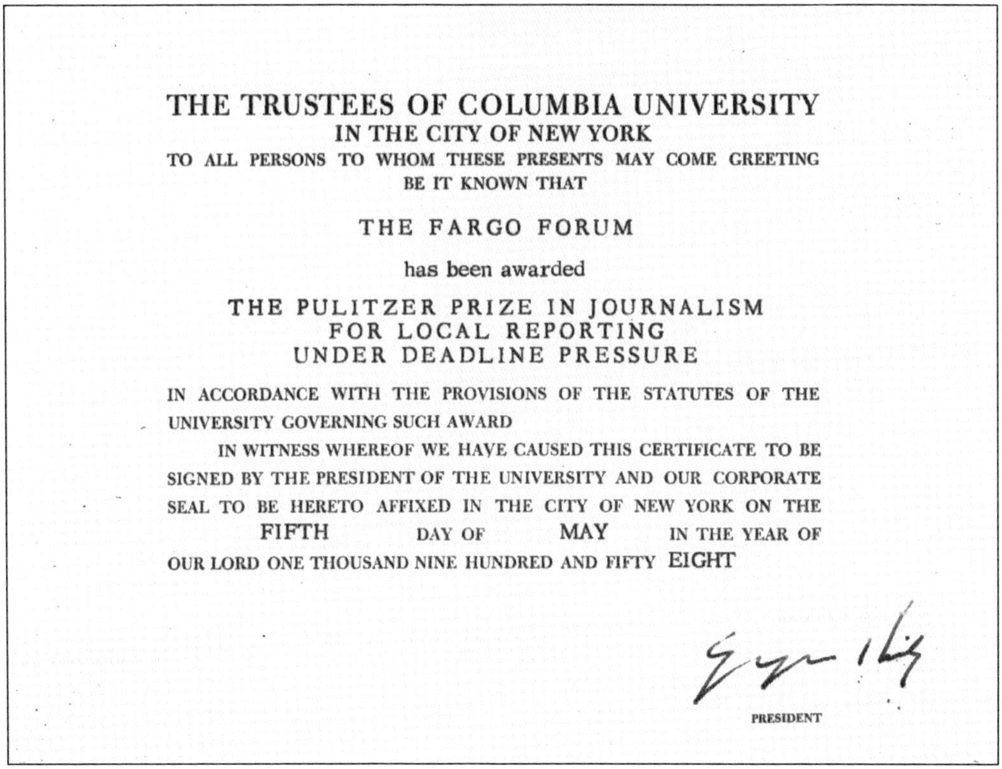

THE TRUSTEES OF COLUMBIA UNIVERSITY
IN THE CITY OF NEW YORK
TO ALL PERSONS TO WHOM THESE PRESENTS MAY COME GREETING
BE IT KNOWN THAT

THE FARGO FORUM

has been awarded

THE PULITZER PRIZE IN JOURNALISM
FOR LOCAL REPORTING
UNDER DEADLINE PRESSURE

IN ACCORDANCE WITH THE PROVISIONS OF THE STATUTES OF THE UNIVERSITY GOVERNING SUCH AWARD

IN WITNESS WHEREOF WE HAVE CAUSED THIS CERTIFICATE TO BE SIGNED BY THE PRESIDENT OF THE UNIVERSITY AND OUR CORPORATE SEAL TO BE HERETO AFFIXED IN THE CITY OF NEW YORK ON THE FIFTH DAY OF MAY IN THE YEAR OF OUR LORD ONE THOUSAND NINE HUNDRED AND FIFTY EIGHT

PRESIDENT

F-M AREA FORECAST

THE FARGO FORUM

Morning Edition

VOL. 24, NO. 301 — FARGO, N. D., FRIDAY MORNING, JUNE 21, 1957 — Sixteen Pages — Price Five Cents

At Least 8 Killed, Scores Injured As Tornado Smashes North Fargo

Bible Words Prophetic Of Fury Of Twister

By ALDEN McLACHLAN

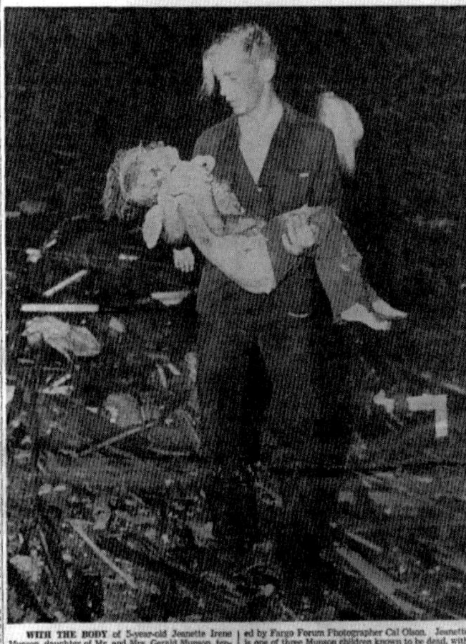

WITH THE BODY of 5-year-old Jeanette Irene Munson, daughter of Mr. and Mrs. Gerald Munson, tenderly cradled in his arms, Richard Shaw, 21, stumbled through wreckage of the tornado as he was photographed by Fargo Forum Photographer Cal Olson. Jeanette is one of three Munson children known to be dead, with two others also believed among those killed. Shaw, 902 20th St. N., is a neighbor of the Munson family.

3 And Possibly 5 Children Of Single Family Among Dead

A tornado struck Fargo about 7:40 p.m. Thursday, killing at least eight persons and injuring scores.

At least three and possibly two more of the dead are children of Mr. and Mrs. Gerald Munson, 818 25th St. N.

With a roar that could be heard through the city, the deadly twister cut a swath three blocks wide from the west city limits to the east city limits on the North Side.

Witnesses said the huge funnel touched down about a mile west of 29th Street North.

It blasted east between 7th and 10th avenues to about 24th street, veering north and then east again.

It smashed through an area between 12th avenue and 15th avenue from 13th Street across the Red River.

Hundreds of homes and cars were damaged.

Shanley high school, the American Lutheran Church and Immanuel Lutheran Church were heavily damaged.

Sections of the Golden Ridge area, west of 24th Street, were virtually destroyed. The bodies of all of the dead were found there.

Most of the homes were without basements and the residents huddled inside catching the full force of the brutal wind.

The identified dead are three children of the Munsons.

They are:

Phyllis Louise, 6.

Jeanette Irene, 5.

Mary Beth, 1.

They were identified by their mother. Another Munson child, Lois Ann, 2½, was hospitalized in critical condition.

The children's bodies were taken from the ruins of their home.

Also at St. John's were the bodies of an unidentified man and woman, found in the same general area.

The body of an unidentified man was taken to Hanson - Runsvold Funeral Home.

Cass Coroner D. H. Lawrence said the bodies of two boys were identified tentatively as Bradley Munson, 10, and Darwin Munson, 12.

He said they were among the six Munson children and their mother reported them missing. She had not viewed the bodies at 2 a.m. today. He said the clothes fit her description.

Mrs. Munson was working and her husband was out of town when the tornado struck.

The coroner said she called home from work when the tornado warnings were flashed and was talking to Phyllis Louise when the twister struck.

He said the girl cried to her mother, "It's coming this way!"

The last the mother heard was her daughter's scream, "It's hitting!" And the phone went dead.

Mrs. Munson was taken to St. John's Hospital and then to the home of her mother, whose name was not immediately available.

The body of a boy believed to be Bradley was brought to St. Luke's where injured were laid on mattresses and cots in the hospital cafeteria as the emergency room became jammed with patients.

A policeman who brought him to the hospital from the Golden Ridge area said he died in the patrol car en route. A splinter had pierced his body near the neck.

The boy believed to be Darwin, died at St. Luke's of head injuries.

Authorities said radio and television warnings that the tornado was approaching sent thousands of residents into basements and probably saved many lives.

Two block-long rows of seven houses each were shattered on two streets, one on 1st Street North, the other several blocks to the west.

As of 11 p.m. injured still were trickling into the hospitals, brought by private cars and by ambulances, some which came from other towns to help.

A priest was on hand at St. Luke's, and was seen administering last rites to at least three of the injured.

Sixty injured had been treated at St. Luke's by Midnight and 16 at St. John's.

Six of those in St. Luke's were in critical condition. The number hospitalized was not available.

Seven persons were admitted at St. John's.

...

TORNADO

(Continued on Page 7, Col. 6)

More Pictures, Stories, Injured List: Pages 5-6-7

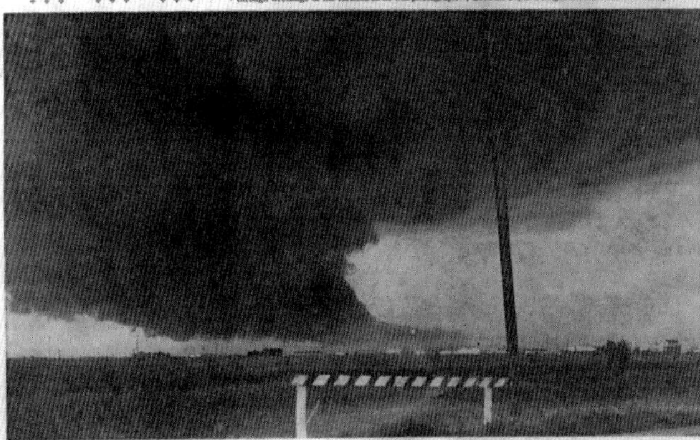

The twister struck down in Fargo Thursday a few minutes after this picture was taken by Fargo Forum photographer Alf Olsen. You are looking northwest from 11th Avenue and 21st Street South.

Here is the front page of the *Fargo Forum* on June 21, 1957. The *Forum* staff dedicated their Pulitzer to the recently retired editor-in-chief H.D. "Happy" Paulson, who worked for the paper for 41 years. Only two other North Dakota newspapers have won a Pulitzer Prize. The *Bismarck Tribune* won in 1938 for self-help in its Dust Bowl columns, and the *Grand Forks Herald* won in 1998 for its coverage of the devastating 1997 Red River flood.

Five

Before and After

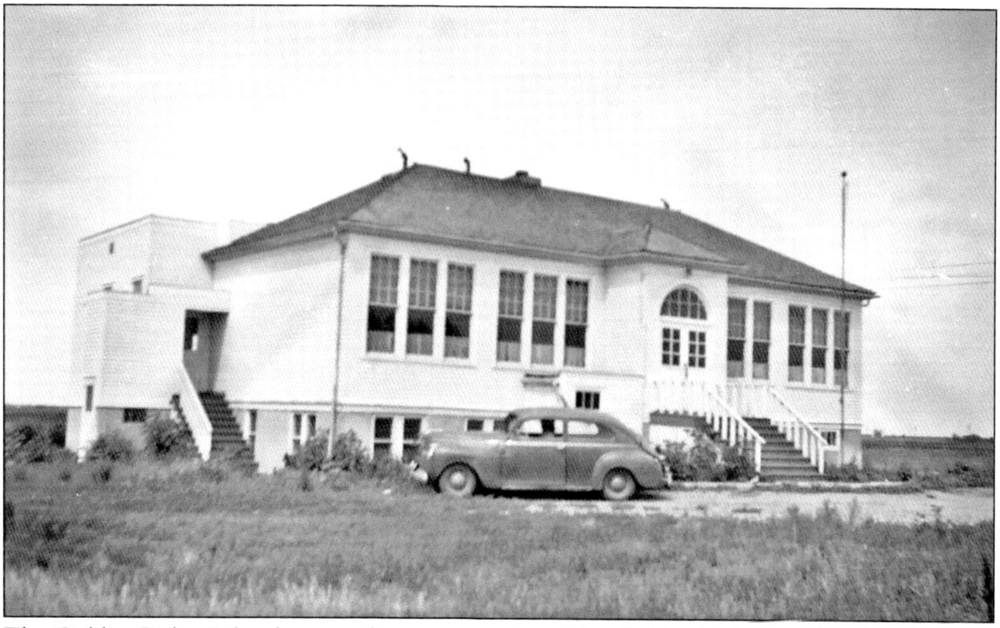

The Golden Ridge School sat on the western edge of the Golden Ridge neighborhood, at 830 Twenty-ninth Street North. It was one of the first buildings struck by the tornado in the Fargo city limits and was completely leveled. All that remained was the block foundation, with much of the debris in neighboring yards. This school was not rebuilt; Madison Elementary School was constructed nearby to serve the neighborhood.

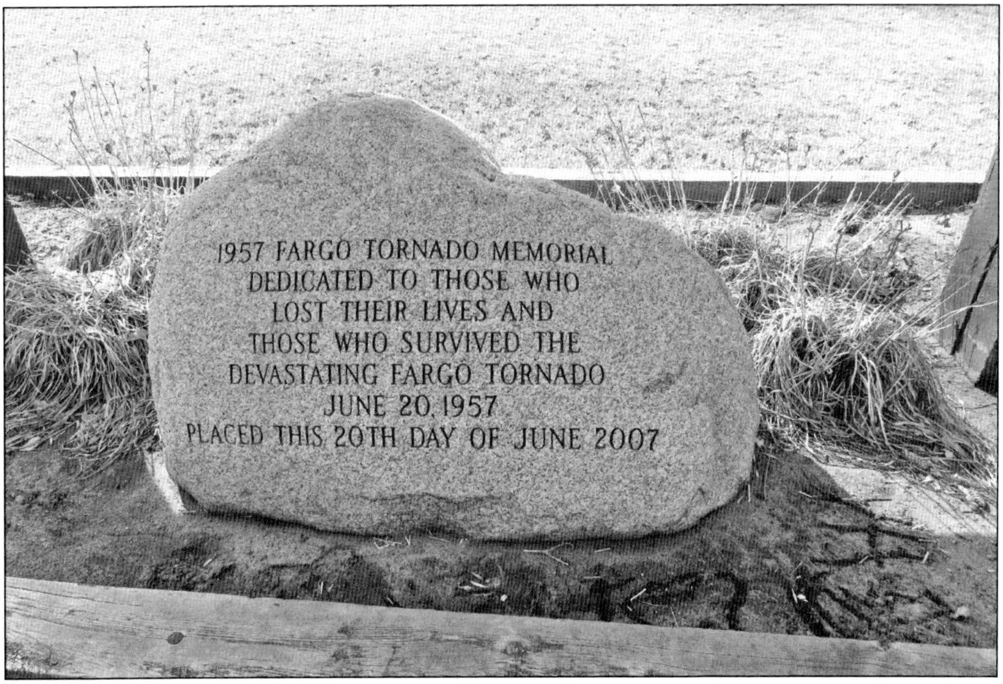

On June 20, 2007, on the 50th anniversary of the tornado, an engraved stone memorial was placed in front of Madison Elementary School in the Golden Ridge neighborhood. Mercedes (Munson) Erickson, mother of the six Munson children who lost their lives, was the guest of honor at the dedication ceremony and received a red rose representing each child.

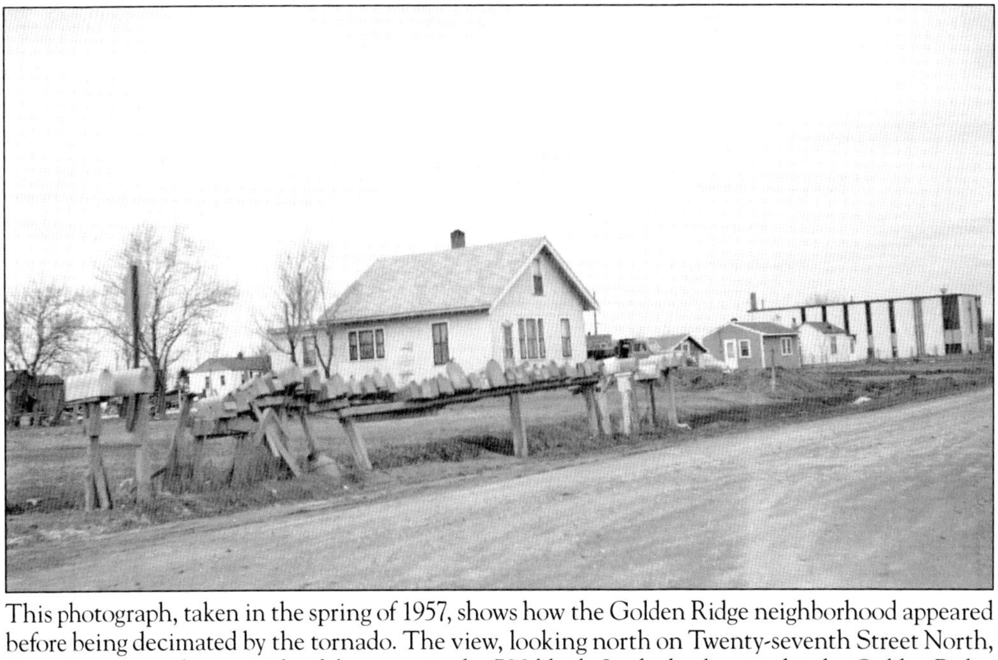

This photograph, taken in the spring of 1957, shows how the Golden Ridge neighborhood appeared before being decimated by the tornado. The view, looking north on Twenty-seventh Street North, shows houses on the west side of the street in the 700 block. In the background is the Golden Ridge Lutheran Church. All structures in this image were completely destroyed by the tornado.

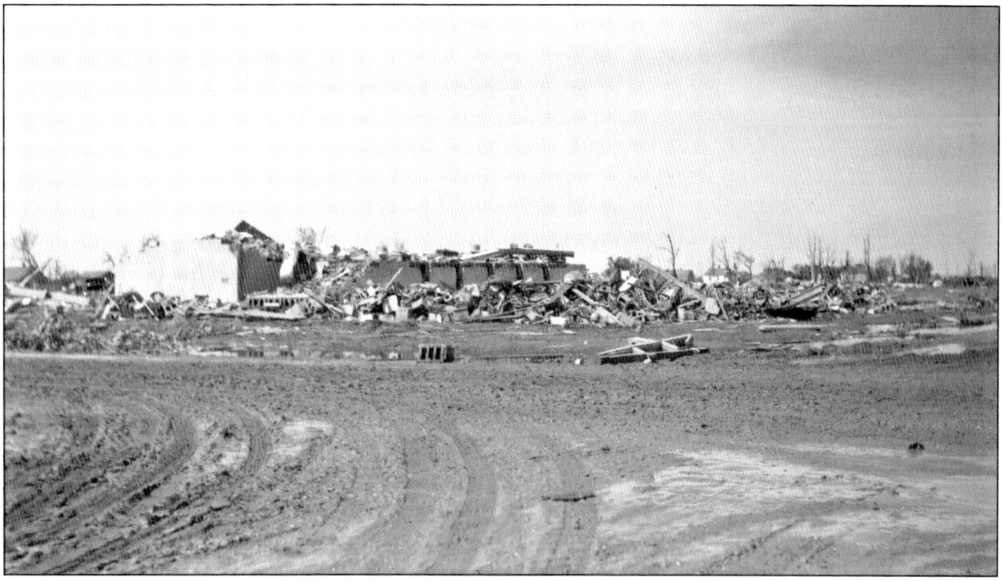

After the tornado, all that was left of the Golden Ridge Lutheran Church was the brick foundation. The church had only stood on the site a year before being destroyed. This view is looking southwest from the intersection of Eighth Avenue North and Twenty-seventh Street North. The Udahl family were charter members of this church.

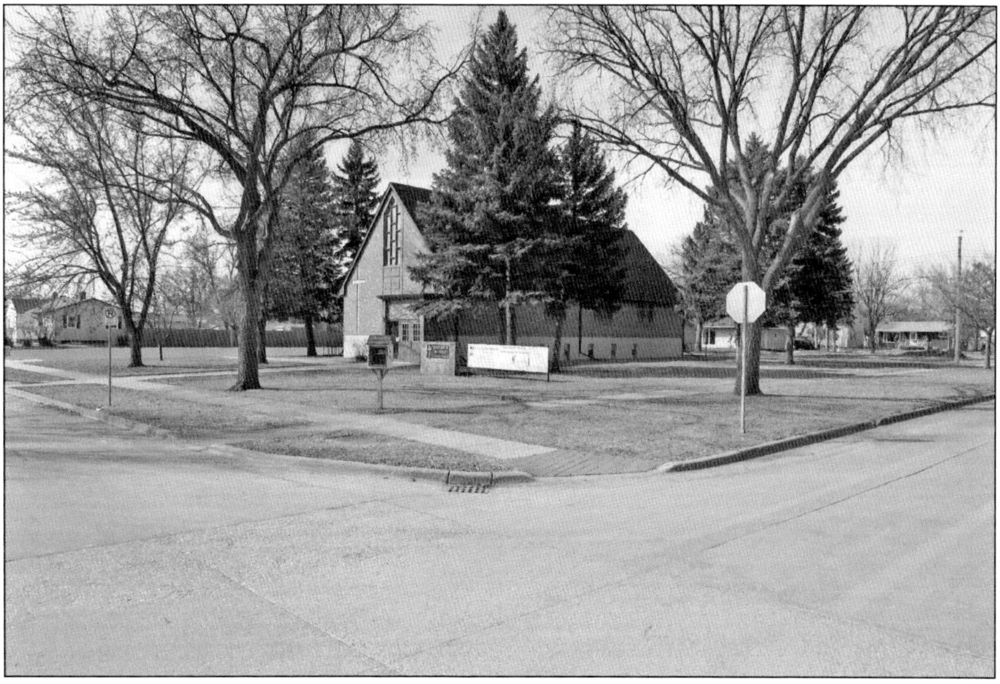

Undeterred by the calamity, 119 parishioners gathered in the ruins of the church's basement to worship on June 30. They began the worship service by singing "Now Thank We All Our God." It was decided to rebuild the church on the foundation of the previous structure. This image, taken from the same vantage point as the previous one, shows the building as it appears today.

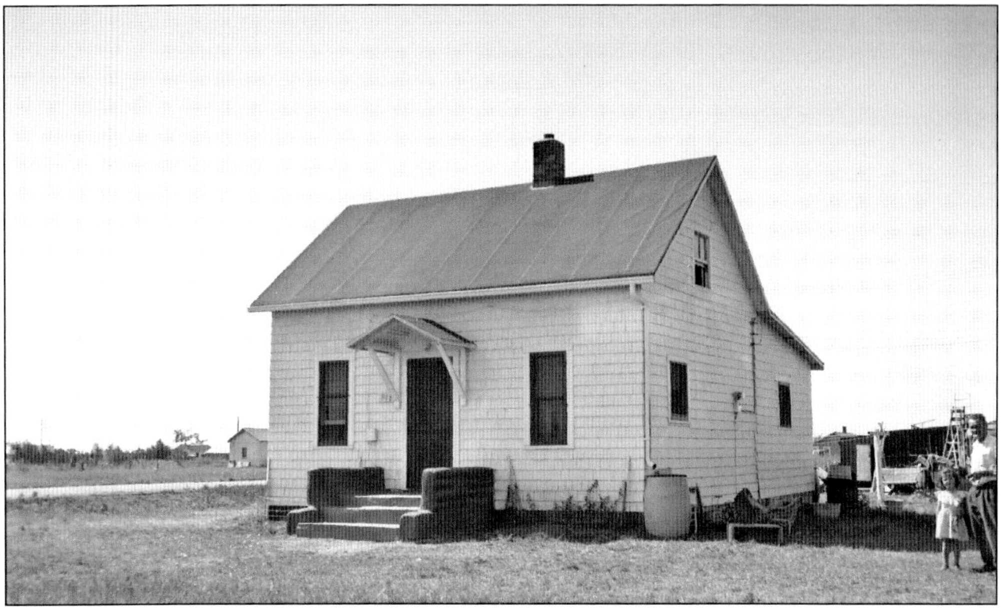

This home, located in the Golden Ridge neighborhood at 802 Twenty-seventh Street North, belonged to Theodore Udahl; his wife, Theresa; and daughter Mary Jean. The Udahls had lived in the house since 1950, when they first came to Fargo. This photograph shows the house as it appeared in 1948.

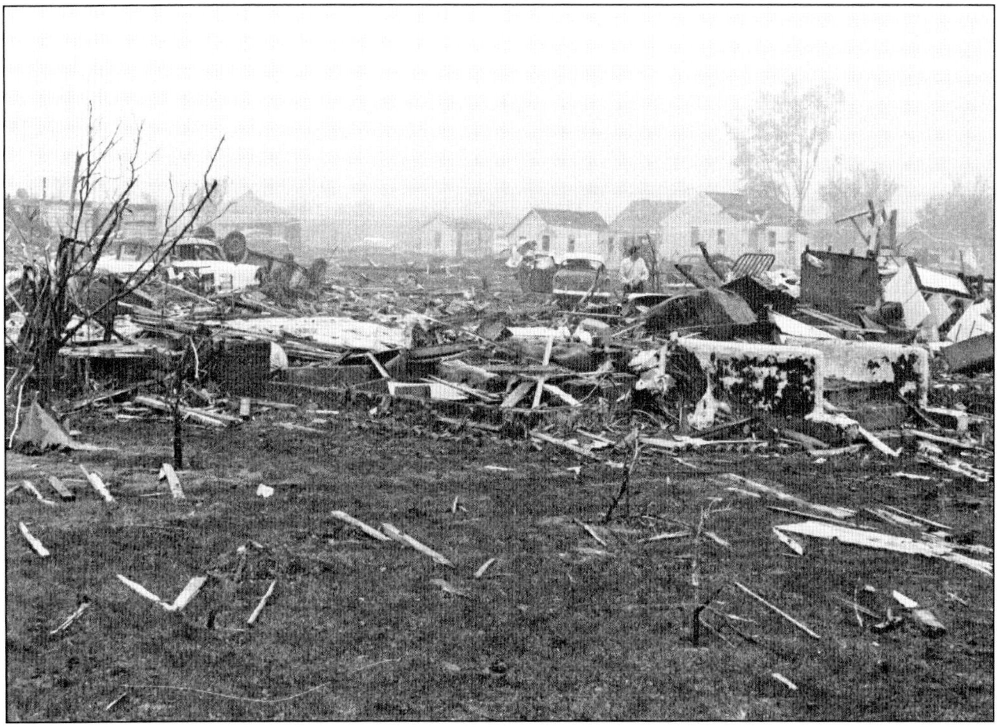

This photograph shows the Udahl home after the tornado. All that is identifiable from the previous image of the house are the front steps, visible at right. All three members of the Udahl family lost their lives at this location. The home did not have a basement for the family to seek shelter in.

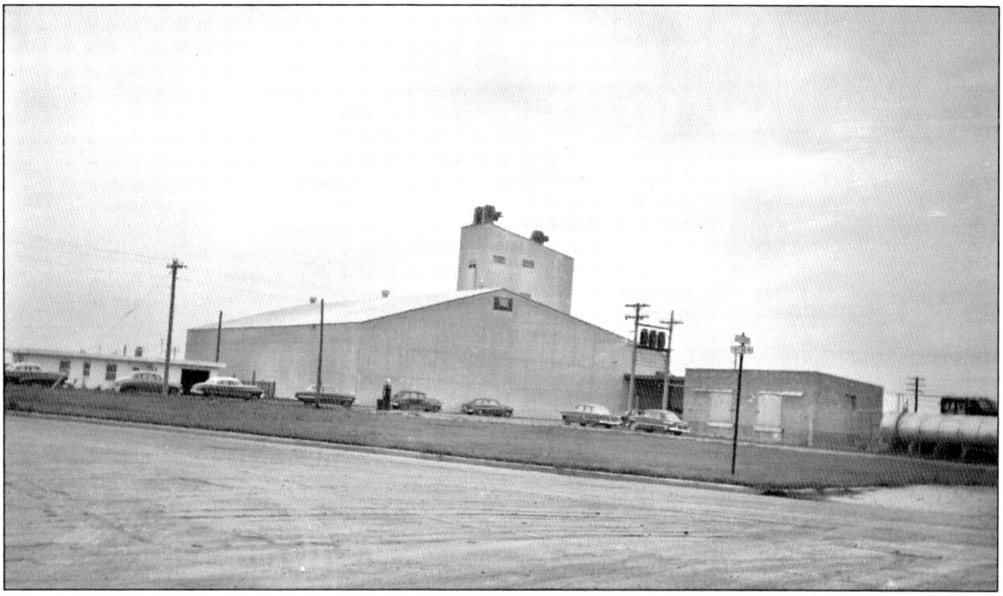

The Peavey Fertilizer Plant, located at 1817 Great Northern Drive, was one of several businesses in Fargo's industrial area destroyed by the tornado. This photograph was taken in 1954, shortly after the $200,000 plant was completed at the intersection of Great Northern Drive and Eighteenth Street North.

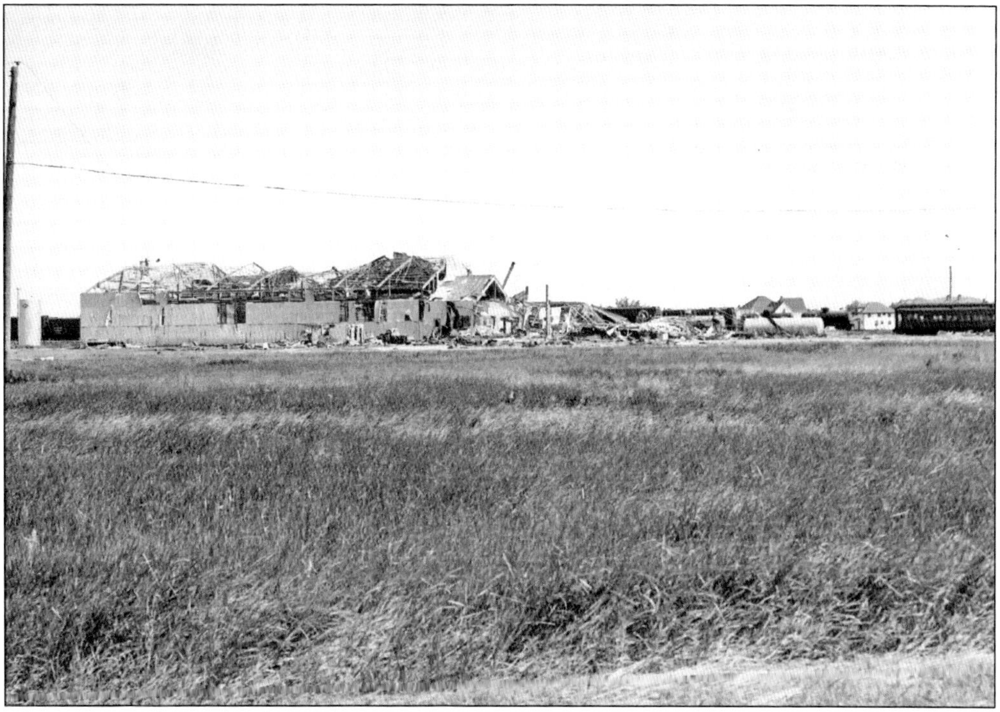

The corrugated metal and steel frame of the Peavey building was no match for the strong winds of the tornado. Much of the roof was peeled off, and sheets of twisted metal littered the surrounding fields and neighboring Great Northern Railroad tracks. Peavey did not replace its facility. In 1959, Shirley-Onstad Inc. built a plumbing supply warehouse on this site.

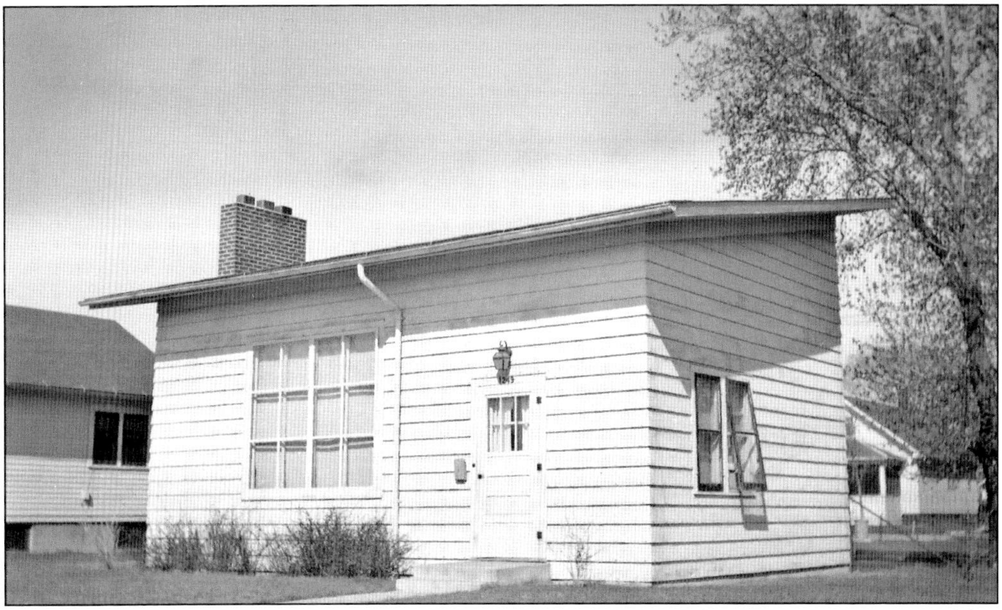

This small two-story home at 1249 Twelfth Street North belonged to Dwain T. Ervin and his wife, Shirley, according to the 1957 city directory. At the time of the tornado, Dwain Ervin was an assistant professor in social sciences at the North Dakota Agricultural College, now North Dakota State University.

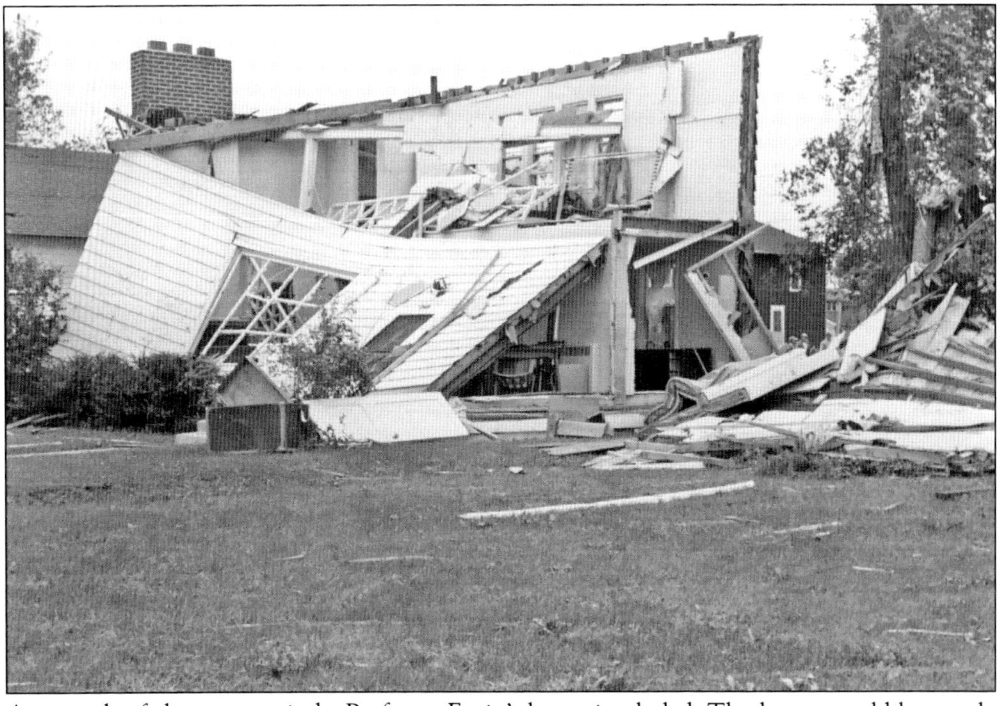

As a result of the strong winds, Professor Ervin's home imploded. The home would be nearly unrecognizable were it not for the front facade, which had been pushed in but was still nearly intact. Due to the proximity of the campus to the path of the tornado, a number of college professors and employees found themselves victims of the disaster.

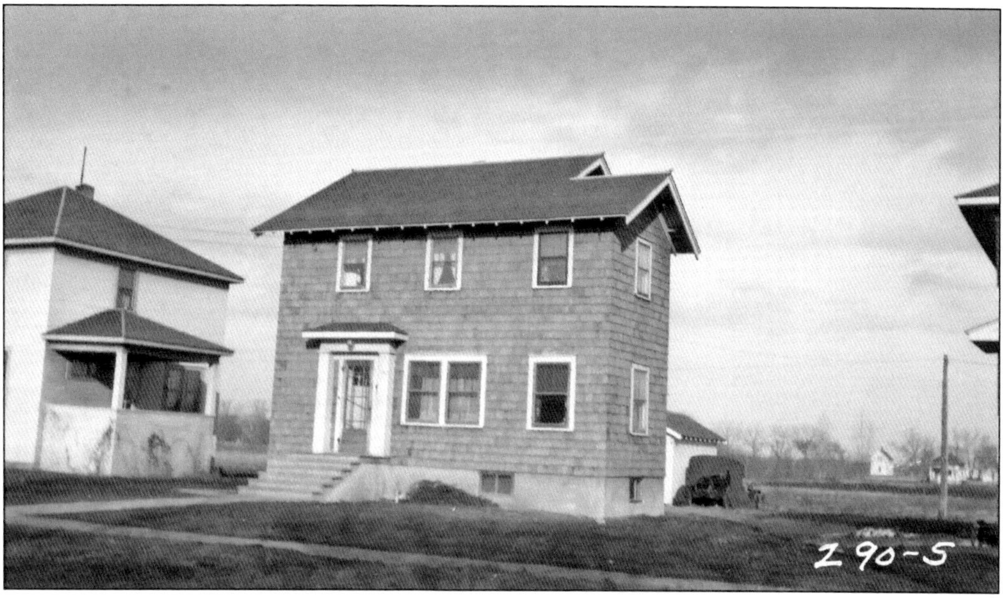

Houses in the 1200 block of Tenth Street North were especially hard hit by the tornado. Evidence of this can be seen in the following images showing two neighboring houses. The house at 1225 Tenth Street North was a two-story, cedar shake–sided, wood frame home before the tornado. It belonged to George E. Peterson Jr.

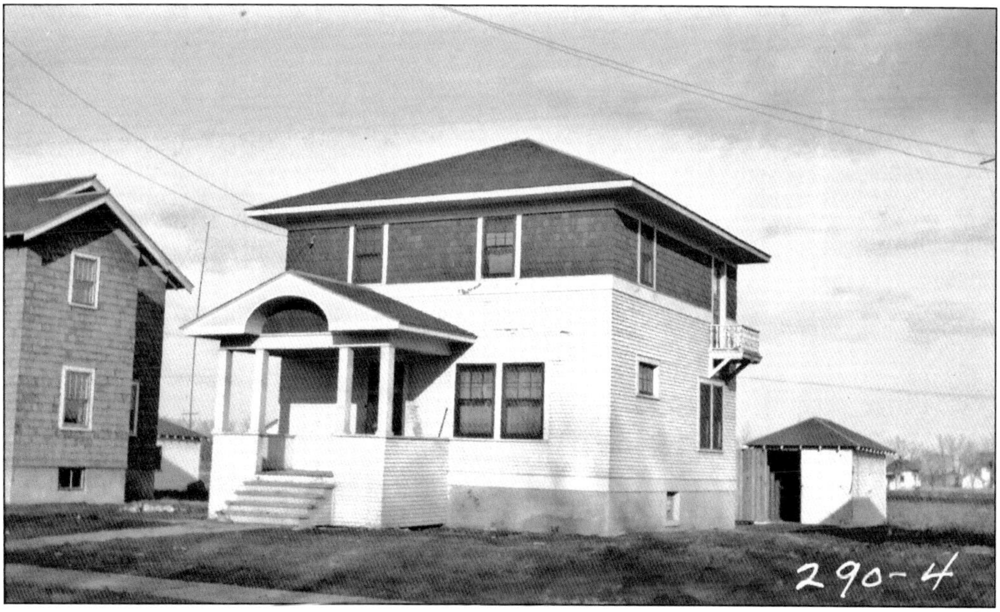

The neighboring house to the south, at 1221 Tenth Street North, was a Cube-style home with a hip roof. Both homes were built in the 1910s. The 1957 city directory listed Orville E. Jacobson and his wife, Mavis, at this address. The Jacobsons worked for the North Dakota Agricultural College.

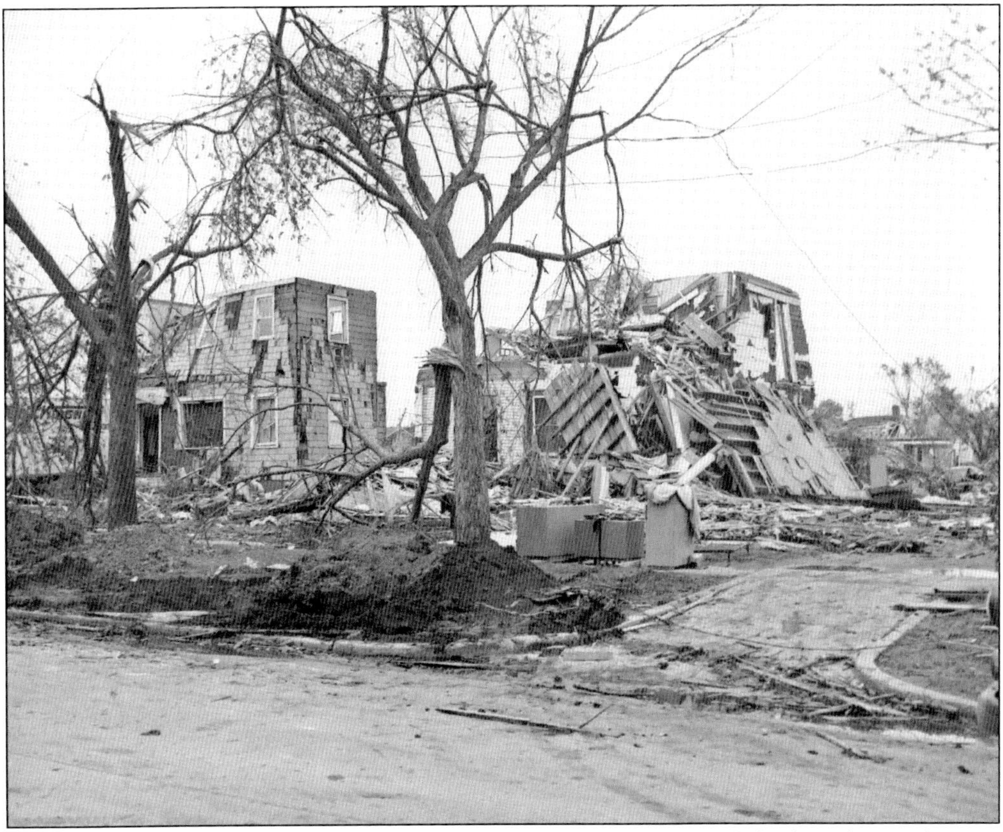

This photograph shows the dramatic and destructive effect the tornado had on the two houses. House number 1225 is on the left, and 1221 is on the right. Both neighbors moved from their properties after the tornado and did not rebuild. Two apartment buildings were constructed on the site in 1959.

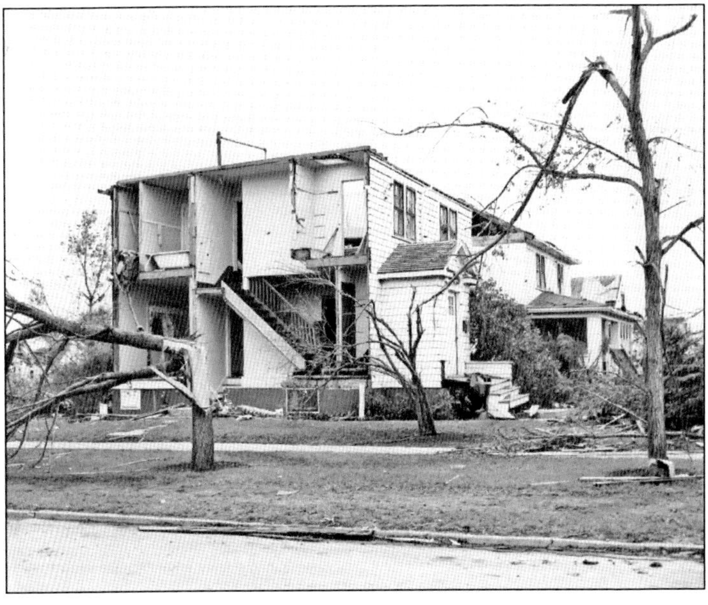

The destruction to the home at 1261 Tenth Street North drew a lot of attention from sightseers and was the subject of many photographs due to the unusual nature of the damage. The strong winds tore the roof off the home and sheared off the entire north wall, exposing the interior like a dollhouse.

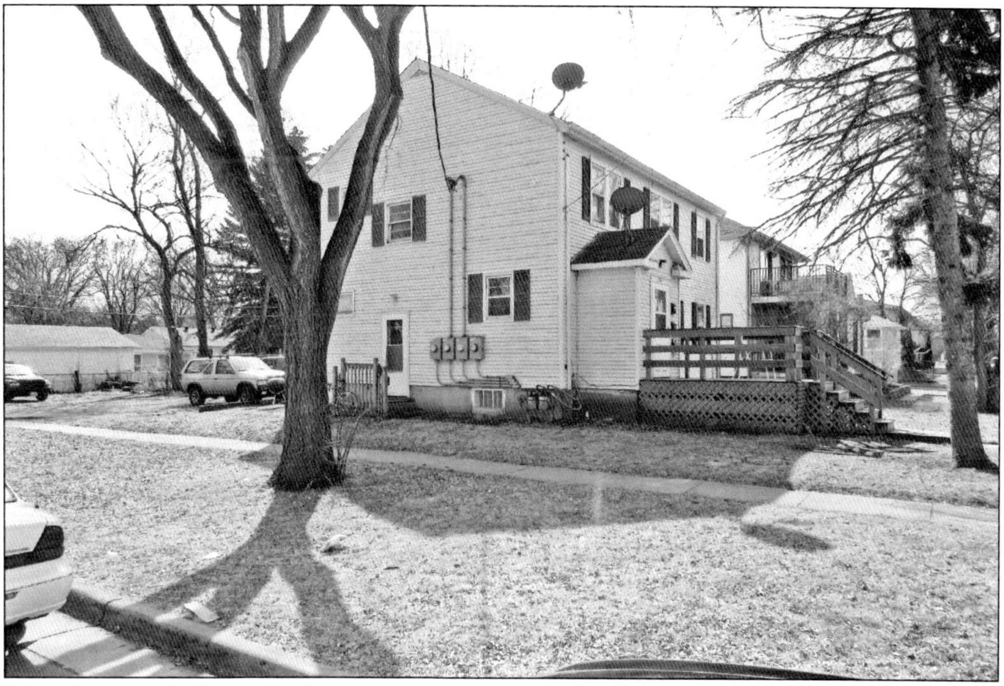

This photograph shows the house as it appears today and was taken from the same location as the previous one. The home has been altered, with the missing wall and roof replaced and an addition built on the far side. But there is no visible evidence of the trauma the structure experienced on June 20, 1957.

The house at 1260 Eighth Street North lost its entire roof. At the time of the tornado, it was home to a widow, Mary Pettinger, and her children Mary Jo and Robert. With the roof being completely lifted off the house and the rest of the structure unscathed, it was popular with disaster sightseers.

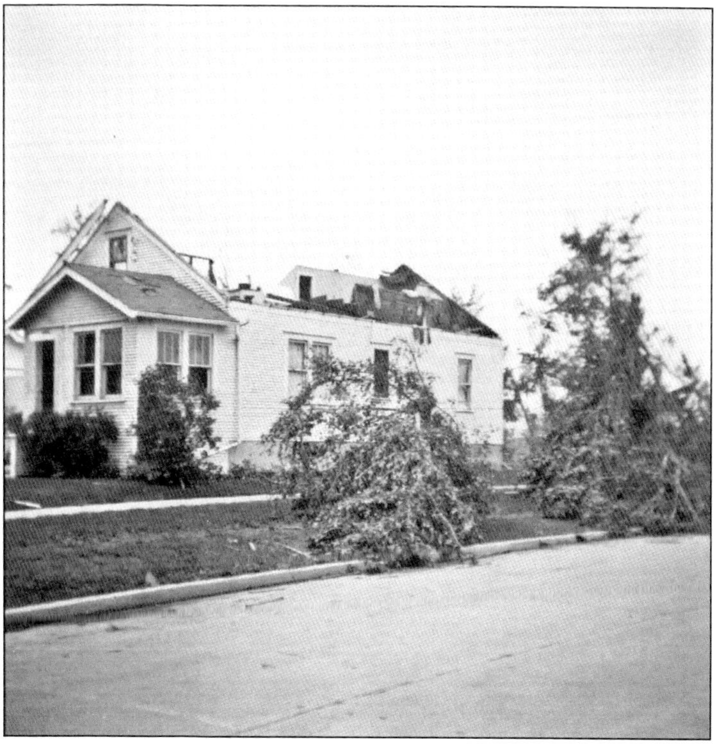

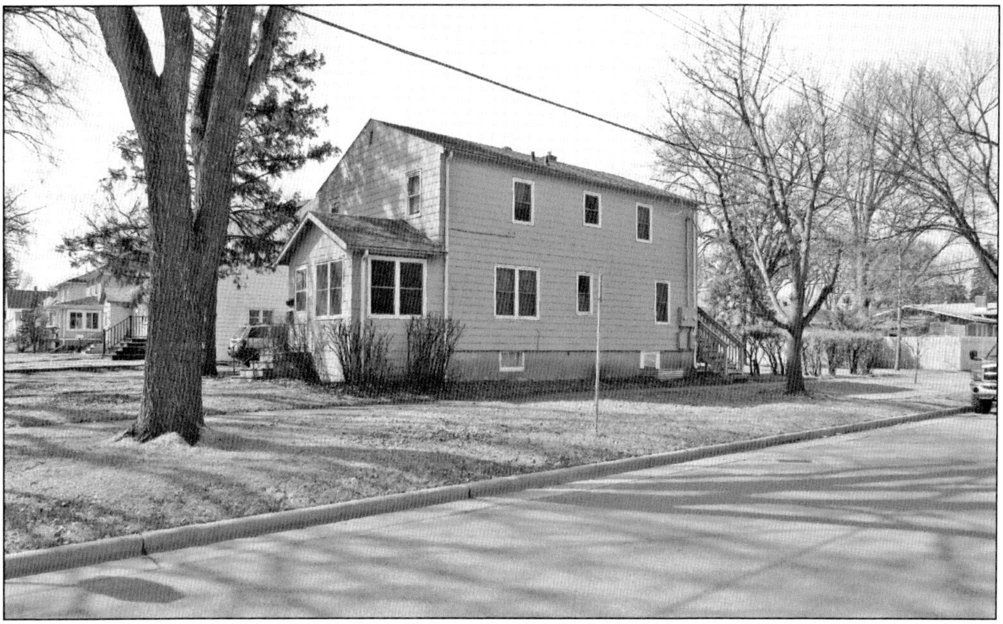

As with many other tornado survivors, Mary Pettinger seemed to have decided that the storm provided her an opportunity to expand onto the second story of the house, as this recent photograph shows. The Pettinger family continued to own the house until the mid-2000s. Pettinger lived to the age of 102.

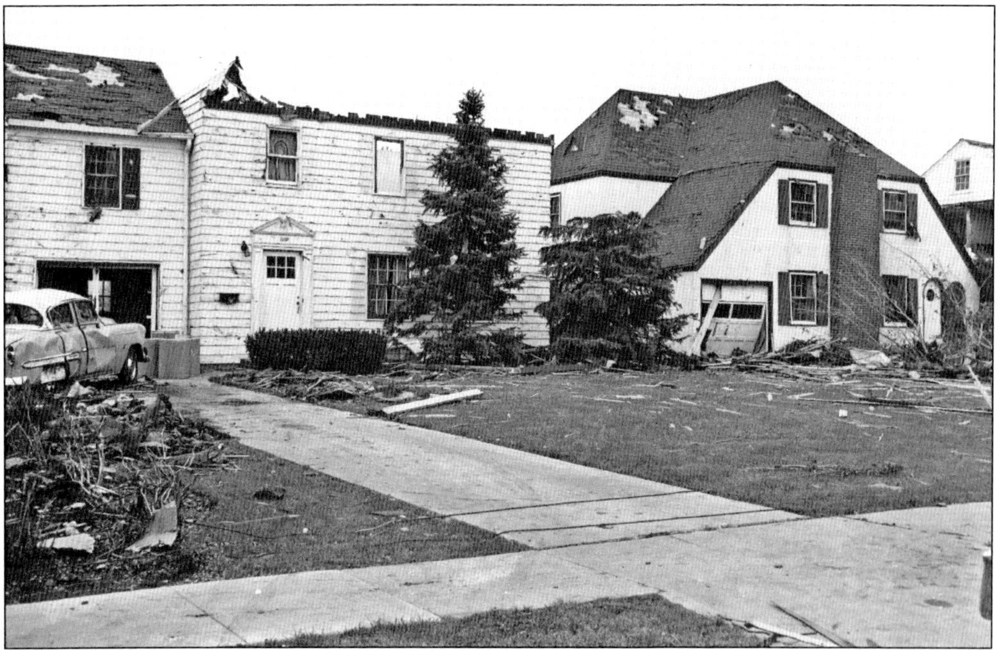

This view from the 1300 block of Broadway exemplifies the mess the tornado left behind. The house at 1309 Broadway, at left, was owned by Arthur F. and Borghild Platt. At the time of the tornado, the Platts were entertaining the O.G. Foss family, who were visiting from Tacoma, Washington. The house at 1305 Broadway was home to the Rev. Robert C. Ouradnik, a Methodist minister to students at the North Dakota Agricultural College.

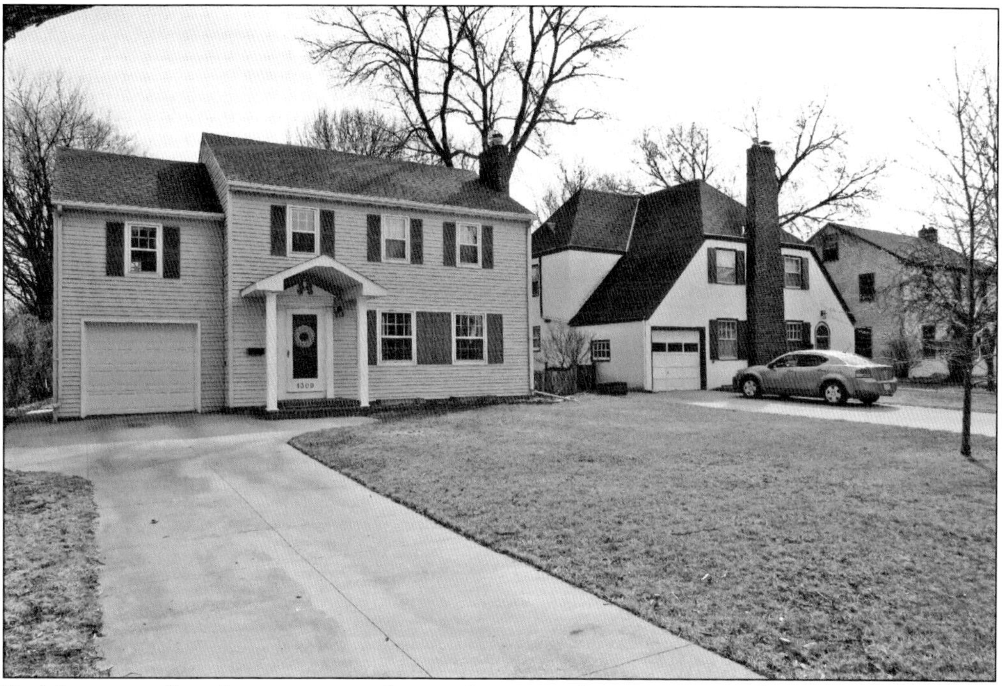

Both houses on Broadway were spared major damage and repairs were made, returning the homes to their pre-tornado appearance. Today, little evidence suggests the beating the houses took in the tornado. But a close look at the Ouradnik house reveals that the brick chimney is a slightly different color where the upper portion was replaced.

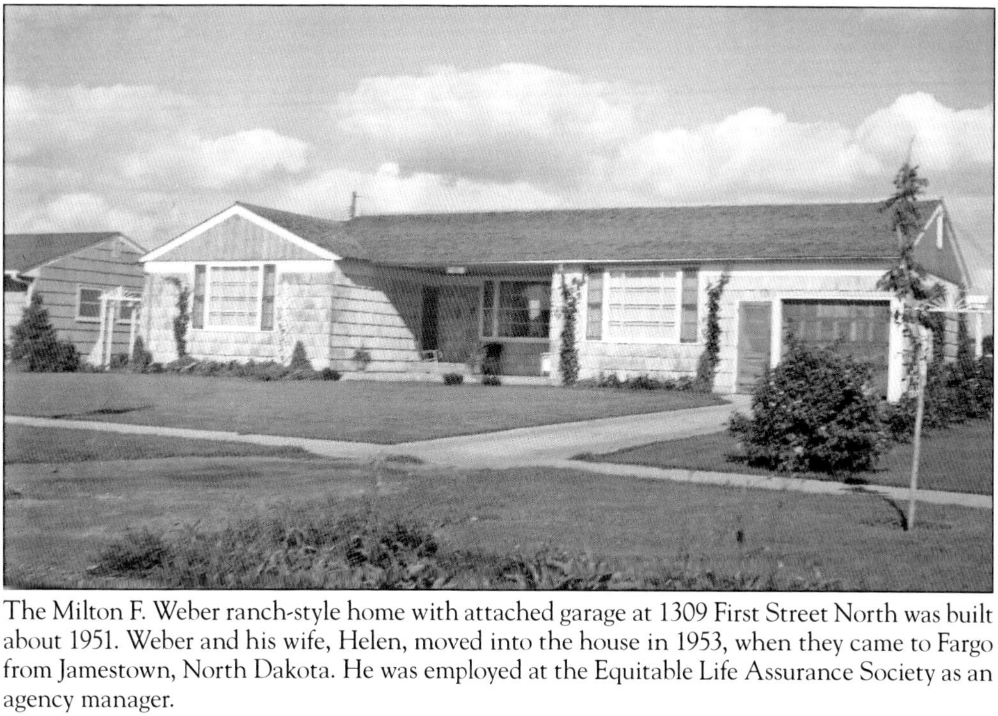

The Milton F. Weber ranch-style home with attached garage at 1309 First Street North was built about 1951. Weber and his wife, Helen, moved into the house in 1953, when they came to Fargo from Jamestown, North Dakota. He was employed at the Equitable Life Assurance Society as an agency manager.

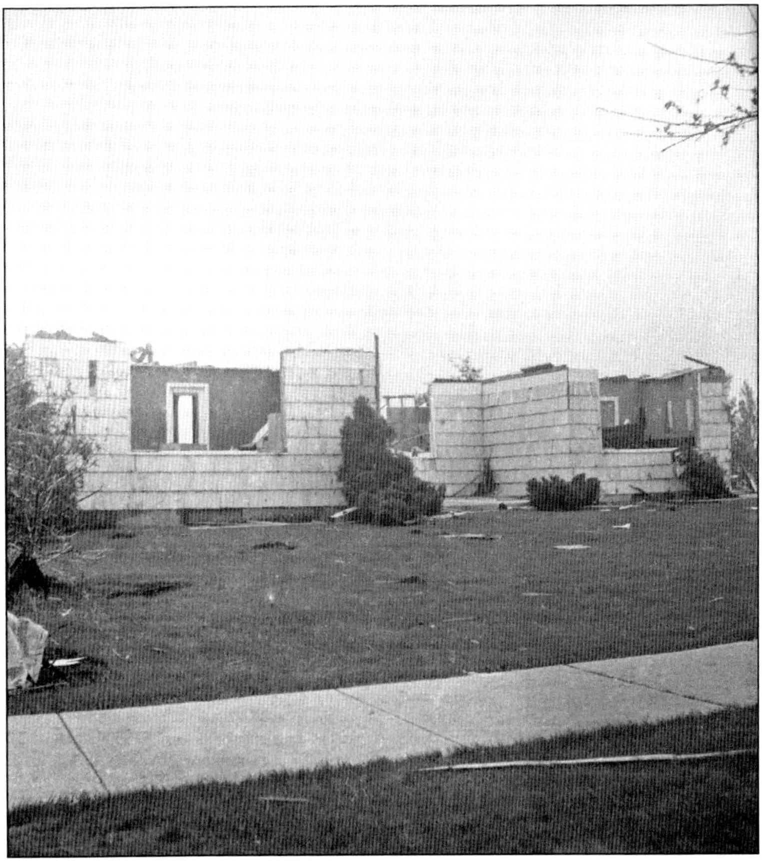

The Webers and their two children were in San Francisco when the disaster happened. The tornado completely removed the roof of their home. A photograph of this home was one of several from this block featured in the *Fargo Forum*. The Webers did not rebuild on the site, and a year later, he was transferred to Minneapolis for his job.

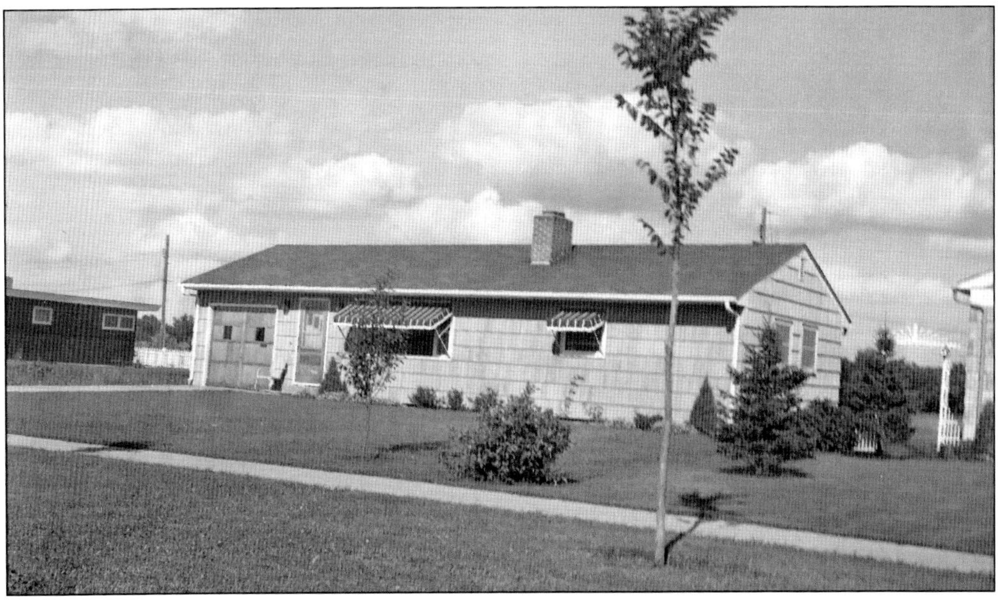

The home at 1313 First Street North was built in 1951 for a Swedish emigrant farmer from Blabon, North Dakota, named Arvid Brag. At the time of the tornado, Brag was a 68-year-old bachelor. He would spend weekends at his home in Fargo and return to his farm during the week.

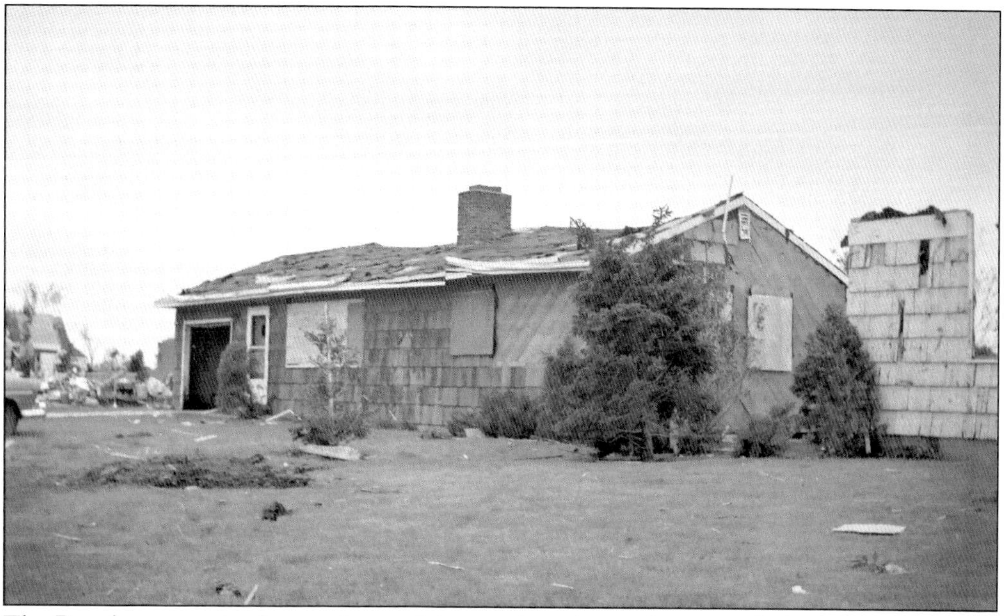

The Brag home received extensive roof damage but ultimately survived the storm, unlike the neighboring homes on either side. Brag made repairs to the home and continued to live there until about 1969. The home is still standing and maintains much of the same appearance as it did prior to the tornado.

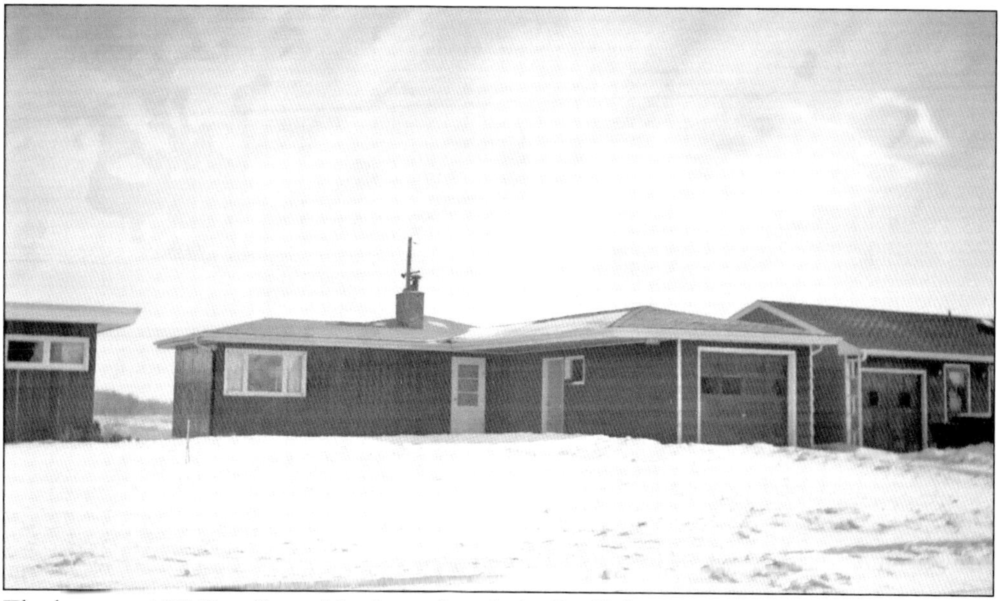

The house at 1317 First Street North was bought by Dr. Hale Aarnes and his wife, Mary, when they arrived in Fargo for him to start his teaching career in the Department of Education at North Dakota Agricultural College. The home was relatively new at the time, having been built in 1951.

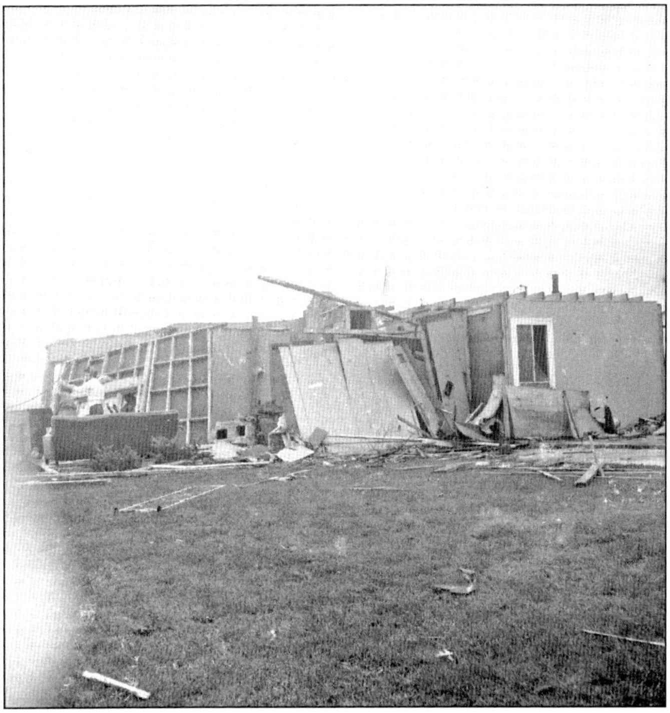

The Aarnes family saw the tornado forming and ran for their basement. Within two minutes, it was upon them. When they emerged from the basement, their home was completely unrecognizable. All exterior walls appear to have been blown away. Two women going through the rubble at left appear to have salvaged a sofa. The Aarneses rebuilt the house on the same footprint as the original structure and lived there until 1968.

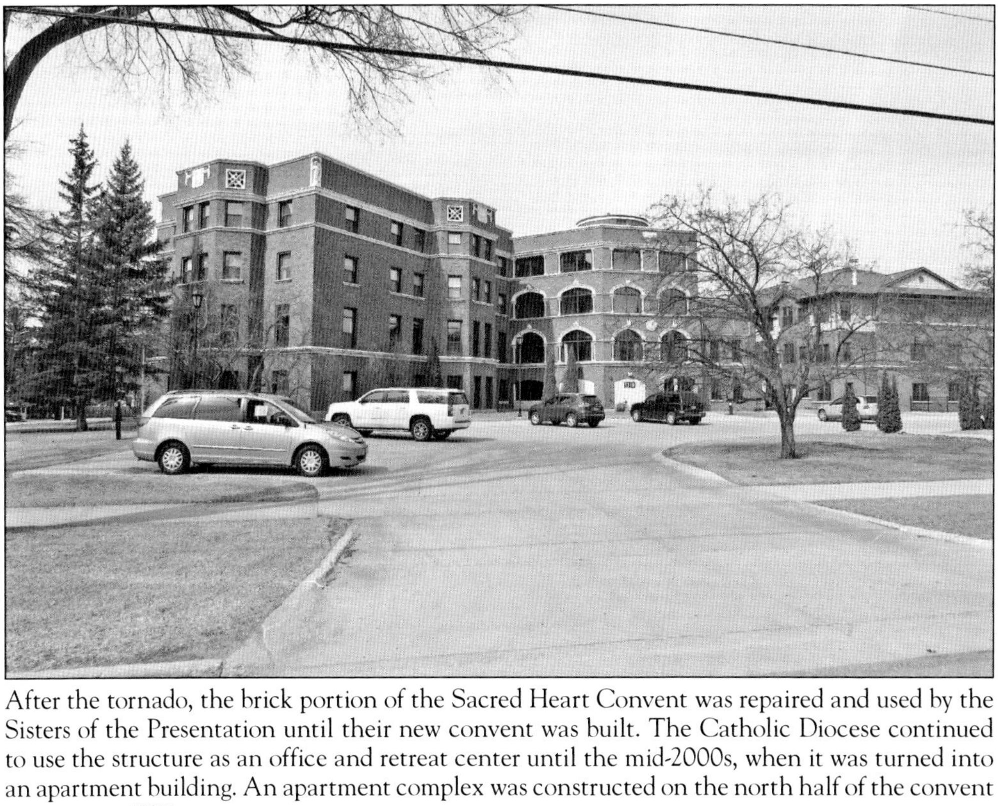

After the tornado, the brick portion of the Sacred Heart Convent was repaired and used by the Sisters of the Presentation until their new convent was built. The Catholic Diocese continued to use the structure as an office and retreat center until the mid-2000s, when it was turned into an apartment building. An apartment complex was constructed on the north half of the convent property in 1972.

Looking south at the north facade of Immanuel Lutheran Church, which sits on the corner of Broadway and Thirteenth Avenue North, this image shows the extensive damage the church suffered from the tornado. Three days after the storm, services were held at Washington School. After that, services were held at Ben Franklin School, with the sermon on June 30 entitled "Rebuilding the Walls of Zion."

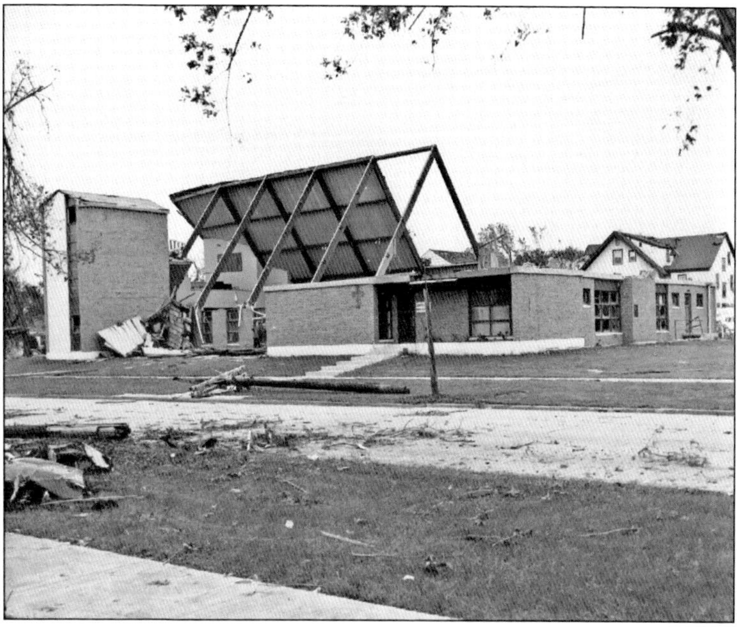

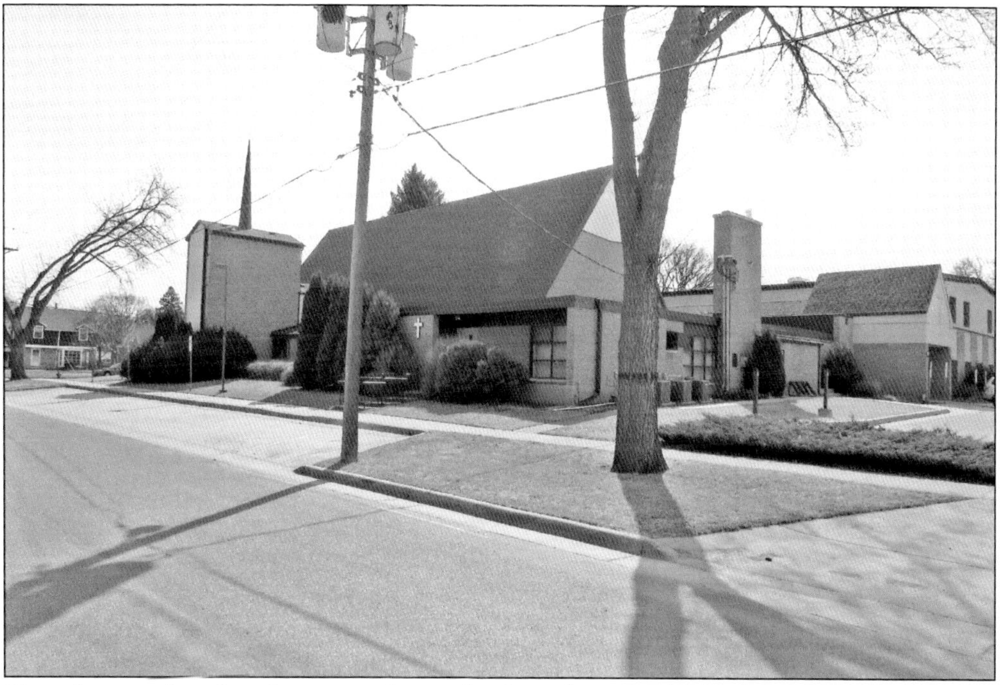

This photograph, taken from a similar angle, shows Immanuel Lutheran Church as it stands today. The congregation was able to raise funds to repair after the tornado and dedicated their new building on March 8, 1958. Additions are seen at right—a parking lot and large two-story gathering hall with Sunday school classrooms.

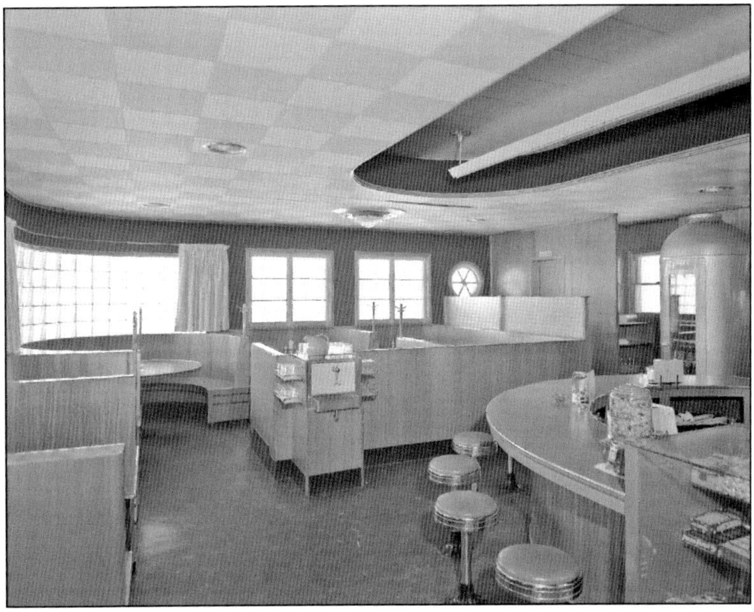

This is an interior view of the Hasty Tasty restaurant showing how the eatery appeared in 1941, around the time of its grand opening. The location of the restaurant, across the street from the North Dakota Agricultural College, made it a convenient and popular place for students, college staff, and faculty to catch a quick meal.

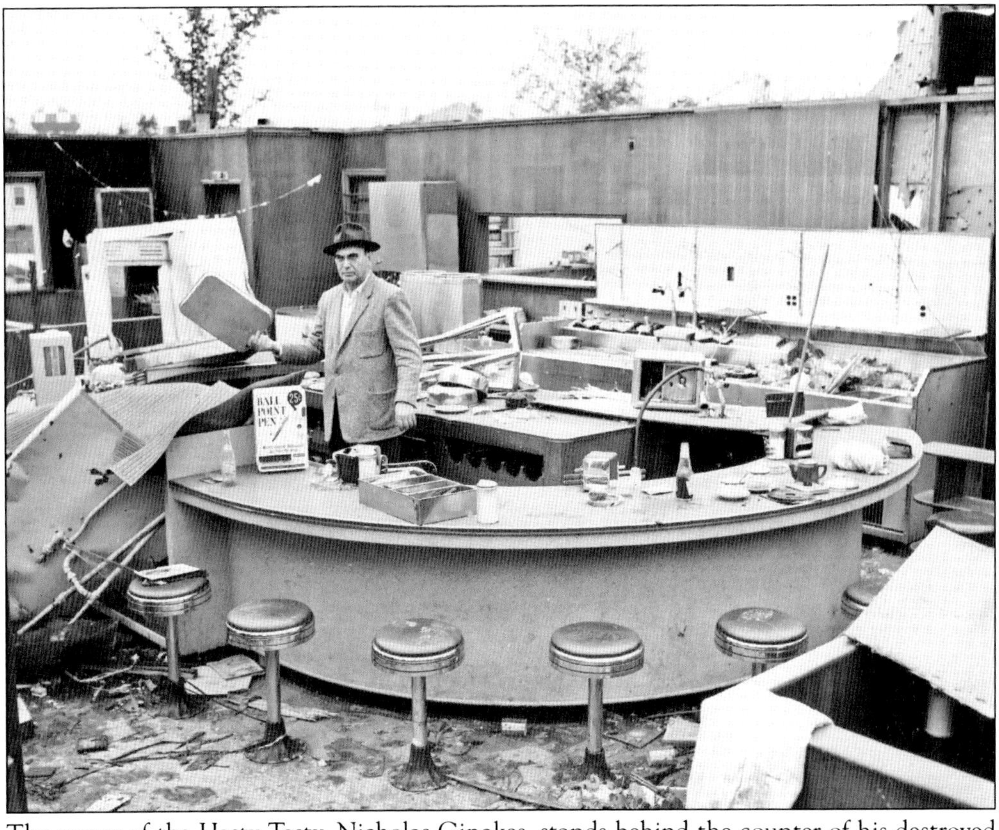

The owner of the Hasty Tasty, Nicholas Ginakes, stands behind the counter of his destroyed restaurant. This image was taken from a similar but slightly different vantage point to the previous photograph. Despite the fact that the roof and much of the building was missing, nothing on the counter, such as condiments, had been disturbed.

The Beta Sigma chapter of Kappa Psi pharmaceutical fraternity at the North Dakota Agricultural College was founded in 1924. The house, at 1249 Eleventh and a Half Street North, served as the fraternity's home from about 1937 to the time of the tornado. The winds removed the roof from the house, exposing the interior to the elements. Boards and plastic sheeting were put in place for protection.

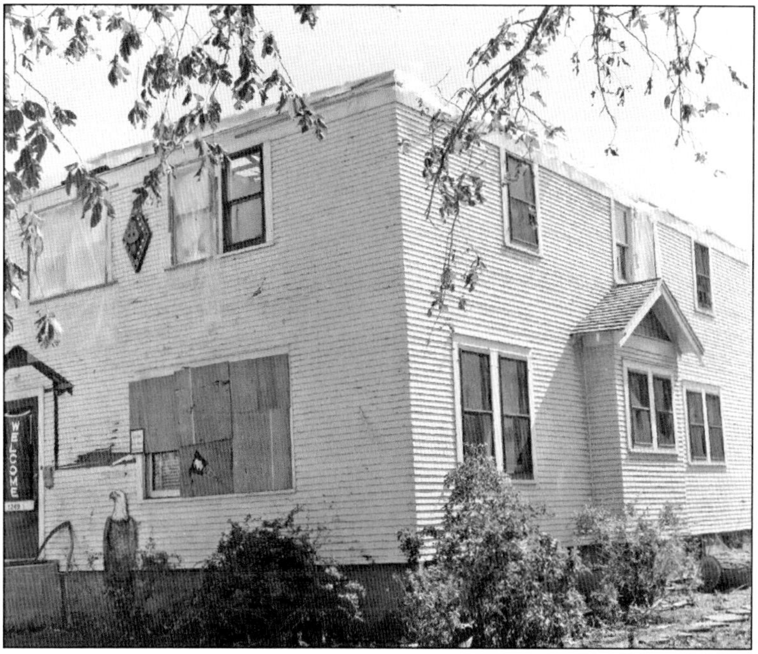

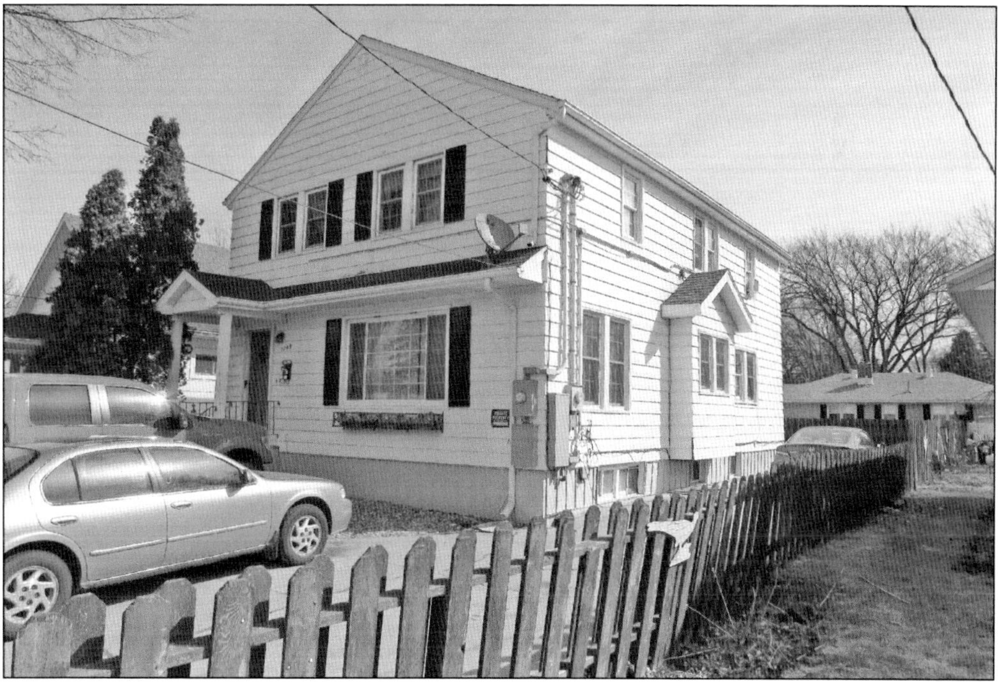

After the tornado, the Kappa Psi fraternity moved from its damaged house to 1343 Thirteenth Street North, today University Drive. The damage to the original fraternity building was repaired, and a new roof was added. The original roof was a jerkinhead style, but, as can be seen from this recent image, the roof was replaced by a plain forward-facing gable. Today, it is a residential property.

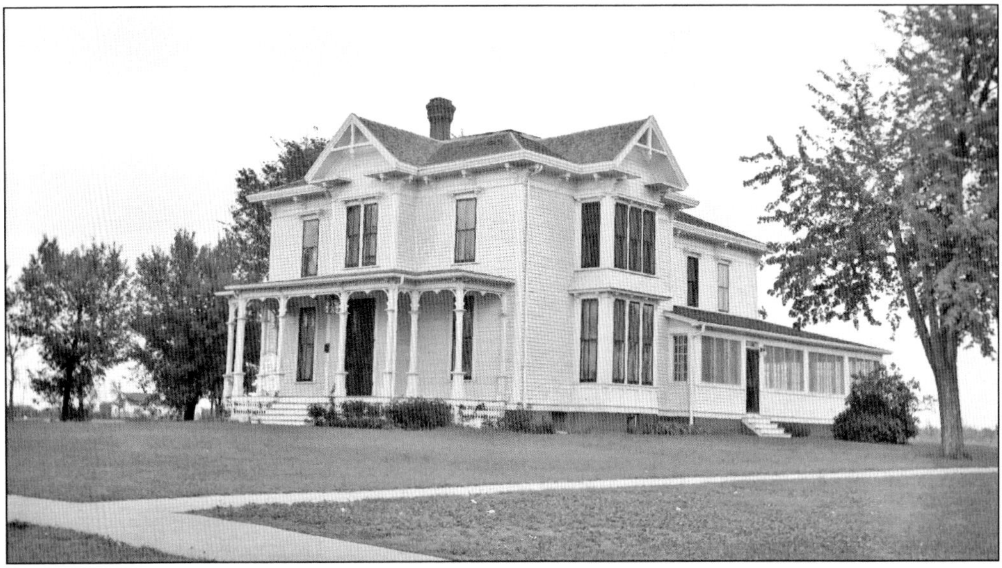

Taken around 1942, this photograph shows the El Zagal clubhouse as it looked before the tornado. Originally built in 1899, the two-story Queen Anne–style Victorian house standing at 1401 Broadway was acquired by the El Zagal Shrine in 1930 to serve as the clubhouse for its nearby golf course.

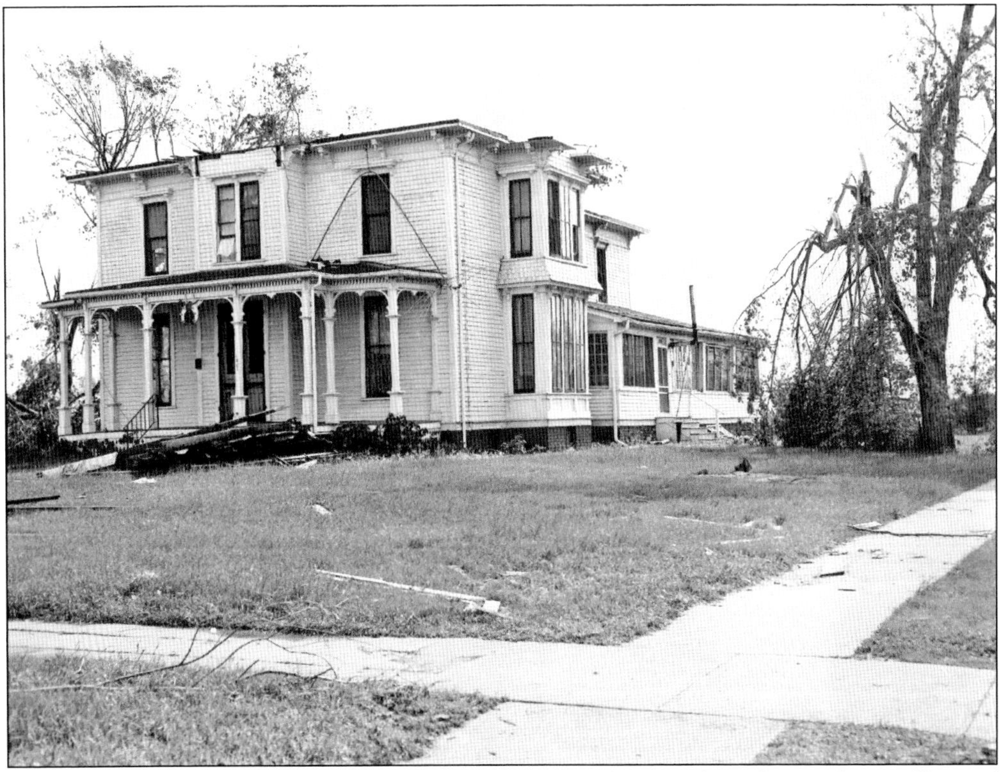

The roof was completely blown off the El Zagal clubhouse by the tornado, and it was damaged beyond repair. In 1960, the Shriners built a new clubhouse three blocks east. The site of the old clubhouse stood empty until a condominium complex was constructed on the site in 1975.

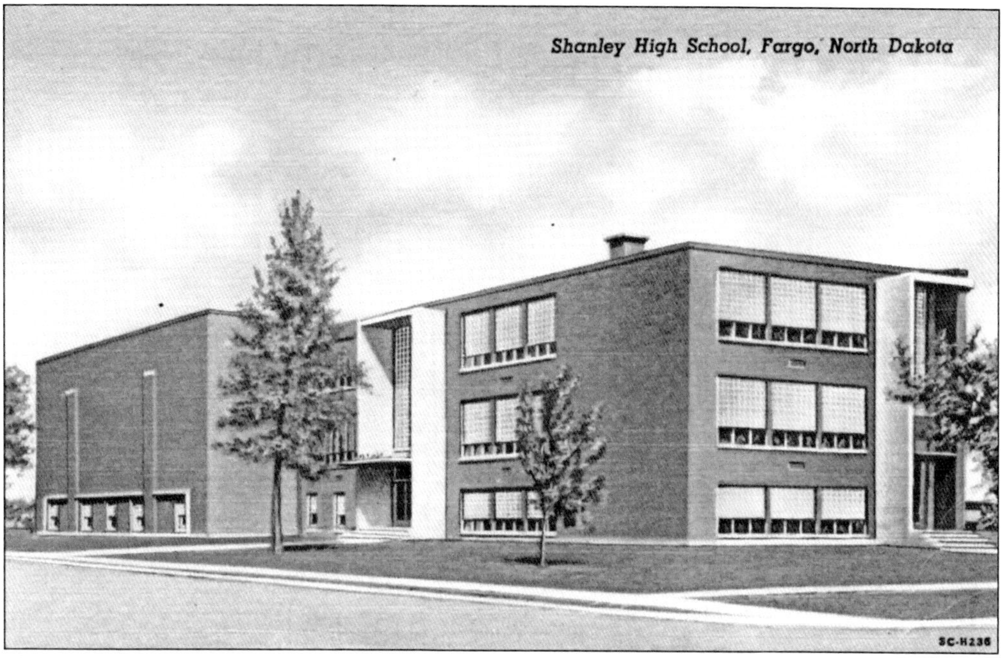

Shanley High School was a private Catholic school located at 705 Thirteenth Avenue North. The school was named after Bishop John Shanley, who was named the first bishop of the Diocese of Jamestown, North Dakota, in 1889, which became the Diocese of Fargo in 1897. The school's first seniors graduated in 1951, and the Presentation Sisters served at Shanley until 1989.

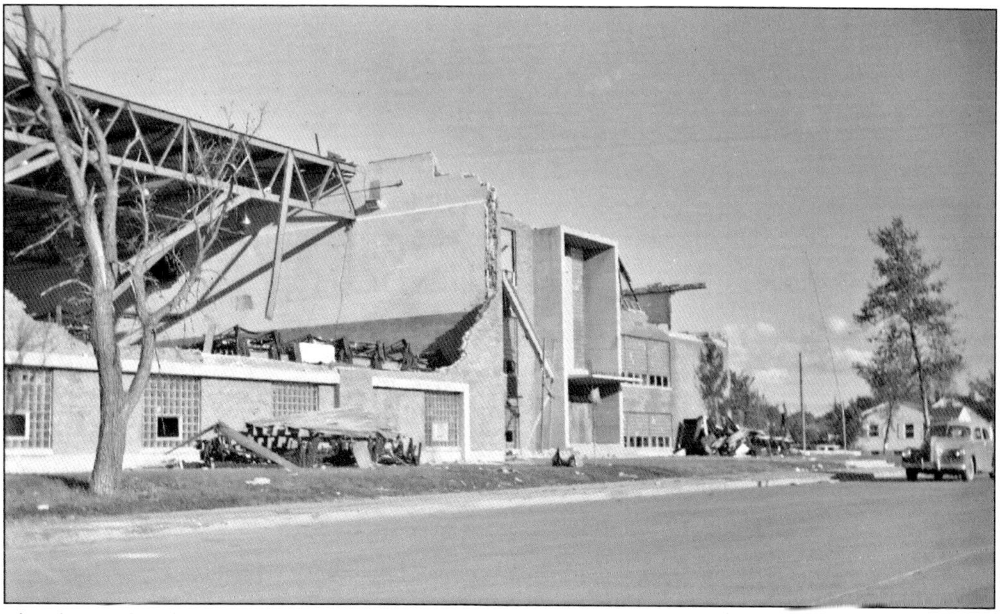
Shanley High School experienced severe tornado damage, which made the school unusable without significant repairs. A large portion of an outer gym wall was missing, and the school's roof beams were exposed. The school was repaired and remained at the same location after the tornado. A new Shanley High School was eventually built and opened in 2002 at 5600 Twenty-fifth Street South. It now serves approximately 330 students.

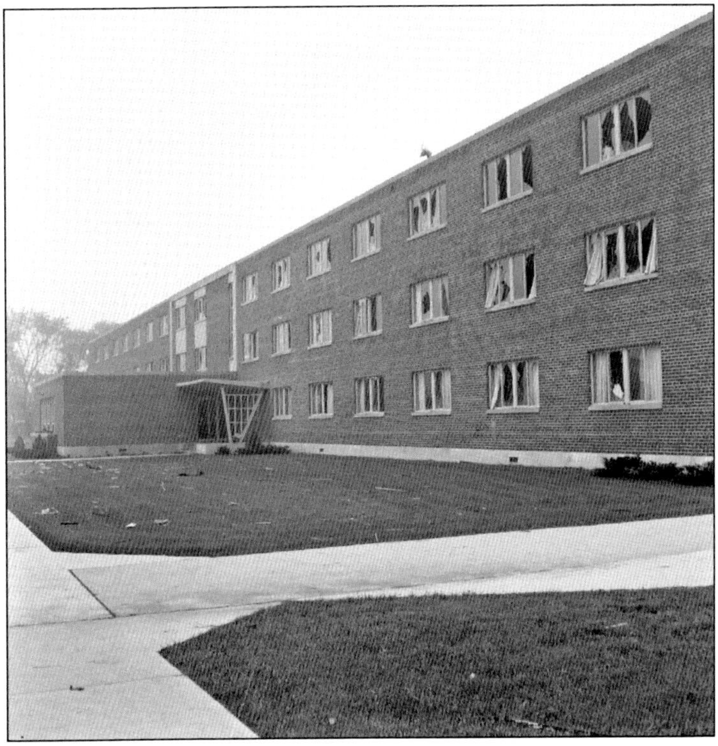

Nearly every window in Dinan Hall, on the North Dakota Agricultural College campus, was blown out by the tornado winds. Evidence of this can be seen in this view of the north side of the building, which was on the opposite side from the actual funnel. Fortunately, school was not in session, and no students were injured by the flying glass.

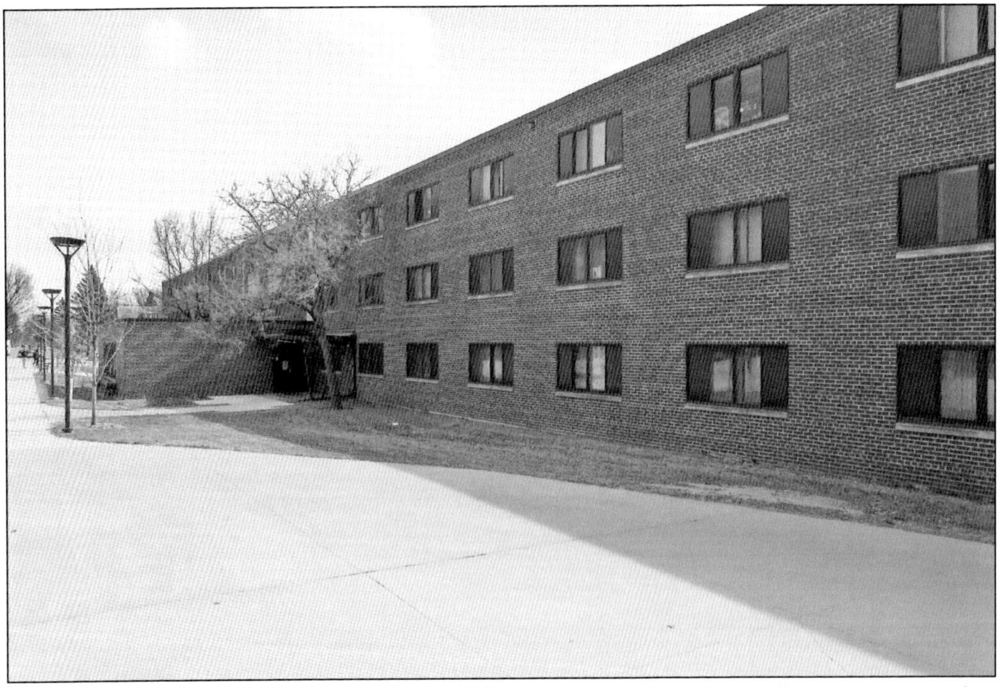

This view from the same location as the previous image shows Dinan Hall as it appears today. The damage the tornado caused has been repaired. At the time of the tornado, the building was only three years old. It was a residence hall for female students and was named after Pearl Dinan, professor of English and dean of women.

One of the buildings that suffered the most severe damage on the North Dakota Agricultural College campus was the Health Center. It was a one-story redbrick Prairie-style structure with a low-pitched hipped roof. It was designed by architect Paul Jones and was built between 1939 and 1940 with labor and funding from the Works Progress Administration and student contributions to the Health Fund.

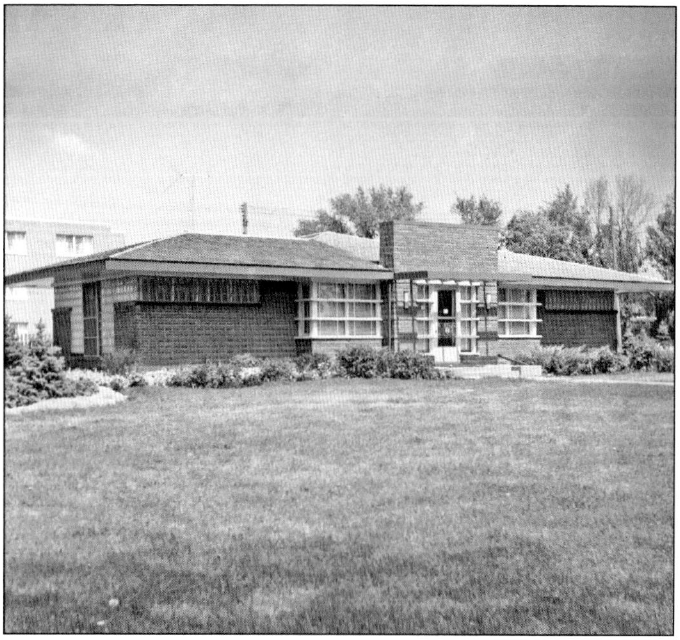

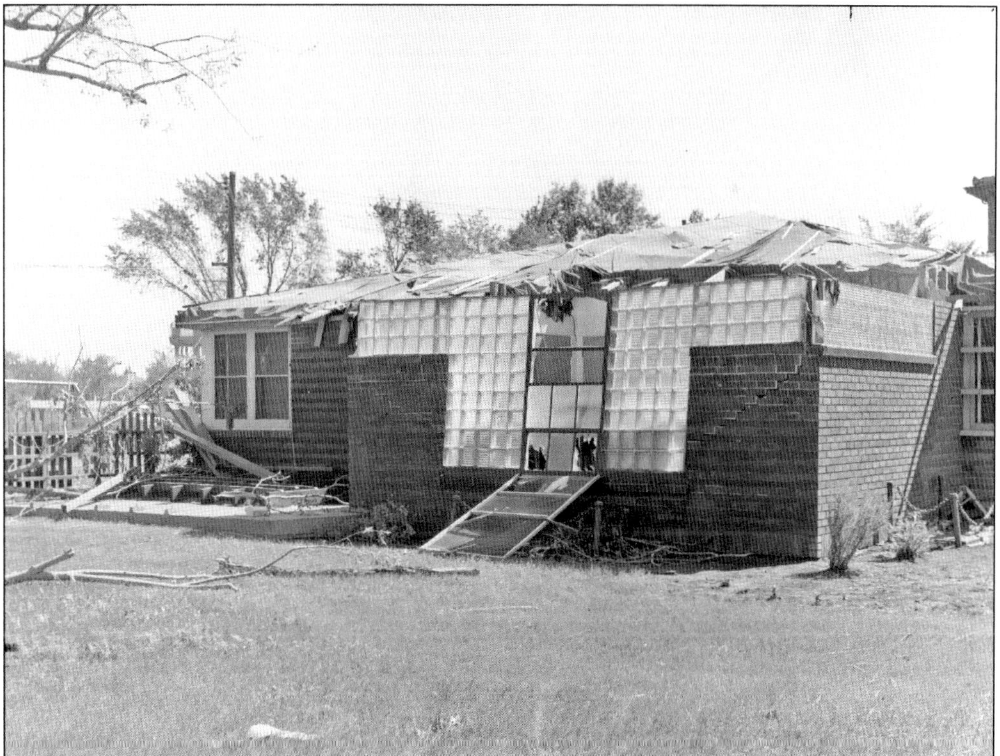

The Health Center lost much of its roof in the tornado. It was repaired, and in 1963, an addition was made to the building. It was renamed the Casper I. Nelson Health Center in 1967, to honor a former faculty member. A new wellness center was built on campus in 2001; the structure was remodeled into classrooms. It was demolished in 2015 to expand the Memorial Union parking lot.

Bibliography

Fargo, N. Dak. Tornado and Minnesota Floods of June, 1957. American National Red Cross. Midwestern area, 1957.

Fujita, Tetsuya. *Research Paper No. 42: A Detailed Analysis of the Fargo Tornadoes of June 20, 1957.* Washington, DC: Department of Commerce, 1960.

Jensen, Ray E. "Fargo, North Dakota F5 Tornado June 20, 1957, How the Public Was Warned: A Personal Account." National Oceanic and Atmospheric Administration, 2009. www.crh.noaa.gov/Image/fgf/pdf/Jensen_Fargp_Warning_paper_11_19_09.pdf

Parsley, Jamie. *Fargo 1957: An Elegy.* Fargo, ND: North Dakota Institute for Regional Studies, 2010.

About the North Dakota State University Archives

NDSU | ARCHIVES

The North Dakota State University (NDSU) Archives, comprised of the Institute for Regional Studies Archives and University Archives, support the research needs of undergraduates, graduate students, faculty, staff, and other scholars at North Dakota State University and beyond. Founded in 1950, the archives has become one of the premier institutions providing access to the history of North Dakota and the northern Great Plains.

In fostering understanding of regional life through research, the mission of the Institute for Regional Studies Archives is to identify, collect, and preserve the historical resources of the region that have lasting value and to promote the use of these materials by the North Dakota State University community, scholars, and the public. Its goal is to provide a research experience for students in the use of primary sources, to advance scholarship, and to further the instructional, research, and public service missions of the university.

The university archives' mission is to appraise, collect, preserve, arrange, describe, and make available important historical, legal, fiscal, administrative, and social records of the university.

The NDSU Archives views providing access to collections and research support, as well as promoting the state and university, as central to NDSU's land grant mission, which states: "We reflect and serve geographically and culturally diverse populations. We share institutional success across the university. We anticipate and welcome growth and service that will occur in ways yet to be conceived. We embrace our unique complexities as a land-grant university on the Northern Great Plains. We remain committed to serving people globally."

The archives houses over 3,000 manuscript collections, over a half million photographs, negatives, and slides, and extensive collections of ephemera and artifacts. The archives' reading room contains over 20,000 books pertaining to every aspect of North Dakota history and over 3,000 rolls of microfilm of the *Fargo Forum*, other North Dakota newspapers, and other primary resources.

Through a nearly 70-year relationship with the NDSU Press, formerly the North Dakota Institute for Regional Studies Press, archival documents and images have been used in dozens of regionally important publications.

Scholars from across the United States and from countries as far away as Iceland, Australia, South Korea, and Russia have visited the archives or used its resources.